Steele at Drury Lane

Steele | AT DRURY LANE

by
JOHN LOFTIS

UNIVERSITY OF CALIFORNIA
PRESS | 1952

Berkeley and Los Angeles

University of California Press
Berkeley and Los Angeles
California

Cambridge University Press
London, England

Designed by Adrian Wilson

Preface

GEORGE A. AITKEN, *by the thoroughness with which he explored the records of Steele's career, established his* The Life of Richard Steele *as the point of origin for all future investigations of the subject. The decisive question about any subsequent book on any aspect of Steele's biography is inevitably, "What does it add to Aitken?" So with this book. I answer that I have examined Steele's theatrical career in the context of early eighteenth-century stage and dramatic history—especially in the context of the dramatic reform movement in which Steele played such a prominent role—as it was impossible for Aitken to do in a general biography. My book is indeed quite as much about the early eighteenth-century theater as about Steele; my subject, as I see it, occupies the middle ground between that of Aitken and that of Allardyce Nicoll in his* Eighteenth Century Drama, 1700–1750, *though mine is, of course, much more limited than theirs.*

My debts are many, but to no one are they greater than to Professor Louis A. Landa, who led me to the close study of Steele that resulted in this book and who assisted and encouraged me throughout my work. With much generosity of time he read my manuscript at several stages of revision and saved me from a score of blunders. Professor Gerald Eades Bentley also read the entire manuscript, making available to me his wide knowledge of the history of the English drama and stage. I am indebted to my colleagues Professors Hugh G. Dick, Edward Niles Hooker, Robert S. Kinsman, John Harrington Smith, and H. T. Swedenberg, Jr., for much sound advice and for many specific suggestions. I owe much, of course, to previous writers on Steele, as my notes will show, but my debt to three of them requires specific statement—

to John Nichols of the eighteenth century, to George A. Aitken, whom I have already mentioned, of the nineteenth, and to Professor Rae Blanchard of the twentieth. To Professor Blanchard I am indeed indebted for personal assistance as well as for the help provided by her writings. My thanks are due to Professor Emmett L. Avery, who over a period of several years answered my queries and supplied me with valuable items of information derived from his own researches in the history of the eighteenth-century stage. To the following scholars I am indebted for a series of helpful suggestions: Professors Alan S. Downer, Reginald Harvey Griffith, Frank Lindsay, John Robert Moore, and Arthur Secord. And finally, I thank my wife for assistance with countless details and for detecting many stylistic weaknesses.

A grant-in-aid from the Pacific Coast Committee for the Humanities made it possible for me to spend the summer of 1949 in England conducting research necessary for this book. The Research Committee of the University of California, Los Angeles, generously supported my work for a period of three years.

I wish to thank the trustees of the Huntington Library and the editors of the Huntington Library Quarterly, the Journal of English and Germanic Philology, Modern Language Notes, Modern Language Quarterly, and the University of California Studies in English for permitting me to reprint previously published material.

J. L.

Contents

Introduction   1

PART ONE:
Backgrounds

1 Politics   11
2 Reform   13
3 Drury Lane and the Tories   25
4 The License   33
5 The Patent   39

PART TWO:
1714–1719

1 Steele in the Management   55
2 Drury Lane under Steele   79
3 Mortgages   91
4 The Censorium   98

PART THREE:
The Dispute
with the
Lord Chamberlain

1 Beginnings   121
2 Suspension   127
3 Reinstatement   149
4 Journalistic Controversy   159

| | 1 | The Genesis of *The Conscious Lovers* | 183 |

PART FOUR: Last Years

	2	*The Conscious Lovers* at Drury Lane	193
	3	Critical Controversy	195
	4	Steele and the Management, 1721–1729	213
	5	Unfinished Plays	230

Conclusion		239
Appendix	Unpublished Documents Relating to Steele's Theatrical Career	243
Index		249

Introduction

DISSATISFACTION with the contemporary English stage reached one of its periodic heights during the early eighteenth century. In nearly every serious discussion of the theater the problem of arresting the decline of drama appeared as an important theme, often as the major one. After the first exchanges of the Jeremy Collier controversy the cry for stage reform was all but unanimous, though there was by no means agreement on what "reform" meant. Doubtless some who denounced stage abuses did so idly, parroting a fashionable attitude, yet in the writings of many there is the ring of sincerity.

Nor was the concern for the state of drama exclusively moralistic. In the Collier controversy, to be sure, the moral issues (frequently identified with critical principles) overshadowed all others, but in the discussions apart from that ill-natured dispute, theatrical principles entirely independent of stage morality were also debated. Professional playwrights and critics as well as churchmen and moralistic reformers were dissatisfied with the manner in which the London stage was conducted. The writings of Dennis, Theobald, Addison, Gildon, Sewell, and Filmer—to name only a few representative figures—reveal a concern with dramatic problems by no means limited to morality. Even in the writings of Steele, where ethical considerations are paramount, there are other major theatrical issues.

Although there was no general agreement on what precisely was wrong and what should be done, most men seriously interested in the stage were willing to pay at least lip service, and in some cases much more, to the idea of more effective control of the London theaters. They believed that more thorough supervision of the stage was required if drama in England was to be restored to its former flourishing condition. But to translate this belief into an effective government of the London stage that could at once curb licentiousness and mercenary exploitation of the drama without stifling the creative impulse of the playwrights with a rigid censorship proved to be, as always, a perplexed problem.

It came to be recognized that the lord chamberlain and his subordinate, the master of the revels, could not, under the existing legislation, effectively supervise the stage.[1] Though theoretically possessing authority to intervene in theatrical matters, the lord chamberlain in practice proved unable to control the theaters' routine operations. The attempts made throughout the reign of Anne (chronicled by J. W. Krutch)[2] to bring the theaters under closer control by the lord chamberlain were largely ineffectual, the theatrical companies remaining substantially independent and continuing to attract sharp criticism. The problem of stage regulation persisted, to be inherited by George I.

It was with this background of dissatisfaction that little more than a month after his arrival in England, George appointed Richard Steele, long famous as a reformer, to the governorship of the leading London company of actors, the Royal Company of Comedians, acting in Drury Lane. Steele held the governorship of Drury Lane until his death in 1729 (except during one stormy period while he was suspended by the lord chamberlain), a position that empowered him to incorporate into the managerial policies of Drury Lane those precepts he had urged for a number of years in his writings. After having written dozens of essays in the *Tatler,* the *Spectator,* and the *Guardian* about drama and the stage in which he revealed himself one of the strongest advocates for the correction of stage abuses, he was given the opportunity—unusual for speculative reformers—of converting his ideas into practice.

That a person of Steele's reputation should have been appointed to Drury Lane attests the contemporary desire for reform and the

---

[1] Cf. P. J. Crean, "The Stage Licensing Act of 1737," *Modern Philology,* XXXV (1938), 239–240.

[2] "Government Attempts to Regulate the Stage after the Jeremy Collier Controversy," *PMLA,* XXXVIII (March, 1923), 153–174; *Comedy and Conscience after the Restoration* (New York, 1924), pp. 166–191.

government's determination that the agitation for reform should not dissipate itself in ineffective protests. Although there were also strong political reasons for his appointment, Steele was made governor of the theater in order that he could supervise the plays presented there; the ministers of George I in the king's name charged him with the duties of a stage censor: "We do hereby command and enjoyn," reads the patent issued to him, "that no new Play, or any old or revived Play, be acted under the authority hereby granted, containing any passages or expressions offensive to piety and good manners, until the same be corrected and purged by the said Governor, from all such offensive and scandalous passages and expressions." The injunction was positive, and it was directed to a man known to be an advocate of a reformed drama, who through experience as a playwright and dramatic critic might be expected to manage judiciously the problems posed by stage regulation. Such powers had been granted to other individuals previously, but never to one who by reputation seemed so well qualified to discharge them. In giving authority to a man with demonstrated ability in accomplishing reform, George I exhibited a seriousness of intent in marked contrast to the attitude of Charles II, who had appointed as stage supervisors men whose own writings were offensive. It was one thing to charge Thomas Killigrew with supervision of the stage, and quite another to give the task to Isaac Bickerstaff.

The concern with stage reform is evident, not merely in his original appointment, but in almost all the major episodes of Steele's career at Drury Lane. In the two periodicals he established during his governorship, the *Town Talk* and the *Theatre*, the need for moral and artistic improvement in drama appears as an insistent theme; he conducted an "academy" (at least informally associated with Drury Lane), one of the avowed purposes of which was to accomplish an "improvement of the public taste in pleasures"; he was suspended from his governorship by the lord chamberlain in 1720 because, among other reasons, he had neglected his duties as stage supervisor; and in a prolonged journalistic controversy provoked by his suspension, he debated with a series of antagonists the major issues raised by the government's attempt to regulate the stage. *The Conscious Lovers,* patently a play in which the didactic purpose is paramount, represents Steele's culminating effort in stage reform, providing as it does a pattern of comedy—exemplary comedy—in which the action and characters are designed as models for and incentives to virtuous behavior.[3] Always the reformer, Steele, "the Censor of Great Britain," brought to Drury Lane an intensified concern for this chief dramatic problem of his time.

At the outset of his career at Drury Lane, several of his contemporaries expressed the hope that his governorship would see the beginning of a new era in theatrical performances. One of them—Sir Richard Blackmore—himself an active exponent of reform, wrote with great enthusiasm about Steele's appointment:

But tho Men who love their Country, born down with a Torrent of profane Libertines, Persons without Taste and Distinction of Vertue and Vice, have almost despair'd of seeing the Comick Poets reform'd, and the exorbitant Liberties of the Stage restrain'd within the Limits of modest Language and decent Behaviour; yet now their Hopes revive, and they promise to themselves a sudden and effectual Reformation of these Abuses, since the Government has plac'd so worthy a Person at the Head of the Actors, and given him ample Authority to rectify their Errors: What a happy Revolution, what a regular and clean Stage may justly be now expected? How free from all sordid and impure Mixtures, how innocent, as well as diverting, will our Comedies appear, when they have been corrected and refin'd by such an accomplish'd Director of the Dramatick Poets? One that has a true and delicate Taste, and who is sensible of the Indecencies and hurtful Nature of our Plays; who has engag'd his celebrated Pen, in defiance of sneering Wits and powerful Libertines, on the Side of Vertue, and has propagated the Esteem of Morals, Humanity, Decorum and Sobriety of Manners; who with great Spirit, Genius, and Courage, to his lasting Honour, has publickly expos'd the Absurdities, Vices, and Follies, that stain and disgrace the Theatre; in which Censure he has not spar'd his own Performances: One who has express'd a warm Zeal on this Subject, and declar'd his generous Intention, if it were in his Power, to cleanse these polluted Places, and not to suffer a Comedy to be presented but what had past a severe Examination, and where all things

---

[3] In my conception of exemplary comedy, I am heavily indebted to John Harrington Smith, *The Gay Couple in Restoration Comedy* (Cambridge, Mass., 1948), pp. 193–232.

which might shock a modest Ear, or be look'd on as repugnant to good Manners, might be expung'd.[4]

Blackmore's strong moral bias led him to a more eloquent statement of the significance of Steele's governorship than most of his contemporaries would have ventured, but he nevertheless reveals something of the general reaction to the appointment. Others shared his hopes. Steele himself, moreover, made brave public promises that he would improve Drury Lane.[5] His appointment was indubitably interpreted as more than an act of political expediency. Prospects seemed bright for the reformers.

Yet sincere and prolonged as was Steele's interest in stage reform, the record of his career at Drury Lane is not one of unwavering adherence to the lofty principles enunciated by Bickerstaff and Mr. Spectator. The disparity between moral conviction and personal conduct was unusually great in Steele's case—as he more than once acknowledged—and his governorship of the theater provides still another example of his conduct falling short of his precepts. This is not to suggest that his advocacy of reform was totally ineffective; without much doubt Drury Lane grew more sensitive to theatrical immorality when he was placed at its head, and *The Conscious Lovers,* perhaps his chief contribution to the theater, served for a long time as a model of what an inoffensive comedy might be. We are compelled to acknowledge, however, that as an administrative head of Drury Lane, Steele did not fulfill expectations.

Steele's promises were not, I would hazard, made hypocritically. For at least the first two seasons of his governorship he took an active interest in the management and no doubt did what he could to improve the quality of performances. Thereafter, unmistakable signs of his neglect appear, his participation in the management subsiding more and more into a concern that he receive his full share of the theater's profits. Not until 1724 did he cease altogether to take part in the theater's affairs, but after January, 1720, he had little to do with the company's policies—politics, ill-health, the

---

[4] *An Essay Upon Wit* (London, 1716), Augustan Reprint Society, Series One, No. 1, 1946, pp. 228–229.

[5] Cf. the *Town Talk,* No. 6.

need for money, and theatrical competition forcing a compromise of his early plans.

Paradoxically, the most interesting episode of his career at Drury Lane coincides with his separation from the active management. In January, 1720, Steele was suspended from his governorship by the lord chamberlain, then the Duke of Newcastle. This event brought into focus the ambiguities of the government's attempt to control the stage. The quarrel between Steele and Newcastle stemmed directly from the ill-defined relationship between patentee and lord chamberlain, a relationship that had been awkward since Charles II granted theatrical patents to D'Avenant and Killigrew. Unlike earlier patentees who submitted peaceably to the authority of the lord chamberlain,[6] Steele protested violently when Newcastle intervened in Drury Lane affairs, and initiated a journalistic campaign that brought his grievances to public review. In the pamphleteering that resulted, contemporary opinion about stage government and the state of drama received a thorough airing. Complicated as it was by political issues, Steele's dispute with Newcastle made more explicit than at any time since the Restoration the precise nature of the government of London theaters.

Steele's career at Drury Lane thus brought attention to issues that transcend his own activities in the theater. As his dispute with the lord chamberlain brought to a focus differences about theater government, so did his dramatic criticism and his most successful play, *The Conscious Lovers,* bring to a focus the sharp critical differences about the satirical comedy of the Restoration. The production of *The Conscious Lovers* occasioned a dispute of scarcely less magnitude than the one that followed Steele's suspension, a dispute in which for the first time the dramatic theory implicit in exemplary comedy was openly debated. Steele's prominence, coupled with the prolonged preparation for the play in his critical writings, combined to give *The Conscious Lovers* a reputation as an archetype of a new form of comedy that was not entirely deserved.[7]

_____

[6] Watson Nicholson, *The Struggle for a Free Stage in London* (Boston, 1906), p. 18.

[7] Cf. John Harrington Smith, "Shadwell, the Ladies, and Change in Comedy," *Modern Philology,* XLVI (1948), 22–33.

Certainly Steele was a pivotal figure in the theater of his day. Chief popularizer of the precepts of Jeremy Collier, he exerted through his dramatic criticism and the example of his comedies perhaps the most potent force in the eighteenth-century revolt against the satirical comedy of Etherege, Wycherley, and Congreve. His appointment to Drury Lane represented an official recognition of his service as a dramatic reformer, as well as an extension of his authority to theater management. He did not distinguish himself as a governor of the theater, but he identified himself with Drury Lane and brought to it disputes that, however troublesome to himself and his colleagues, are highly informative to historians of the stage. Despite his dereliction of duty, his was a memorable career in the eighteenth-century theater.

Part One | BACKGROUNDS

1 | Politics

IN VIEW of party feeling in the England of 1714, it would be naïve to assume that the appointment of Steele to the governorship of Drury Lane was entirely a disinterested attempt to improve the condition of the stage. Steele's appointment was prompted by political considerations quite as much as by concern for the state of drama, just as later his activities as governor of the theater were conditioned by his political fortunes. By placing Steele at the head of Drury Lane, the king could repay a political obligation as well as perform a service to the theater.

Few Whigs in the fall of 1714 were more unequivocally entitled to party rewards than Steele, who through the last troubled years of Anne's reign had demonstrated an uncompromising loyalty to the Whig cause and the Protestant succession. He had always been an active Whig, finding it difficult to suppress his enthusiasm for the party principles (even in the *Spectator* he and Addison had incorporated in the person of Sir Roger de Coverley a mild but perceptible satire of the traditional Tory virtues), but it was in his political tracts and pamphlets that he had rendered his most substantial service to the house of Hanover and to the Whig party.

A brief review of these political writings will make evident the strength of his claim to favors from George I.[1] He issued his first political pamphlet, *The Englishman's Thanks to the Duke of Marlborough*, on January 4, 1712, a mere five days after that nobleman was deprived of all offices by Queen Anne. The ecstatic praise Steele heaps on Marlborough appears deeply sincere in the light of the particularly inopportune time he chose for the letter. But it

---

[1] Steele's political tracts have been admirably edited by Rae Blanchard: *Tracts and Pamphlets by Richard Steele* (Baltimore, 1944).

was not until 1713, when the country was aroused over the question of the demolition of the French port of Dunkirk—a possible port of debarkation for a French-supported invasion by the Pretender James Edward—that Steele became a leading participant in political pamphleteering,[2] calling attention so frequently to the threat offered by the port that "Dunkirk" became a byword with which the Tory journalists taunted him. In four numbers of the *Guardian*, in *The Importance of Dunkirk Consider'd*, in repeated numbers of the *Englishman*, in *The Crisis*, in *The French Faith Represented in the Present State of Dunkirk*, and finally in *Mr. Steele's Apology for Himself and His Writings*, he made and repeated his charges and warnings. His warnings were unheeded by those in power, but his vigilance helped to prevent the harbor's use against England when she was exposed to a formidable enemy.

In the *Englishman* (first series), a periodical that ran to fifty-seven numbers, Steele confined himself almost entirely to matters immediately connected with the Hanoverian succession. In the first number he explained that Nestor Ironside had given over the *Guardian* because the nation was in too serious a condition for the "railleries of poets and philosophers"; his successor, the Englishman, would occupy himself more appropriately with the distressing condition of the world. And the Englishman kept his word, urging, in addition to the demolition of Dunkirk, the removal of the Pretender from Bar le Duc (because it was dangerously close to England) and the establishment of an open understanding between the Elector of Hanover and Queen Anne.

For such bold writing in opposition to the Tory government, Steele did not escape unpunished. Basing their charge on two numbers of the *Englishman* (Nos. 46 and 57) and on *The Crisis* (in which Steele reviews the legislation designed to insure a Protestant succession), the ministry accused him of sedition. Steele's own full, if not always unbiased, account of the ensuing proceedings against him appears in his longest political pamphlet, *Mr. Steele's Apology for Himself and His Writings*, written before the death of the queen but not published until King George was safely on the throne. The pamphlet has several informative autobiographical

---

[2] Cf. John Robert Moore, "Defoe, Steele, and the Demolition of Dunkirk," *Huntington Library Quarterly*, XIII (1950), 279–302.

passages, but most of it is devoted to a detailed account of the preliminaries and the actual hearing of Steele's case before the House of Commons, with the full text of his three-hour address in defense of himself. He relates that he had the honor to stand between Walpole and Stanhope before the bar, both of whom acted as counsels for the defense, a circumstance indicating the importance attached to the trial. The trial was openly recognized as a party contest, and, with the Tory majority functioning, Steele was, as he had anticipated, censored and formally expelled.

When he published *Mr. Steele's Apology* on October 22, 1714, little more than a month after the king landed in England, Steele could not have been unaware of the advantages to be gained by recalling to everyone's mind the services he had performed for the house of Hanover. It is true that the pamphlet was written—but not published—before Anne died; his motive in writing it perhaps had nothing to do with the hope of reward for his party sufferings. The pamphlet nevertheless provided an appropriate medium for tactfully emphasizing his claims to the bounty of the new monarch. Even before it appeared, however, the king began repaying his debt to Steele. Four days before the publication of the *Apology,* Steele received what was to prove his largest single reward for his political services—the governorship of Drury Lane.

2 | Reform

WHATEVER the combination of motives leading to Steele's appointment, the event was received hopefully by many who desired a more carefully supervised stage. Sir Richard Blackmore's sanguine prophecy has already been noted, and at least two of Blackmore's contemporaries recorded similar reactions to the appointment. "It were to be wished our Stage was Chaster," wrote Lady Cowper, "and I cannot but hope, now it is under Mr. *Steele's*

Direction, that it will mend."[3] Thomas Brereton, after a conventional lament for the condition of the stage (including a blast at Jeremy Collier and his partisans), expressed hope for it from "the apt Genius of the polite Person who has the Direction of it at present."[4] From one of Steele's reputation, obviously much was expected.

Blackmore, Lady Cowper, and Brereton doubtlessly based their expectations on Steele's essays, in which he had shown himself at once a reformer and a devoted friend of the theater, precisely the combination desired by the less extreme of the critics of the stage. Several years earlier Edward Filmer had objected to Collier that not satirical attacks but sympathetic guidance would be effective in amending the theater.[5] Filmer made no reference to Steele, but the principle he enunciated is evident in the satisfaction at Steele's appointment. From at least the time of Dennis's *Usefulness of the Stage* (June, 1698) it was recognized that Collier attacked not merely stage abuses but the stage itself: if the theater were to be affected by Collier's precepts without being destroyed, a compromise had to be reached. Uneasy compromises had already been attempted (among them the appointment of Vanbrugh and Congreve to the Haymarket in 1705),[6] but perhaps none that promised so well as the appointment to the governorship of the principal London theater of the man who, more than any other, had popularized the complaints of the reformers.

Testimony is abundant to the efficacy of Steele's attempts at reform. John Gay's praise in *The Present State of Wit*[7] is the most famous, but there are many other statements, including one by Cibber. "While the world was under the daily correction and authority of your *Lucubrations*," he wrote, "their influence on the publick was not more visible in any one instance, than the sudden

---

[3] *The Diary of Mary Countess Cowper, Lady of the Bedchamber to the Princess of Wales, 1714–1720* (London, 1864), entry for February 15, 1715, pp. 46–47.

[4] Dedication to *Esther: or Faith Triumphant* (London, 1715).

[5] Preface to *A Defence of Plays* (London, 1707).

[6] Krutch, *Comedy and Conscience*, pp. 185–189.

[7] *The Present State of Wit* (London, 1711), Augustan Reprint Society, Series One, No. 3, 1947, pp. 3–4.

improvement (I might say reformation) of the Stage that immediately followed them. . . ."⁸ And the allusions to Steele as "the Censor of Great Britain" are, of course, legion. It is unnecessary to labor the point: in the eyes of his contemporaries Steele, during the decade following the establishment of the *Tatler*, was the most famous and most effective reformer of the age.

Repeatedly in his periodicals—especially in the *Tatler*—Steele denounced stage abuses (those Collier had specified), but he did so with a novel moderation and tact, presenting his precepts forcefully but without arousing the antagonism of the playwrights, actors, and theater-goers of London. It was his particular gift, in Gay's famous phrase, to "make virtue fashionable." Where Jeremy Collier provoked resentment and indignation, Steele, without sacrificing essential principles, won a sympathetic hearing by virtue of being more temperate. He more shrewdly gauged his audience. Collier assailed plays that could be considered immoral only by puritanical standards; Steele attacked plays of a more extreme kind, such as *The Man of Mode*, avoiding the absurdities to which Collier's zeal extended. Steele's graceful humor was always a protection from the ridicule that other reformers suffered. Dramatists and stage managers were willing to accept reprimands from a sophisticated member of their own group.

Yet Steele's genial campaign for stage reform was not universally applauded. The more extreme of the reformers charged that the good accomplished by his moral criticism was more than annulled by the impetus his writings gave to theater attendance, regarded by extremists as inescapably evil. Here, of course, we come to the impassable barrier between Steele and the more devoted of the followers of Collier. Steele insisted vehemently that the stage could be made a powerful agent for propagating Christian virtue; the extremists were unwilling to allow the existence of the stage.

Representative of the illiberal attitude is a pamphlet by Defoe that merits special attention because of its clear formulation of the extremists' position. It voices at the same time objections to Steele which, when considered, serve to explain why friends of the stage were grateful to him. In intent this pamphlet, *The Fears*

⁸ Dedication of *Ximena, or the Heroick Daughter* (London, 1719).

of the Pretender Turn'd into the Fears of Debauchery with a Hint to Richard Steele, Esq. (1715), is a dissuasive from the playhouse, including an indictment of Steele as the individual chiefly responsible for the growth in popularity of plays. Defoe acknowledges Steele's service to the nation in exposing many petty vices, and he asserts that because of this service Steele is entitled to forgiveness for misdeeds of an ordinary nature. However,

It can never be forgiven him, either by God, or Man, till he Repents of, and Reforms it; that he did more by recommending the Play-Houses, to promote the present Madness of the Age, in running up the Humour of following Plays to such an Extream, as we now see it, than all the Agents Hell ever employed before. . . .

Here, what he pleas'd to mention, was ever admir'd; and for the *Spectator* to give a good Word to a Play, was to fill the House. In process of Time, his Name was put to the Prologue and Epilogue, to push a Play into the World; and for a grave Person, in an Antik Dress, with a Comick Gravity, to sit in a Box, and suppos'd, tho' but in Banter, to be the *Spectator,* was sufficient to draw the whole Town to the Theatre.

By these Things, it is not to be imagined, what Number of People, from City and Country, (who could Entertain themselves before, with Innocent Diversion, and good Company, and had no Opinion of the Play-Houses,) were drawn in by Crowds, to follow the Stage; and Plays were represented in such a Manner, in so many Particulars, as that it was not doubted, but the Stage would go farther to settle our Vertue than the Pulpit, and we should be Play'd out of Vice and Profaneness, sooner than Preach'd out of it.[9]

The extremists, then, for whom Defoe is a representative spokesman, did not accept Steele as an ally; they regarded him rather as himself an offending playwright with the added guilt of having increased enormously the popularity of the theaters. Even his attempt to make the stage a moral agent aroused objections.

But Steele, on his side, warmly acknowledged his allegiance to the reformers' chief, Jeremy Collier, declaring in his *Apology* that he wrote *The Lying Lover* in the "severity" required by Collier— though the play was damned for his efforts.[10] His dramatic criticism and comedies, indeed, offer indisputable proof of the strength of his attachment to Collier; in reading *A Short View* after a pro-

---

[9] Pp. 20–21.

[10] In *Tracts and Pamphlets,* pp. 311–312.

longed study of Steele's writings, one feels that he is reading Steele's source book, so strikingly similar are many of Collier's and Steele's complaints about the stage. That the reformers, of whom Collier was merely the most conspicuous,[11] influenced Steele strongly has, of course, always been common knowledge, but perhaps it has not always been realized how direct and circumstantial that influence was.

Nowhere is Steele's similarity to Collier more clearly evident— or more significant—than in his denunciations of the conventional "fine gentleman" of Restoration comedy, a character whom he, like Collier, insisted occasioned emulation rather than a merited contempt. The specific grounds for their objection to the character are virtually the same, as a comparison of a well-known passage from each of their writings will reveal. First, Collier's denunciation of Valentine in Congreve's *Love for Love*:

Valentine in *Love for Love* is (if I may so call him) the Hero of the *Play;* This Spark the *Poet* would pass for a Person of Virtue, but he speaks to late. 'Tis true, He was hearty in his Affection to *Angelica*. Now without question, to be in Love with a fine Lady of 30000 Pounds is a great Virtue! But then abating this single Commendation, *Valentine* is altogether compounded of Vice. He is a prodigal Debauchee, unnatural, and Profane, Obscene, Sawcy, and undutiful, And yet this Libertine is crown'd for the Man of Merit, has his Wishes thrown into his Lap, and makes the Happy *Exit*. . . .

To sum up the Evidence. A fine Gentleman, is a fine Whoring, Swearing, Smutty, Atheistical Man.[12]

Turn now to Steele's criticism of Dorimant in Etherege's *The Man of Mode:*

I will take for granted, that a fine Gentleman should be honest in his Actions, and refined in his Language. Instead of this, our Hero, in this Piece, is a direct Knave in his Designs, and a Clown in his Language. *Bellair* is his Admirer and Friend; in return for which, because he is forsooth a greater Wit than his said Friend, he thinks it reasonable to

---

[11] For a discussion of Collier's relationship to earlier literary criticism, see J. E. Spingarn, ed., *Critical Essays of the Seventeenth Century* (Oxford, 1908–1909), I, lxxxi–lxxxvii.

[12] *A Short View of the Immorality and Profaneness of the English Stage* (London, 1698), pp. 142–143.

perswade him to Marry a young Lady, whose Virtue, he thinks, will last no longer than till she is a Wife, and then she cannot but fall to his Share, as he is an irresistible fine Gentleman. The Falshood to Mrs. *Loveit*, and the Barbarity of Triumphing over her Anguish for losing him, is another Instance of his Honesty, as well as his good Nature. As to his fine Language; he calls the Orange Woman, who, it seems, is inclined to grow Fat, *An Over-grown Jade, with a Flasket of Guts before her;* and salutes her with a pretty Phrase of, *How now, Double Tripe?*

. . . I take the Shooe-maker to be, in reality, the Fine Gentleman of the Play: For it seems he is an Atheist. . . .[13]

Steele extends ideas already explicit in what Collier had written. Nor is this similarity inconsequential, for here we are at the crucial point of Steele's criticism of Restoration comedy: his rejection of the satirical theory by which Restoration dramatists sought to justify their presentation of depraved characters, characters such as Dorimant. Like Collier, he believed that Restoration dramatists had made adultery, irreverence, and profanity attractive by endowing witty, sophisticated, and successful characters with those vices, denying, as did Collier, that the debauched characters aroused feelings of revulsion in the spectators. It is but a step from the denunciation of the heroes of Restoration comedy, represented by Dorimant, to the exposition of the admirable qualities of a new type of hero for comedy, later to be personified by Bevil, Jr., the exemplary young protagonist of *The Conscious Lovers;* indeed, John Dennis accused Steele of writing the *Spectator*, No. 65, to prepare the way for that play.[14] Steele's conception of a fit hero for comedy may be accurately described as one possessing the antithesis of the moral qualities of Dorimant (and, with some reservations, of Valentine).

Although it was not until *The Conscious Lovers* that Steele revealed his rival to Dorimant, even in his early comedies he scrupulously avoided the characters to which Collier had taken exception, self-consciously preventing any confusion of moral values. In *The Funeral* (1701), as he himself observed, although there are comic incidents that move laughter, "Virtue and Vice

[13] The *Spectator*, No. 65.

[14] *A Defence of Sir Fopling Flutter*. In Edward Niles Hooker, ed., *The Critical Works of John Dennis* (Baltimore, 1939–1943), II, 244.

appear just as they ought to do."[15] Lord Hardy and Campley, the sympathetic and successful leading characters, are sometimes misled by high spirits into bold remarks, but they are thoroughly admirable young gentlemen, revealing a Christian sensitivity to the afflictions of others. Campley's clandestine gift to Hardy is a magnanimous act of benevolence; Hardy's generosity and filial devotion anticipate the perfection of Bevil, Jr. In *The Lying Lover* (1703) Steele's method is somewhat different (partly, perhaps, because he followed Corneille's *Le Menteur* very closely), but again his didactic technique is direct rather than satiric. In Young Bookwit, vice and folly are totally unsuccessful, virtue only offering a reward; his unhappy prison experience produces reflections on misconduct that cannot be misunderstood. Steele approached the satiric manner of Restoration comedy most closely in *The Tender Husband* (1705), the merry pranks that enliven the play providing a strong contrast to the sober, reasonable behavior of the "conscious lovers." Never, however, is there any serious confusion of values; the ridiculous characters are easily recognizable as such, whereas vicious characters do not exist. Captain Clerimont and his sister-in-law, Mrs. Clerimont, their playful intrigues notwithstanding, are fundamentally honorable, as are without exception all the characters who appear in the play—even Pounce, the scheming lawyer, proves to be a benevolent brother.

It is, of course, in *The Conscious Lovers* (1722) that Steele's revolt against the Restoration attitude toward moral qualities comes to its climax. For several years before his appointment to Drury Lane he was planning and talking about the play; his plans for it were known to his friends for some time before 1714. However, that play, occasioning a large-scale critical controversy as it did, must receive separate and more extensive treatment.

Steele's affinity with Collier is revealed not in his dramatic characters alone but in several aspects of his comic theory, as in his distrust of laughter and ridicule. In answering the critics who would make delight rather than instruction the chief end of comedy, Collier had suggested, in terms anticipating Steele, that laughter and madness are near allied: "...certainly Mirth and Laughing, without respect to the Cause, are not such supreme Satisfactions! A man has sometimes Pleasure in losing his Wits.

[15] *Mr. Steele's Apology*, in *Tracts and Pamphlets*, p. 339.

Frensy, and *Possession*, will shake the Lungs, and brighten the Face; and yet I suppose they are not much to be coveted."[16] In the same vein Steele charged Restoration dramatists with the fault of misdirected ridicule, with making virtue ridiculous; it was they, he insisted, who had made matrimony odious to fashionable people by laughing at it.[17] Nor did he confine his objections to ridicule of improper subjects. Curious as it appears from a writer of his unquestioned gift for humor, he persistently expressed a distrust of laughter itself (while creating several delightfully comic characters), insisting, in theory at least, on the superiority of the more severe pleasures.[18] His indictment of laughter in the epilogue to *The Lying Lover* links it, as Collier had done, to insanity:

> For laughter's a distorted passion, born
> Of sudden self-esteem and sudden scorn;
> Which, when 'tis o'er, the men in pleasure wise,
> Both him that moved it and themselves despise. . . .

As late as the preface to *The Conscious Lovers*, in justifying the inclusion of a pathetic event in comedy, he wrote of "a joy too exquisite for laughter."

It will be enough to mention one more similarity of detail between Collier and Steele. In a passage with which Steele would have agreed without reservation, Collier reproached the dramatists for encouraging dueling:

What is more Common than Duels and Quarelling in their *Characters* of Figure? Those Practises which are infamous in Reason, *Capital* in *Law*, and Damnable in Religion, are the Credit of the *Stage*. Thus Rage and Resentment, Blood and Barbarity, are almost Deified.[19]

Subdue the tones and we could mistake the writer for Steele, in whose writings the condemnation of dueling is so characteristic as to serve as an identifying theme.

Steele's service to Collier and the legion of his fellow reformers was that of a popularizer; indeed, as well as such an intangible matter can be determined, he was the person most influential in

---

[16] *A Short View*, p. 162.
[17] Cf. the *Tatler*, No. 199.
[18] Cf. *ibid.*, No. 15.
[19] *A Short View*, p. 283.

gaining a sympathetic hearing for their complaints. Not Addison, as has sometimes been asserted,[20] but Steele is entitled to that distinction. In the *Tatler*, of which Steele was the entrepreneur, more than in the *Spectator*, under Addison's leadership, the stage and its abuses came under scrutiny; the relevant essays within these periodicals, moreover, were more often than not from Steele's pen. Addison supported the reformers (conspicuously in the *Spectator*, No. 446), but his writings on stage abuses were less numerous and less compelling than his collaborator's. Beyond the partnership, no one appears to challenge Steele's position.

Strong ally of the reformers though Steele was, there always remained one major difference from the extremists among them—Steele insisted on the usefulness of the stage. It must be remembered that in Steele's essays in defense of the stage he was answering the many highly articulate reformers who would deny it existence. Because the arguments advanced by the opposition have largely disappeared, it is sometimes forgotten that Steele's arguments, their genial tone notwithstanding, were originally controversial. Consider, for example, the following passage from the *Guardian* in contrast to the indictment of the stage by Defoe previously quoted:

The love of virtue, which has been so warmly roused by this admirable piece [*Cato*] in all parts of the theatre, is an unanswerable instance of how great force the stage might be towards the improvement of the world, were it regarded and encouraged as much as it ought. There is no medium in this case, for the advantage of action, and the representation of vice and virtue in an agreeable or odious manner before our eyes, are so irresistibly prevalent, that the theatre ought to be shut up, or carefully governed, in any nation that values the promotion of virtue or guard of innocence among its people. Speeches or sermons will ever suffer, in some degree, from the characters of those that make them; and mankind are so unwilling to reflect on what makes for their own mortification, that they are ever cavilling against the lives of those who speak in the cause of goodness, to keep themselves in countenance, and continue in beloved infirmities. But in the case of the stage, envy and detraction are baffled, and none are offended, but all insensibly won by personated characters, which they

[20] Notably by Alexandre Beljame, who credits Addison with some of Steele's essays: *Men of Letters and the English Public in the Eighteenth Century*, English edition (London, 1948), 230–246.

neither look upon as their rivals or superiors; every man that has any degree of what is laudable in a theatrical character, is secretly pleased, and encouraged, in the prosecution of that virtue without fancying any man about him has more of it.[21]

Here is not mere affirmation of the moral usefulness of the stage but a penetrating explanation, the more effective because not extravagant, of the means by which moral teaching is conveyed. Steele acknowledges the danger of an improperly conducted stage, a danger that is a correlative of the stage's potency as an agent for the dissemination of ideas. He is moderate and reasonable, but his studied logic reveals an argumentative purpose.

Perhaps equally effective in his defense of the stage was Steele's espousing the cause of the actors—his insistence that theirs was an honorable profession, entitled to the respect and gratitude of society. The social status of actors had risen since the Restoration (partly as a result of the example afforded by Thomas Betterton), but it was still low enough to invite contempt; the profession was at best a semirespectable one, carrying a stigma that only the most conspicuous success could overcome. Although related to the general disesteem for the theaters, the contempt for the players was more far-reaching, some of the firmest of the defenders of the theater as an institution—John Dennis, Aaron Hill, George Sewell, and Charles Gildon among others—regarding them as little better than hired menials. That an actor should presume to alter the work of a playwright, to set up for a playwright himself, or to manage a theater was matter for satire. This at the time when the actor-managers were emerging as the dominant force at Drury Lane. With Steele, an intimate of Cibber and Wilks from the first years of the century, matters were emphatically otherwise, as he abundantly demonstrated in his essays. Why are not the actors more esteemed? he inquires in the *Tatler*. "If the merit of a performance is to be valued according to the talents which are necessary to it, the qualifications of a player should raise him much above the arts and ways of life which we call mercenary or mechanic."[22] The player, who by his talents adds immeasurably to the effect of a dramatic performance, properly should enjoy the appro-

---

[21] No. 43.
[22] The *Tatler*, No. 182.

bation of those to whose pleasure and improvement he contributes. Few of Steele's essays are more applauded than that in the *Tatler* in which, with an appropriate dignity, he describes Betterton's funeral in Westminster Abbey, allowing the occasion to suggest a meditation on Betterton's career. "Such an actor as Mr. Betterton," Steele observes, "ought to be recorded with the same respect as Roscius among the Romans."[23]

Steele's praise of the actors meant tangible profits to them as well as improved social status, and most of them were no doubt more grateful for the larger crowds on benefit nights than for the more kindly regard of the quality. Betterton, Cibber, Wilks, Doggett, Mills, Estcourt, Hart, and Mohun, among others, enjoyed direct notices in Steele's periodicals, and we have it on Cibber's authority that the notices were effective.[24]

So far Steele has been considered as an enlightened champion of theatrical reform. He was that beyond dispute. Yet a word of qualification is required. Steele was extraordinarily persistent in urging the amendment of theatrical abuses (to the point of monotony), but his dramatic criticism is not so exclusively dominated by the theme of reform that purely aesthetic principles are totally submerged. His didactic preoccupation is seldom obscured, but it is not always dominant, many of his discussions of Restoration comedy—the chief provocation for Collier's attack—revealing no animus but rather a penetrating interest in dramatic merits. He specifically commends some of the plays that Collier had condemned—*Love for Love,* for example[25]—and ignores the moral issues. Throughout his career Restoration comedy formed a large part of the repertory of the London theaters, and he showed no inclination to condemn it wholesale. On the contrary, he praised, with varying degrees of enthusiasm, many of the plays considered most characteristic of the type: *The Old Bachelor* ("a comedy of deserved reputation"), *The Way of the World, The Constant Couple, Epsom Wells* and even *The Country Wife.*

This last play raises special problems that Steele was forced to

[23] No. 167.

[24] R. W. Lowe, ed., *An Apology for the Life of Mr. Colley Cibber* (London, 1889), II, 162.

[25] The *Tatler,* No. 1. Cf. also Addison in No. 120.

consider,[26] but it is significant that he did not condemn it as he later did *The Man of Mode.* He acknowledged in Wycherley's play, as he did not in Etherege's, the satirical intent of the action. He was tolerant even of Horner. "The character of Horner, and the design of it, is a good representation of the age in which that comedy was written. . . ," he wrote, allowing the historical argument to excuse the representation of a depraved and, we may add, successful character. By way of qualification he remarked that such a character as Horner would not be accepted from a playwright of Steele's own age because of the change for the better in the conception of the "fine gentleman." Steele's historical defense of Horner resembles the argument Dennis later employed in answer to Steele's denunciation of Dorimant. Dorimant was recognized by Etherege's contemporaries, Dennis asserted, as a dramatic portrait of the Earl of Rochester and hence was a faithful representation of a gentleman of Charles II's court, the authenticity of the portrait justifying it.[27] At this later time Steele did not agree. If confronted with his inconsistency, perhaps he would have insisted that Wycherley's satirical intent was more clearly marked than Etherege's. At any rate he seems to have been less scrupulously sensitive to the portrayal of a debauched character in 1709 than later.

His dramatic criticism betrays, then, a lack of a thoroughgoing consistency. As his essays are the result of reflections scattered over a number of years, many of them suggested by the performances of plays, it is not surprising that his emphasis shifts—now toward aesthetic qualities, now toward moral values. If a trend is discernible (and it can be detected only indistinctly), it is in the direction of increased piety as he grew older. His "Commendatory Verses" for *The Way of the World,* at the turn of the century, and a laudatory prologue for Vanbrugh's *The Mistake,* in 1705, reveal him publicly associated with comedies by playwrights who had felt the sting of Collier's attack; his early plays are less obviously pious than his last one; his journalistic commendation of specific plays, most of which were Restoration comedies, occurs with greater frequency in the early numbers of the *Tatler* than anywhere else in

---

[26] The *Tatler,* No. 3.
[27] *A Defence of Sir Fopling Flutter,* in Hooker, *Dennis,* II, 248.

his writings. Progressively through his several series of essays, he wrote more about dramatic theory and less about individual plays, his theory betraying his moral bias more clearly than his critical judgments. This trend toward a heavier didacticism is partly to be associated with his preparing the way over a number of years for *The Conscious Lovers,* a preparation that included an exposition of the theory of exemplary comedy with its openly didactic intent. However, the fact of the growing moral concern helps to explain why ideas in an essay written in 1709 are inconsistent with some expressed later.

These inconsistencies to the contrary, Steele was at all times unmistakably on the side of the reformers, and he was considered an ally by the large number of them who believed that the stage, under proper regulation, could support Christian morality. Hence the expressions of satisfaction at his appointment to Drury Lane. It was possible to detect in the appointment, through the haze of political expediency that conditioned it, a triumph for the sympathizers with Jeremy Collier. Because of "his publick services to Religion and Vertue" as well as "his steady adherence to the true interest of his country,"[28] George I deemed Steele a fit man to govern the Theatre-Royal.

3 | # Drury Lane and the Tories

IT IS in no way surprising that Steele was made governor of Drury Lane in the fall of 1714, when his party came back into power; he was both well qualified for the position and entitled to political rewards. However, it appears that his qualifications for the post were recognized even before the accession of George I— recognized, in fact, by his political opponents, the Tories led by Robert Harley. He was offered the theater (presumably Drury Lane) during the last years of Anne's reign through the comp-

---

[28] These phrases appear in Steele's patent, issued January 19, 1715.

troller of her household, Lord Lansdowne, Jacobite Tory and one of the "occasional" peers about whom Steele wrote bitterly in March, 1713.[29]

Our knowledge of this offer comes chiefly from the dedication of a sermon to Steele by David Scurlock (a cousin of Lady Steele) in 1720 during Steele's suspension from Drury Lane, a dedication in which Scurlock holds up Steele as an example of the virtues extolled in his sermon—notably, unselfish devotion to the public interest. In elaborating his point, he recalls the ingratitude Steele has encountered in recompense for his faithful service to his party:

In the meantime, I hope, Sir, painful experience will reduce you *to think of your family, at least, as belonging to the Nation,* and not to give up yourself, as you have formerly, in resigning your employments and income, for the sake of such friends as take from you what those you used like adversaries offered you. Consider what an appearance you must make to so elegant and generous a gentleman as the Lord Lansdowne, who offered you the theatre in your own way, without solicitation, in the last reign, now it is torn from you, in spite of the strongest instrument by which Power could give it you, in this?[30]

Steele himself alluded to this offer in a petition he addressed to the king in 1715 (requesting that he be named master of the charterhouse). Steele wished to show the indebtedness of the crown to him—to point out (as Scurlock did later) the ingratitude he had experienced for his service to the house of Hanover before Anne's death:

Qu'il entra dans la Chambre des communes quoiqu'il sçut que son Zele l'avoit rendu si odieux, qu'il en seroit chassé; et qu'il ne le fit que dans la Vue d'allarmer la nation en lui faisant connoitre par la liberté de ses discours, le Danger ou elle etoit, en donnant occasion à quelques membres de l'attaquer sur ce qu'il avoit ecrit.

Qu'on lui avoit offert ci-devant la direction du Theatre, parce qu'on le connoit capable de Rectifier les Representations qui s'y font.[31]

Que sous le Reyne de Votre Majesté il a presenté une Tres Humble Requête pour avoir la direction du Theatre qu'il avoit refusée auparavant.

_____

[29] In *A Letter to Sir M.[iles] W.[arton] Concerning Occasional Peers.*

[30] Quoted from George A. Aitken, *The Life of Richard Steele* (London, 1889), II, 246–247.

[31] Italics mine.

Votre Majesté a eu la Bonté de Lui en accorder une Patente, mois [sic] le Revenu de cet emploi est fort incertain.[32]

The offer was made then, according to Steele, because it was known that he was capable of reforming the stage. Is it possible that the zeal for reform was strong enough to overcome party prejudice?

In view of Steele's interest in the theater and in reform and his usual need for money, it would at first seem curious that if he was offered the theater during the reign of Anne he did not take it. But a closer examination of the available evidence suggests that, Steele's statement to the contrary, the offer was a political one, which he refused for political reasons.

In the paragraph in which he mentions Lord Lansdowne, David Scurlock urges Steele "not to give up yourself, as you have formerly, in resigning your employments and income, for the sake of such friends as take from you what those you used like adversaries offered you." He refers to Steele's resignation of his commissionership of stamps and his pension as gentleman-usher to the late Prince George of Denmark, both in the summer of 1713, just before his election to a seat in the House of Commons. Steele wrote to the lord treasurer, Harley, on June 4, 1713, announcing his intention to seek a place in Parliament, and requesting, in order to be eligible for election, that his resignation as commissioner of the stamp-revenue be accepted.[33] Harley, apparently not anxious to be rid of him, did not act immediately, and Steele had to write again on July 30, 1713.[34] His resignation was accepted in time, however, for him to be elected on August 25. Steele resigned his pension the same summer. He wished to avoid any obligation to the ministry, which he felt compelled to attack in his writings and which he was now openly to oppose in Parliament. In *The Importance of Dunkirk Considered*, published in September, 1713, he mentioned the taunts hurled at him by the *Examiner* for criticizing the queen's policy, or more properly that of her ministers, while

[32] Blenheim MSS. Aitken, *Life*, II, 76. Aitken fails to note this allusion to the early offer of the theater: cf. *ibid.*, II, 247.

[33] Rae Blanchard, ed., *The Correspondence of Richard Steele* (London, 1941), pp. 79–80.

[34] *Ibid.*, p. 82.

"eating her Bread";[85] by clearing himself of any obligation to the ministry led by Harley, he could more easily defend his reputation for personal integrity.

Now Lord Lansdowne, who—according to David Scurlock— offered Steele the theater, was in the Tory ministry under Harley.[86] Following the sweeping Tory victory of the autumn of 1710, George Granville was appointed secretary of war. He performed his duties satisfactorily, gave faithful attendance to St. John and Harley, and grew in favor and influence with the party and with the queen. Early in 1712 he was created Baron Lansdowne as one of the twelve whom Harley persuaded the queen to ennoble in order to insure a Tory majority in the House of Lords. Although he was the most generally acceptable of the new lords—he was the actual head of an old family in which two titles had recently become extinct— along with the others he had to undergo ridicule directed at the mass production of peers; and he could scarcely have been un- aware of Steele's strictures in *A Letter to Sir M.[iles] W.[arton] Concerning Occasional Peers* (March, 1713). As the pamphlet was issued anonymously, however, he may not have known who wrote it. Lansdowne's influence grew, and in June, 1712, he was given the more important post of comptroller of the household in exchange for his secretaryship of war. Two months later he was made a member of the privy council, which was to have the all- important task of naming the queen's successor.

But why should a man in Lansdowne's position make an offer of the theater to a vociferous member of the opposition, above all to one who had written a pamphlet on the tender subject of occa- sional peers? We may only surmise. We do know that Lansdowne was himself a poet and dramatist and that he was a liberal friend to other poets and dramatists. Testimony to his generosity at about the time of the offer to Steele is an impressive list of dedications and literary compliments to him from, among others, Pope, Young, and Dennis. That he was a magnanimous and generous patron of men of letters cannot be doubted; and from the facts

---

[85] In *Tracts and Pamphlets*, p. 99.

[86] I have taken the facts of Lansdowne's career from Elizabeth Handa- syde, *Granville the Polite: The Life of George Granville Lord Lansdowne, 1666–1735* (London, 1933).

available it appears that his generosity extended to his political opponent, Steele.

Although a prominent officer in the royal household, Lansdowne did not, of course, have supervision of the stage—as always, that responsibility was the lord chamberlain's. Nevertheless, he had influence in theatrical affairs, as shown by an appeal addressed to him by Barton Booth for assistance in gaining admission to partnership in the Drury Lane management. Booth's letter, dated December 16, 1712, reveals Lansdowne's contemporary reputation as an influential intermediary in procuring theatrical favors:

> I Know the Worth, and honour of the Vice Chamberlain, but not being so well Known to Him, as to your Lordship, I have humbly begg'd of You to be my Patron, and Advocate to him; and I am well assurd, he has ever had a just, and true Regard for your Lordship.
>
> I must beg leave to tell your Lordship, that you are an Honour and an Ornament to Dramatic Poetry in Particular. The Knowledge of that naturally inclind me to beleive, your Lordship woud readily endeavour to help an oppressd actor, who has had the good fortune to please the Town, and sometimes your Lordship, whose Judgement I would willingly stand or fall by.[37]

The letter is the more relevant to Steele's case because of its date— the offer to Steele probably came within a few months of December, 1712, certainly not much more than a year from that time.

But what about political considerations? Would Harley have agreed to Steele's appointment? And was Swift, who always maintained that he influenced the ministry to favor Whig authors, in any way responsible for the offer to Steele—or even aware of it? The offer came from Lansdowne, but it is not at all likely that he could have made it without the full approval of Harley. What then is the probability that the approval was given? The theater was an important political gift, which would not have been offered casually to an active member of the opposition.

It is known that Robert Harley was moderate in his treatment of the opposition; he was conciliatory toward the Whigs to an extent that aroused the anger of the extreme elements in his party.[38] And among the Whigs whom he courted, whose support

[37] British Museum, Additional MS 38607, fol. 9.

[38] See George Macaulay Trevelyan, *England Under Queen Anne* (London, 1934), III, chaps. 6, 7.

he particularly wished, were the poets and authors. He was eager to secure the allegiance of men who were capable of performing journalistic service for his ministry. He was shrewd enough, as everyone knows, to attract Jonathan Swift to his side. Is it not possible that Harley was angling for the services of Steele also—that the theater was offered to Steele as a sort of tacit bribe for his support, or perhaps even his silence?

It is, indeed, known positively that Steele turned down some attractive offers from Harley's ministry. In a letter written in 1715 to the Duke of Newcastle, Steele, in recounting his sufferings in the Whig cause, observes: "I do not insist upon what offers I have refused...."[39] More convincingly, Colley Cibber (himself a manager of Drury Lane during Anne's last years) wrote in a dedicatory epistle to Steele in 1719:

It gives but a melancholy reflection to know, that while in the late reign you were warmly supporting our staggering hopes of the Protestant Succession, the enemies of it, then in power, were subtle enough to offer you a security of fortune only to be *silent*—An uncomfortable account—that even the *forbearance of a virtue* should be worth more than the *use* of it.[40]

Cibber does not assert that Steele was offered the theater, but his allusion to the ingratitude of the present ministry as compared with the liberality of the former one, to which Steele was a professed enemy, is remarkably like Scurlock's allusion to Lansdowne's offer.

What is known of the relations between Harley and Steele offers no obstacle to believing that the minister was eager for the journalist's support. John Forster, the nineteenth-century biographer of Swift, remarked that "Harley doubtless would have been glad to get Steele back, or any part of him back, on any terms ...,"[41]

[39] *Correspondence*, p. 102.

[40] Dedication of *Ximena*. J. Oldmixon in *The Life and Posthumous Works of Arthur Maynwaring* (London, 1715), p. 193, recalls Steele's authorship of the *Medley*, No. 23, adding that Steele "was then [1711] courted by the Treasurer to come into his Interests, but Mr. *Steele* prefer'd those of his Country, even to his own, and frequently attack'd those hated Ministers with his Pen, under other Names when he did not think fit to make use of his own, while he was Commissioner of the *Stamp-Office*."

[41] *The Life of Jonathan Swift* (New York, 1876), I, 301.

and such certainly seems to have been the case. Swift took credit for intervening with Harley for Steele, for making it possible for him to keep his commissionership of stamps, but it is apparent that Steele believed Swift had not helped him. "They laugh at you," Steele wrote bitterly in May, 1713, in answer to Swift's assertion that it was he who had kept Steele in his employment, "if they make you believe your interposition has kept me thus long in my office."[42] Two months earlier George Berkeley, in describing to Sir John Percival the academy Steele planned to conduct in York Buildings, suggested indirectly but positively Steele's good relations with Harley. "He [Steele] tells me he has had some discourse with the Lord Treasurer relating to it [the academy], and talks as if he would engage my Lord Treasurer in his project, designing that it shall comprehend both Whigs and Tories. . . ."[43] Steele apparently did not gain Harley's support—the plans for the academy came to nothing until 1715—but Berkeley's remark is nevertheless convincing evidence that Steele was on good terms with the Tory lord treasurer early in 1713.

The extant letters of Steele to Harley are testimony to the amicable relations between them. "The generous treatment which I have had from your Lordship," Steele wrote in August, 1712, "exacts all that I am capable of doing, for the advancement of anything more immediately under your administration."[44] In his letter resigning his commissionership, written in June, 1713, Steele remarks: "When I had the honour of a short conversation with you, you were pleased not only to signifie to me that I should remain in this Office, but to add that if I would name to you one of more value which would be more commodious to me, you would favour me in it."[45] Small wonder that Steele mocked at Swift's claim that he had prevented his dismissal. Since Harley, then, made a strong show of friendship to Steele—a stronger one than Swift realized—it seems likely that he would have given his approval to Lansdowne's offer, if indeed he did not suggest it.

[42] *Correspondence*, pp. 72–73.
[43] Benjamin Rand, ed., *The Correspondence of George Berkeley and Sir John Percival* (Cambridge, 1941), p. 112.
[44] *Correspondence*, p. 59.
[45] *Ibid.*, p. 79.

One additional matter is relevant. Queen Anne was actively concerned about the immorality of the stage. By no means did she wish to close the theaters, and she seemed inclined to encourage the men of the theater themselves rather than outsiders to accomplish the reforms. Yet throughout her reign she made efforts to bring the stage under control. There were a series of attempts, none completely successful, as I have already said, at legal reform of the stage. One of the attempts may have included the appointment of Steele to the governorship of Drury Lane.

How much of our knowledge of this early offer of the theater is fact; how much supposition? What is the probable date of the offer? We know that the offer came from Lansdowne, who was in the ministry from 1710 until the death of Anne, but was comptroller of the household and very close to the queen only from June, 1712, until her death. Harley was on good terms with Steele at least until the summer of 1713, and he was, in all probability, eager to secure his journalistic support or at least his silence. Cibber wrote that Harley's ministry made some remunerative offer to Steele. We know that during the reign of Anne the stage was in chronic need of reform and that Steele had a wide reputation as a reformer. Not until the summer of 1713, when his political interests were intensified, did Steele feel any apparent reluctance about accepting or holding Tory gifts; had the theater been offered to him before then, probably he would have accepted. In March, 1714, he was expelled from the House of Commons for writings he published in January and February of that year, his expulsion establishing a date after which the offer could scarcely have been made. The date indicated, then, by our knowledge of Steele's life is 1713. It is corroborated by what we know of Lansdowne's activities at the time and by David Scurlock's mentioning the offer of the theater in conjunction with Steele's resigning his pension and his employment under the Tory ministry.[46]

A note from Steele to his wife, written April 22, 1713, provides

[46] The only evidence that does not suggest 1713 is Oldmixon's statement that Steele was courted by the treasurer at the time he wrote a number of the *Medley*—that is, in 1711. Steele himself in June, 1713, alluded to Harley's "courting" him, as though an offer had recently been made. Probably Harley tried for several years to gain Steele's allegiance.

very tentatively a more exact dating of the offer. "I have met with Doggett and We shall fall into a discourse which will turn to account. I shall dine with him at some Eating House...."[47] Thomas Doggett was at the time one of the actor-managers of Drury Lane.[48] In view of Steele's phrasing and the date (only a month after Berkeley's indirect statement about the Harley-Steele friendship), it is likely that the meeting was in some way connected with the ministry's offer of the theater.

4 | The License

WHEN the death of Queen Anne terminated the license authorizing the Drury Lane company to present plays, the actor-managers had been in virtually complete control of the theater's internal affairs for about three years. Following a series of managerial revolutions—chronicled in Cibber's *Apology*—they came to undisputed power in 1711, when they were successful in depriving their partner Owen Swiney of any active share in the management. They compelled him to accept a stipend of £600 a year rather than a portion of the profits. In 1712 William Collier, a Tory lawyer with influence at court, replaced Swiney as the silent partner in the company and received an increased stipend of £700, but he took no more part in the business of the theater than had Swiney. Since coming to power, the actor-managers had also experienced a change in their own ranks, Barton Booth replacing Thomas Doggett. Doggett, who with Robert Wilks and Colley

[47] *Correspondence*, pp. 285–286. In her note appended to this letter, Professor Blanchard suggests that this meeting was connected with the offer mentioned by Scurlock.

[48] Aitken mistakenly commented that Doggett had withdrawn from the Drury Lane management before this note was written: cf. *Life,* I, 376n. Actually Doggett did not withdraw until the following winter—when Booth gained admission to the partnership.

Cibber formed the original triumvirate, retired soon after Booth in the fall of 1713 forced the managers to accept him as a partner. The number of active managers thus remained at three, although Doggett retained a disputed claim to a share in the profits and stage properties.[49]

The theater management under the actor-managers was not without internal conflicts, but it was stable enough for their substantial talents to be efficiently employed in their dual capacities. They were then in their prime as actors—all four of them (if both Booth and Doggett are included) were already distinguished. Their acting skills, moreover, were complementary, allowing them to work together without rivalry for roles. In their business affairs they were cautious and methodical; they conducted their affairs according to an established routine that gave the theater a reputation for dependability.[50] In short, the actor-managers, whatever their later shortcomings, began their long domination of Drury Lane in a manner that promised well for both drama and their mutual profit.

This promising start was described many years later by Cibber, but it also attracted contemporary notice. Charles Johnson, in the flush of gratitude to the actor-managers for a successful performance of one of his plays, described quite specifically their service to the stage:

... I think those Gentlemen, who are honour'd with their Names in the Royal Licence, behave themselves worthy the Favour they Receive; They have at great Expence given the English Stage a Propriety and Elegance it never knew before, and added to the Beauties of the Poet the just Decorations of the Scene; in order to this they have within themselves Incourag'd the Diligent, and Discountenanc'd the Idle; They have indeavour'd by the best Copies from the best Authors, to revive in us a Taste for Tragedy; but I doubt we are not reform'd enough, nor they rich

---

[49] For an account of the rise of the actor-managers, see Richard Hindry Barker, *Mr. Cibber of Drury Lane* (New York, 1939), pp. 79–98.

[50] A document in the Public Record Office (L.C. 7/3) entitled "Rules and Regulations for the Management of the Theatres," drawn up during the last years of Anne's reign, provides an informative account of the actor-managers' weekly routine. It reveals that they operated the theater according to a systematic plan.

enough, yet to purchase it. As to the Incouragement they give those Gentlemen who write, I am an Instance No body who has the least Claim to Merit can want it....[51]

Johnson's enthusiasm for the actor-managers was conditioned by the substantial service they had done him in performing his play to advantage. Though others joined in praising them, his was decidedly not a unanimous view. Nevertheless, there is no reason to question his statement that the actor-managers had introduced a new polish to stage performances—that they had employed stage settings more effectively than before and had improved the discipline of the actors. Johnson mentions only indirectly "the Favour they Receive." However, there is no dispute about the prosperity of Drury Lane after the actor-managers came to authority—the profits were handsome.

Such then was the flourishing condition of Drury Lane when Steele entered the management. The reformers, it is true, were loud in their complaints about the theater's performances, yet at least some of the partisans of the stage saw in the emergence of the actor-managers a potent force for improved drama.

The actor-managers themselves invited Steele to join them. Cibber relates that during the months immediately following the queen's death when plays were not acted, he and his colleagues, realizing that they would be compelled to continue paying the stipend of £700 a year to some courtier, if not to Collier then to someone else, determined to find a more suitable associate than the Tory lawyer. They applied to Steele, Cibber asserts, because they knew his high pretensions to favor at court and because they acknowledged themselves indebted to him for many journalistic favors, "there being scarce a Comedian of Merit in our whole Company whom his *Tatlers* had not made better by his publick Recommendation of them."[52] The managers were grateful for this assistance in the past, and they hoped that it would be continued— they would gain much if in another periodical Steele would again

---

[51] Preface to *The Successful Pyrate* (London, 1713). Cf. also the preface to Charles Shadwell, *The Humours of the Army* (London, 1713) and the preface to Susanna Centlivre, *The Wonder: A Woman Keeps a Secret* (London, 1714).

[52] *Apology*, II, 162–163.

write about the stage. They knew, moreover, the advantages of associating themselves with one in Steele's fortunate political position; players frequently needed just such an advocate with the court as Steele could be.[53] Their motives are thus perfectly comprehensible, combining gratitude with the expectation of substantial profit.

Steele was ready enough to oblige the actor-managers when they suggested that he apply for the license. He would certainly have welcomed the substantial income to be expected from Drury Lane, as well as the close association with the theater.

At the begining of the negotiations, there seems to have been a discussion of the terms of the proposed partnership, but the reports of the agreement reached are conflicting. The reports date from a later period, being in fact parts of testimony offered in a lawsuit between Steele and the managers. In September, 1725, Steele entered suit against the managers in an unsuccessful attempt to regain a part of the theater's profits that since 1720 the managers had withheld from him on the grounds that he had ceased to assist them in conducting the company's business. In the subsequent litigation he and the managers presented depositions in which they reviewed from their separate points of view their relations at Drury Lane. According to the managers, Steele, when he entered the management, "faithfully promised and agreed to attend the [word illegible] meetings and Consultations of the sd Company and to write plays and other performances and to Instruct the Younger Actors and to sollicite ye people of quality and other persons of Distinction to come to the sd Theatre and to Use his Utmost Endavours to promote the Interest thereof. . . ."[54] Steele denied that he had promised to attend the company's meetings or to instruct the young actors, not being qualified to give such instruction, but he acknowledged that he had promised to write plays for the theater, to solicit people of quality and distinction in behalf of the theater, and, more generally, to do his utmost to support it.[55] Of these conflicting reports Steele's is the more

---

[53] Cf. *The Laureat: or, The Right Side of Colley Cibber, Esq.* (London, 1740), p. 84.
[54] P.R.O., C11/2416/49.
[55] *Ibid.*

plausible. There is no inherent implausibility in his promising to attend the company's meetings, as the managers asserted, but it appears incredible that a person who had never appeared on any stage should promise to teach acting. Tradition, moreover, would have counted for something in Steele's relations with the managers. The managers obviously expected (and received) more assistance from Steele than they had received from their previous courtier-partners, yet they would scarcely have expected, in view of their experience with Collier and Swiney, that Steele would perform routine theatrical chores. Probably, as Steele maintained, there was merely a general agreement that he should do all he could, through his writing and his personal associations, to advance the theater's interests.

At any rate, matters having been determined between Steele and the actor-managers, Steele applied for assistance to the Duke of Marlborough,[56] who immediately obtained the license from the king. A memorandum in Steele's handwriting is testimony to the ease with which it was procured: "Message from the King to know whether I was in earnest in desiring the Playhouse or that others thought of it for me—If I likd it I should have it as an earnest of His future favour."[57] Steele was in earnest, and on October 18, 1714, the license passed, signed by the Duke of Shrewsbury, then lord chamberlain.

A letter of Steele's suggests that he may have gained the Duke of Marlborough's assistance with the license through the mediation of the duchess,[58] though there was reason enough for the duke himself to be grateful to Steele for his previous journalistic support. Steele had identified Marlborough with the Whig cause and championed him in his writings with a zeal that combined ad-

[56] Cibber, *Apology*, II, 164–165.

[57] Blenheim MSS. Quoted in Aitken, *Life*, II, 48.

[58] The duchess had mentioned Steele approvingly several times in her letters from Holland and Belgium, when she and the duke were there in retirement following their break with the queen: *Letters of Sarah Duchess of Marlborough* (London, 1875), pp. 79, 88, 95. There is no evidence to support Willard Connely's assumption that Steele engaged in a mild flirtation with the duchess (then a countess) in 1702. See Connely, *Sir Richard Steele* (New York and London, 1934), p. 68.

miration for the man with a sincere belief in the principles of government he ostensibly represented. However, it is a meeting with the duchess to which Steele refers in a letter to his wife, written September 8, 1714: "I shall dine at Cleland's [a Scotch friend of Steele's] in order to see Lady Marleborough as soon as she is at Leisure after dinner. I have spoken to two or Three of the Justices and I think all will do Well."[59] The "Justices" were the regents in control of the government until the arrival of the king.

The license that Steele, with the aid of Marlborough, obtained is in no way exceptional; the powers granted are the usual ones in such documents. Steele and the four actor-managers (Doggett's name is included)[60] were given authority

. . . to Act and Represent in any Convenient Place during Our Pleasure and no longer, and in such manner as any three or more of them shall think proper, all Comedys, Tragedies, and all other Theatricall performances (Musicall Entertainments only excepted) Subject to such Rules and Orders for their good Government therein, as they shall receive from time to time from the Chamberlain of Our Household. . . .[61]

The grant was thus to subsist only during the royal pleasure; nor were the powers conveyed to be independent of the lord chamberlain. Unlike the later patent, the license made no distinction between the positions of Steele and the actor-managers, assigning equal authority to them all.

[59] *Correspondence,* p. 306.

[60] In a deposition of May, 1715, Steele asserted that it had been within his power to leave out Doggett's name or that of any other of the actor-managers' from the license, "the benefitt thereof being granted att the sole Instance and in favour of this Defendant [Steele] only. . . ." P.R.O., C11/6/44.

[61] Aitken prints the full text of the license: *Life,* II, 48.

5 | The Patent

THE EARLY part of the Drury Lane season of 1714–1715, the first of Steele's managership, was unusually successful; the city was crowded with people attracted to London by the accession of the new monarch, and the theater's audiences were proportionately larger.[62] The previous season had been good, but the fall of 1714 surpassed precedent, the theater's total profits between the opening on September 21 and December 17, 1714, amounting to £1,700.[63] Steele had reason to be pleased with the association he had formed—though he did not share in the extraordinary profits because he was receiving a fixed stipend.

Such prosperity was not to continue uninterrupted. From the beginning of the season the company was plagued with legal disputes, and in December it encountered a formidable rival when John and Christopher Mosier Rich reopened the handsomely redecorated Lincoln's Inn Fields Theatre. The Drury Lane managers, Steele among them, were driven to court litigation to protect themselves from their legal antagonists and to a prolonged series of dramatic innovations to meet the serious competition offered by Lincoln's Inn Fields.

One of the legal disputes affected no less than the managers' tenure in the Drury Lane playhouse. William Collier, the Tory lawyer whom Steele had displaced in the theatrical license, held a lease for the theater from a group of intermediaries, who in turn leased from the Duke of Bedford. Collier had not assigned his

[62] Cibber, *Apology*, II, 165.
[63] Drury Lane profits from November 23, 1713, until February 21, 1716, are recorded in some detail in P.R.O., C33/335 (master's report of December 17, 1716, settling the financial problems posed by Doggett's withdrawal). Barker discusses the company's fortunes during these years: *Cibber*, pp. 99–110.

lease to the actor-managers; and when he found himself excluded from the theater's profits, he appealed to the courts for an ejectment of the company. Wilks, Cibber, and Booth in turn secured an injunction against the ejectment proceedings until their differences with Collier could come to a court hearing. The injunction was granted, with the provision that they pay their rent (£3 12s per diem) directly to the intermediaries, who were lessees from the Duke of Bedford. Here apparently the matter rested. We hear no more from Collier, possibly because he could not afford the expense of continued litigation.[64]

Simultaneously with this dispute the three actor-managers and Steele were engaged in a legal controversy with Thomas Doggett, who, though he had withdrawn from all participation in the company's activities in the fall of 1713, insisted that he was entitled to a share of the company's profits. Because the litigation was initiated before Steele came into the management, his part in it was small; he was compelled, however, to answer Doggett's bill.[65] Doggett had brought suit against the other managers before the death of Queen Anne. Wilks, Cibber, and Booth had replied with a countersuit, attempting, according to Cibber,[66] to discourage Doggett by prolonging the litigation. Certainly their strategy succeeded in delaying a settlement; the suit and countersuit dragged on, often before the court.[67] Steele answered Doggett's complaint briefly in May, 1715, stating merely that Doggett had not worked with the other managers since the new license passed, and referring judgment to the court. In a final settlement, reached on March 6, 1716, the court decided against Doggett, decreeing that if he still refused to sign the articles of agreement by which the managers had governed their affairs since Steele's patent was granted, he was to receive £600 for his share in the theater's stage

---

[64] Barker summarizes the affair: *Cibber,* p. 102.

[65] P.R.O., C11/6/44. Doggett's name was included, as I have noted, in the license granted in October, 1714—as Steele later asserted, at his, Steele's, request (*ibid.*)—and his name was also mentioned in the theatrical patent granted to Steele in January, 1715. Steele also named Doggett in the deed by which he assigned to the actor-managers part of his authority in the patent, though Doggett did not execute the deed.

[66] *Apology,* II, 149–150.

[67] P.R.O., C11/6/44; C11/2342/26.

properties, with interest figured at 15 per cent, and was thenceforth to be excluded from all profits.[68]

Though thus excluded from any future share in the profits, Doggett was by the terms of the settlement entitled to a fifth part of those already accrued—a substantial sum. In an attempt to reduce the amount due him, Steele (who by this time had exchanged his stipend for a share) and his three colleagues resorted unsuccessfully to a stratagem that the colleagues later employed successfully against Steele. They deducted from the income of the theater a pound a day each in payment for their own services; in other words, they paid themselves salaries in addition to their shares of the profits. The master who inspected the company's books to see that the court's decision was carried out disallowed this deduction, forcing Steele, Wilks, Booth, and Cibber to consider their "salaries" as part of the company's profits and as such subject to division with Doggett.[69]

Much more troublesome, more costly, and certainly more persistent than all these legal entanglements were the problems that confronted Steele and the actor-managers arising from the competition provided by Lincoln's Inn Fields Theatre. When Steele came into the management, Drury Lane held a virtual monopoly on drama in London. Except for occasional performances in the theater at the Haymarket (usually operas), in theatrical booths, and in semiprivate "great rooms," only at Drury Lane could plays be seen. On December 18, 1714, however, that theatrical monopoly was broken when John and Christopher Mosier Rich, acting under the authority of a patent inherited from their father, Christopher Rich, reopened Lincoln's Inn Fields.

During the last years of Anne's reign, Christopher Rich had been prevented by an order of silence from exercising his patent— one that represented the combined grants of Charles II to D'Avenant and Killigrew. However, George, remarking that Rich's patent seemed to be a lawful grant and that there had formerly been two theaters in London, lifted the order of silence[70] not

---

[68] P.R.O., C33/327, fol. 226 (chancery decree). The master's report terminating the affair was presented on December 17, 1716: C33/335.

[69] P.R.O., C33/335.

[70] Cibber, *Apology,* II, 165–166.

long after his accession—though Rich died before he was able to take advantage of the favor. His two sons inherited his patent and his rights to Lincoln's Inn Fields (which the father had hopefully redecorated before Anne died), promptly opened the theater, and initiated a theatrical rivalry that was to outlive Steele.

Almost immediately the Drury Lane company felt the rivalry in the form of seriously reduced profits. After the spectacularly successful autumn during which profits amounted to £1,700, profits for the entire remainder of the season (after Lincoln's Inn Fields opened) amounted only to £820.[71] Audiences flocked to the new theater, attracted by its handsome appointments, its location, and the vaudeville-type entertainments in which John Rich specialized. Drury Lane losses were somewhat abated by the patronage of the royal family (including a handsome gift from the Prince of Wales), but the company's fortunes nevertheless declined disastrously.

Nor was the competition between the theaters for audiences only. When Lincoln's Inn Fields opened, seven or eight actors left Drury Lane in one day to join Rich, occasioning an acute shortage of performers at Drury Lane which forced the company to postpone some of its best plays.[72] The Drury Lane managers naturally considered such tactics from their new rival unfair; and, in their attempt to gain redress, they appealed, it appears, to the lord chamberlain, the Duke of Shrewsbury. At any rate, a notice in the *Weekly Packet* on the day the new theater opened (December 18) suggests that the lord chamberlain planned to intervene: ". . . it is said, that some of the Gentlemen who have left the House in Drury Lane . . . are order'd to return to their Colours, upon Pain of not exercising their Lungs elsewhere. . . ." But there is no indication at all that the lord chamberlain took action. On the contrary, in what seems to be an allusion to this episode, Steele complained a year and a half later (when there was again trouble about actors transferring from one company to another): "My Lord Chamberlain denyed to protect the Late License, and sent me to the Law-

[71] P.R.O., C33/335 (master's report of December 17, 1716, on Doggett's withdrawal).

[72] Cibber, *Apology*, II, 169.

yers."[73] Certainly the actors who joined Rich at Lincoln's Inn Fields were not penalized.

In this episode may be observed a beginning of the friction between the Drury Lane management and the lord chamberlain which culminated five years later in Steele's suspension. When the lord chamberlain refused to punish the actors who left Drury Lane, Steele, it seems, went to "the Lawyers"—though with no apparent success. Attempting to go over the lord chamberlain's head, he also prepared a petition to the king (no record exists of his actually presenting it) in which he requested that His Majesty would "forbid actors or actresses of either house to pass over to the other without the express permission of the Lord Chamberlain."[74] Steele complained that some of the actors of his company had been enticed away and that the remainder demanded higher wages. Futile though his efforts proved to be in this instance, Steele was thus already in the second month of his managership assuming an active share in conducting the company's affairs, and already he was finding dependency on the lord chamberlain irksome.

The rivalry with Lincoln's Inn Fields soon produced a change in Steele's relations with his brother managers as well as with the lord chamberlain. When the actor-managers were faced with greatly lowered profits, Cibber reports, they held a conference with Steele, explaining to him that since his stipend of £700 a year was subject to the condition upon which William Collier had received it—namely, Drury Lane's being the only company permitted to act—they could no longer pay it to him. As an alternative they suggested that the fixed stipend be exchanged for an equal share with the actor-managers in the company's profits. To this Steele readily agreed, acting in the entire affair, so Cibber reports, in a thoroughly affable and coöperative manner.[75]

At this same conference Steele introduced another matter of the highest importance to himself and his colleagues—a proposal to petition for a theatrical patent. Steele told Wilks, Booth, and Cibber that at the time of the "desertion" of the Drury Lane actors to Lincoln's Inn Fields he had been advised (presumably by the

[73] *Correspondence*, p. 112.

[74] H.M.C., *Eighth Report* (London, 1881), Appendix, pt. 1, p. 24a.

[75] *Apology*, II, 172.

lawyers whom he consulted) to obtain in place of the license, which subsisted only during the royal pleasure, a theatrical patent. This he could easily do, he explained, if the actor-managers were willing that the patent be granted to him alone, with the understanding that he would assign shares in it to them after it was granted. Cibber reports that he, Wilks, and Booth were highly pleased at the proposal, because a patent would free them from their abject dependency on the lord chamberlain and his subordinates. Thus a desire for independence from the lord chamberlain motivated the actor-managers as well as Steele. They accordingly urged him to present his petition without delay.[76]

This decisive conference probably occurred late in December, 1714, or early in January, 1715—the endorsement on Steele's petition for the patent is dated January 10. The petition itself emphasizes anew the need for stage reform. Observing that the theater has "for many years last past been very much perverted to the great Scandall of Religion and Good Government," Steele requests a more permanent authority in order that he can "remedy so inveterate an evil. . . ."[77] Curiously, Steele implies that he might have had the patent earlier, presumably at the time when he received the license; he had not wished, he asserts, "this Favour in so ample a manner as your Majtie was graciously disposed to bestow it upon him" until his association with the theater showed him that he could conduct it to His Majesty's satisfaction. Steele specifically requests that the duration of the patent be limited to his lifetime and three years after his death. Great inconveniences had arisen, he comments in an oblique stroke at John Rich, from the continuance of such grants in perpetuity to the heirs of patentees. Quite naturally he said nothing in the petition about his desire for independence from the lord chamberlain.

The petition was endorsed by Lord Townshend, secretary of state for the northern division:

His Majesty is graciously pleased to refer this Petition to Mr. Attorney or Mr. Sollicitor General to consider thereof and report his Opinion what his Majesty may fitly do therein whereupon his Majesty will declare his further Pleasure.

---

[76] *Ibid.*, II, 173.

[77] P.R.O., L.C. 7/3; *Correspondence*, pp. 524–525.

Steele later asserted that, whereas this endorsement specifies either the attorney *or* solicitor general, he arranged for the petition to be sent to *both* these officers in order that there might be no doubt about its legality. He wished to make sure that the grant to him would not be an infringement upon that held by John Rich and his brother.[78]

Northey and Lechmere, the attorney and solicitor general, asked for the actor-managers to signify their willingness that the license held jointly be replaced by a patent to Steele only, though whether such a statement was an absolute prerequisite to the granting of the patent is a disputed point.[79] Whether necessary or not, however, the actor-managers signed the statement immediately, whereupon Northey and Lechmere rendered their opinion, on January 12, 1715, that the letters patent could be legally granted "Subject to Such Regulations as have been Usual in Grants of ye like Nature."[80] The phrasing of their opinion echoes Steele's statement about the need for reform of the stage.

This legal opinion prepared the way for the next step required by the elaborate legal machinery: the royal warrant for the patent. The warrant, dated January 14, 1715, and signed by Townshend, was directed back to Northey and Lechmere, instructing them to prepare the patent itself and informing them of the powers to be granted.[81] Again repeating Steele's phrases about the desirability of stage reform, the warrant authorizes the patent, "provided that the Authority of the Said Patents be not participated by or assigned to any other Persons than those Named in Our present Licence," that is, to no one other than Cibber, Wilks, Booth, *and Doggett* (who is mentioned earlier in the document as a participant in the license). Steele is to be granted full authority to "keep a company of Comedians for Our Service to exercise and act Tragedies, Comedies, Plays, Operas" either in the Drury Lane playhouse or in any other he and his associates shall erect in London or

---

[78] *The State of the Case,* in *Tracts and Pamphlets,* pp. 599–600.

[79] In their subsequent lawsuits with Steele the managers insisted that their consent was necessary; Steele insisted it was not. P.R.O., C11/2416/49. Cf. also Cibber, *Apology,* II, 174.

[80] P.R.O., L.C. 7/3. See below, p. 243.

[81] P.R.O., L.C. 7/3. See below, pp. 244–245.

Westminster. It is significant that operas are to be permitted; in the license the company was expressly forbidden to present musical entertainments. Northey and Lechmere are instructed, however, to include in the patent "all Such Powers, Authoritys, Clauses, Regulations and Provisoes as have been usual in Grants of the like Nature, and as you shall think necessary in this behalf." Steele was to be granted no extraordinary or unprecedented powers.

After these preliminaries the patent itself passed the great seal on January 19, 1715. In compliment to Steele, Lord Chancellor Cowper declined his customary fee on the occasion.[82] The other incidental expenses were paid from the theater's treasury.[83]

The powers conveyed by the patent were similar to those Charles II had granted to Killigrew and D'Avenant; indeed, Steele later asserted that "there is nothing in it, as to the bestowing part, from the Crown, but what are meer transcripts of the Patent given by King CHARLES II to Sir WILLIAM DAVENANT."[84] One important difference, however, did exist: the former grants were perpetual ones; the one to Steele was limited to his lifetime and three years after his death. Steele, of course, had requested this limitation; had he wished, probably he could have obtained a grant in perpetuity. At any rate, five years later he wrote that though he might have had the patent for himself and his heirs, "I made a conscience and scruple of asking for my heirs an office that required a very particular turn and capacity to execute."[85] Otherwise the patent he asked for and received was, in legal essentials, almost identical with the earlier ones.

Steele printed his patent in the *Town Talk*, No. 6, remarking that it was free of the tautologies usual in such documents. The patent is indeed gracefully written, and it contains in addition to the usual legal formulas some interesting observations on the state of the drama and the need for stage reform. It is especially informa-

---

[82] Cibber, *Apology*, II, 174.

[83] P.R.O. C11/2416/49 (deposition of Steele, executed June 23, 1726, in answer to the managers' bill of complaint against him). For a memorandum of expenses apparently incurred in obtaining the patent, see John Loftis, "Steele and the Drury Lane Patent," *Modern Language Notes*, LXIV (1949), 19–21.

[84] The *Theatre*, No. 8.

[85] *Ibid.*

tive in revealing the efficacy of the pamphleteering of Jeremy Collier and his fellow reformers; the preamble to the patent chronicles the current stage abuses (the abuses that are the stated reason for Steele's appointment) in terms suggesting unmistakably *A Short View*. The proper use of the stage has been perverted, it is charged,

... instead of exhibiting such representations of human life as may tend to the encouragement and honour of Religion and Virtue, and discountenancing Vice, the English STAGE hath been the complaint of the sober, intelligent and religious part of our people; and, by indecent and immodest expressions, by prophane allusions to Holy Scripture, by abusive and scurrilous representations of the clergy, and by the success and applause bestowed on libertine characters, it hath given great and insufferable scandal to Religion and good Manners...."

Here are precisely the complaints voiced by Collier. Dramatists are profane, they are contemptuous of the Bible and of the clergy, and they present debauched characters in an attractive light, rewarding rather than punishing them. Such an explicit statement in an official document provides unequivocal evidence of the force of the reform movement.

Incongruous as it may seem, in Steele's patent there is an implied statement of a controversial principle of dramatic criticism: the authority of the crown is enlisted in support of poetic justice. Such at any rate seems to be the drift of the charge that "success and applause [are] bestowed upon libertine characters." Certainly Steele interpreted the patent as a mandate to him to rid the stage of the offending characters—the witty, attractive, and successful libertines who had aroused Collier's wrath. "The fine gentleman is not absolutely obliged to wrong his friend in the most unpardonable instance, that of his bed; nor is the fine lady of course to like him best, who lavishes his youth among the abandoned of her sex," he observed in the *Town Talk* after quoting the patent, commenting on the changes in drama to be expected from the grant to him. Thus, indirectly, in the patent itself may be found support for exemplary comedy, support that, of course, came originally from the reformers. When the presentation of vicious characters became reprehensible, the exemplary method remained the logical alternative.

Immediately upon receiving the patent, Steele assigned equal shares to the actor-managers, as he had promised when they acknowledged their willingness that the grant be made to him only. In the entire transaction he acted with generosity and with complete honesty, making no effort to employ his political position to the detriment of his colleagues and, indeed, refusing to take advantage of a mistake made by Cibber that might have been costly. Because Steele was compelled to leave London the day after the patent passed (in order to stand for Parliament in Burroughbridge, Yorkshire), he and the actor-managers signed in haste articles of partnership drawn up by Cibber, in which through an oversight Steele was granted an equal share with the actor-managers in the stage properties. When he returned to London, however, he consented in a second agreement to pay his partners £1,200 for the share.[86]

The powers conveyed to Steele and assigned in part by him to the actor-managers were great, but they were not clearly defined; just as fifty-three years earlier when theatrical patents were granted to D'Avenant and Killigrew,[87] no clear distinction was made between the authority of the patentee and his assigns and that of the lord chamberlain. As the earlier grants occasioned disputes, so also did this one. The ambiguity of Steele's relationship with the lord chamberlain caused trouble from the beginning.

Smarting under the lord chamberlain's refusal to intervene in their dispute with Lincoln's Inn Fields, Steele and the actor-managers all but declared their independence from that officer when they received the patent; theirs was a separate authority, they maintained, supported by a royal grant. The patent, they believed, freed them from dependency on the lord chamberlain and his subordinates, even in such matters as the licensing of new plays. "The Patent granted by his Majesty King *George* the First to Sir *Richard Steele,* and his Assigns, of which I was one," wrote Cibber, "made us sole Judges of what Plays might be proper for

[86] Cibber, *Apology,* II, 174–175.

[87] For an account of trouble caused by the ill-defined nature of the grant conveyed by D'Avenant's and Killigrew's patents, see Allardyce Nicoll, *A History of Restoration Drama, 1660–1700* (Cambridge, 1928), pp. 270–271; 275–276. Leslie Hotson, *The Commonwealth and Restoration Stage* (Cambridge, Mass., 1928), pp. 204–206; 210–213. Arthur F. White, "The Office of Revels and Dramatic Censorship During the Restoration Period," *Western Reserve University Bulletin,* XXXIV (1931), 7–11.

the Stage, without submitting them to the Approbation or License of any other particular Person."[88] When, immediately after the patent passed the great seal, the master of the revels (a subordinate of the lord chamberlain) demanded his usual licensing fee for a new play, Cibber waited on him, requested that he give evidence of his authority over a patent company, and, in the absence of such authority, refused to pay the fee.[89] For nearly five years the Drury Lane company neither submitted their new plays to the master of the revels nor paid the fees. In defying the subordinate, Cibber, of course, defied the authority of the lord chamberlain himself.[90]

Nor was this refusal to submit new plays to the master of the revels the sole instance of the managers' defiance of the lord chamberlain in the weeks immediately after the patent passed. A more decisive act, an open refusal to obey a direct order from the lord chamberlain, grew out of a dispute with Sir John Vanbrugh. Several years earlier a large quantity of stage properties had been removed from Vanbrugh's theater, the Haymarket, to Drury Lane in one of the several managerial exchanges that occurred during the last years of Anne's reign. The actor-managers had at first paid £200 a year for the properties, a sum later reduced to £100. For more than a year before the patent was granted, however, they had refused to pay anything. Vanbrugh consequently appealed to the lord chamberlain. Equity in the case was obscured by the complex series of managerial exchanges that had taken place since the properties were removed from the Haymarket. Nevertheless, the Duke of Shrewsbury (the lord chamberlain) issued an order to the Drury Lane managers that they pay Vanbrugh £100 a year,[91] the order, dated January 14, 1715 (just five days before the patent passed), being signed by the duke himself. Cibber, acting for the Drury Lane managers, replied with an unequivocal refusal in a letter written three days *after* the patent passed, the audacious tone of

[88] *Apology*, I, 276–277.

[89] *Ibid.*, I, 278.

[90] This fact was noted in a letter of legal advice to the lord chamberlain written in January, 1720. P.R.O., S.P. 35, vol. lxxiv, No. 43 (10).

[91] P.R.O., L.C. 5/156. The dispute between Vanbrugh and the managers is described in a series of documents in L.C. 7/3. See also Barker, *Cibber* pp. 102–103.

which bears witness to the confidence he felt in the strength of the patent:

When we had first the Honour of Her Majts. licence, Sr John Stanley persuaded us to do something in favour of the Opera, in consideration of our being the Sole Company then permitted to Act, and we hoping it would recommend us to the Court did Spontaniously pay severall hundred pounds to the Opera. But when our licence was broke into by the Addition of Mr Booths name, we thought ourselves no longer under that obligation and have never paid it since nor recd any Order about it till now, which at this time seems as reasonable to be sent to the other Company as ours, Especially since the best part of theirs are made up of our Actors, when we cannot get an Order to oblige them to return to us. And farther neither the late Licence nor his Majts Letters Patents (by virtue of which we now Act) nor any agreement whatsoever obliges us to continue such payments. . . .[92]

The boldness of the allusion to the lord chamberlain's refusal to enter the dispute between Drury Lane and Lincoln's Inn Fields reveals the intensity of the managers' resentment.

That Shrewsbury should have tolerated such a reply is curious—but he took no direct action. Only after the Duke of Newcastle became lord chamberlain were reprisals taken.

In the early months of 1715, then, Steele found himself governor of Drury Lane by the authority of a royal grant strong enough to permit him and his colleagues, at least temporarily, to defy a powerful officer of the royal household. The grant was important and remunerative—it proved to be the largest single gift he received from his party. But it was by no means his only reward for his service to the Protestant succession. On January 12, 1715 (the day the attorney and solicitor general rendered their opinion on his patent), he was awarded a present of £500 from the king; in February he was elected to Parliament through the patronage of a Whig lord; in April he was knighted; in June, 1716, he was appointed a commissioner for the forfeited estates in Scotland. Yet these favors notwithstanding, Steele believed himself ill-used by his party and his sovereign; he believed that the rewards, of which Drury Lane was the principal, were inadequate recompense for his faithful service to the Whig party and to the house of Hanover.

---

[92] P.R.O., L.C. 7/3. Quoted in Barker, *Cibber*, p. 103.

His letters bear witness to a deep resentment at what he considered the party's ingratitude. On May 25, 1715, four months after the patent passed, he wrote to his patron (the Earl of Clare) expressing bitterness at the financial losses he had endured for the Whigs. He will do no more, he declares, "without knowing the terms. . . . As for my Patent for the Playhouse I shall make it appear next Winter that it was a great Service to the Crown that I accepted it."[93] In another letter to Clare, written July 19, 1715, he insists that "care of me is not to be taken, except I passe through sollicitations, which will take up more of my time, and quiet of mind than it is Worth."[94] His resentment evidently increased as the years passed. In an undated letter to Lady Steele, conjecturally assigned to March, 1717, he speaks openly of his disappointments:

I am talking to My Wife, and therefore may speake my Heart and the Vanity of it, I know, and you are witnesse, that I have served the Royall Family with an unreservednesse due only to Heaven, and I am now, (I thank my Brother Whiggs) not possessed of twenty shillings from the favour of the Court. The Play-House it had been barbarity to deny at the Player's request and therefore I do not allow it, a Favour.[95]

What then did Steele expect? Why, in view of the seemingly liberal rewards he received, was he disappointed?

Apparently Steele anticipated a high ministerial post. He was mentioned for one before the king's arrival in England,[96] and his close friend and collaborator Addison, who had been more restrained than he in his support of the Whig cause, received such a reward. For Steele, however, the appointment never came. He continued to be active in Whig politics—he was a member of Parliament until two years before his death. But he was disap-

[93] *Correspondence*, pp. 101–102. The "next Winter" Steele wrote the *Town Talk*, in which he stated emphatically that he intended to reform the theater. Probably his "great Service to the Crown" was his reforming mission.

[94] *Correspondence*, p. 105.

[95] *Ibid.*, pp. 331–332.

[96] Aitken, *Life*, II, 37.

pointed that his chief gift from the king proved to be the relatively humble one of the governorship of Drury Lane.[97]

---

[97] Thomas Salmon, in *The Chronological Historian* (London, 1747), II, 45, remarked about Steele's appointment to Drury Lane: "About this time the celebrated Mr. Steele, to his great mortification, was made Governor of the Playhouse, when he expected a post among the first Ministers of State, on the merit of his immortal libels, particularly *The Crisis*, published in the reign of Queen Anne." (Quoted from Aitken, *Life*, II, 55n.)

Part Two | 1714-1719

1 | Steele in the Management

EMBOLDENED by their successful defiance of the lord chamberlain, Steele and the actor-managers made more ambitious plans for Drury Lane than previously. No longer, they believed, were they subject to the caprices of the chamberlain or of court favorites who might interest themselves in the affairs of the theater;[1] hence they could hazard larger expenditures with reasonable assurance that their money would yield a return. During the first summer after the patent was granted, they redecorated the theater. The following fall the opening was delayed because the work was not completed in time for the usual date.[2] Larger expenditures were made in staging individual plays—an elaborate production of *All for Love,* for example, costing the unprecedented sum of £600.[3] Drury Lane had not yet heard the lord chamberlain's last word; nevertheless, the managers confidently went their way for the time unmolested.

What part was Steele taking in the theater's affairs? Enjoying the fruits of the Whig victory, he was again in Parliament and was busy in many enterprises other than Drury Lane—one of which was the academy in York Buildings. He was no mere figure-head, however, at Drury Lane. Though not in close daily association with the theater, as the actor-managers were, he assumed for a time a measure of responsibility for the company, taking a part in directing the theater's affairs. Precisely how large a part must now be determined.

Steele retained a nominal association with Drury Lane until his

---

[1] Cf. *The State of the Case,* in *Tracts and Pamphlets,* p. 604.

[2] Cibber, *Apology,* II, 175n.

[3] *Ibid.,* II, 175.

death in 1729, but he was active in the management only until January, 1720. Earlier, he was in fact a partner of the actor-managers; later, he merely shared their profits. After he was suspended by the lord chamberlain in January, 1720, he did not, even following his reinstatement in May, 1721, resume his previous close relationship with his colleagues—partly because of his poor health. After January, 1720, he was frequently too ill to manage his affairs; after 1724, almost always so. Taking advantage of Steele's absence from the theater, the actor-managers, on January 28, 1720, began to deduct from the theater's clear profits £5 a day, which they divided in payment for their own services'—precisely the stratagem they, with Steele, attempted unsuccessfully to employ against Doggett. The date this deduction began is a significant one in Steele's relationship with Drury Lane in that it marks the end of his active participation in the management. Thus the present inquiry into his Drury Lane activities can be limited to the years 1714–1720.

Steele himself recorded in general terms the theory of his relationship with the actor-managers, describing the principle by which he conducted his share of the theater's business. It is necessary, he wrote, to have at the head of a company of actors men who understand by personal experience the requirements of theatrical production. A company of actors

. . . cannot possibly be governed, as to their oeconomy, their accommodation on the Stage, their salaries and assignments of their parts, but by themselves and those of acknowledged superiority amongst them. He that should attempt to govern them but by a regulation formed upon this plan, would find himself at the head of an army of officers, each of whom would not only think himself, but really be, as to the mechanic part of the ordonnance amongst them, superior to his General. . . .

The Patentee [Steele himself] therefore, in my humble opinion, did like a wise man, and a great politician, in becoming but a sharer and director with relation to the expence, and reserving the character of Governor only with regard to the morality of the Stage.[5]

---

[4] The date when the managers began this deduction has previously been given as June 18, 1723 (cf. Aitken, *Life*, II, 303; *Correspondence*, p. 171n). For my reasons for assigning this earlier date, see below, pp. 214–215.

[5] The *Theatre*, No. 7.

Therefore, Steele's participation should not be looked for in the day-to-day business of the theater. He was not qualified by training for the duties of stage management, nor, with his many other interests and responsibilities, had he the time for them.⁶ As the distinguished partner of the actor-managers, he concerned himself with the exceptional rather than with the routine—with major problems affecting the company's policies and prosperity (though not exclusively with those affecting the morality of the stage, as he here implies).

A close inquiry into just what he did at Drury Lane is limited by the serious paucity of theatrical records. Still, there are scattered sources of reference available.

Paradoxically, our most complete information about Steele's support of Drury Lane comes from the period after he left the management altogether. As a consequence of the actor-managers' deduction from the profits, Steele in 1725, then in retirement in Wales, initiated a lawsuit against them. The actor-managers soon thereafter introduced a countersuit, charging Steele with neglect of the theater's affairs.⁷ In the records of the resulting litigation, which was protracted over a period of three years, appear the most direct available statements about Steele's sharing the burdens of the management.

According to the actor-managers' testimony in a deposition sworn on January 11, 1726, Steele neglected altogether the affairs of the theater after January 28, 1720, although, they insisted, by the terms of their partnership he was equally obligated with them to carry on the company's business. What is particularly informative about the testimony, however, is the managers' insistence that until 1720 Steele performed his share of the work. When they invited him to join them in the management, they asserted, Steele expressed gratitude, promising to attend to the business of the

---

⁶ Steele's name, for example, does not appear with the actor-managers' on the many tradesmen's bills submitted to Drury Lane that are preserved in the Folger Shakespeare Library, the British Museum, the Enthoven Collection, and elsewhere.

⁷ For an account of the circumstances leading to Steele's suit and the managers' countersuit, see below, pp. 213–229. Aitken reports the successive stages of the litigation: *Life,* II, 303–317.

theater—specifically, to attend the company's meetings, to write plays and other performances, to solicit people of quality in behalf of the theater, and to do what he could to attract audiences. They asserted also, as we have already observed, that Steele promised to assist in instructing the younger actors—a curious promise, if it were in fact made. After insisting vehemently that Steele owed them these obligations, the managers state unequivocally that "the sd. Sr. Rich. Steele pursuant to his said promise and agreement with yr. Oratrs. of Entering into the sd. partnership did for some time Continue to attend the business of the sd. Company & to assist yor. Oratrs. in the management thereof untill the 28th day Janry 1719/20 since which he the sd. Sr. Richd. Steele hath altogether absented himself from the business of this theatre. . . ."[8] Until January, 1720, then, Steele performed his duties to his colleagues' satisfaction—and the duties, as enumerated by them, were important ones. They emphatically did not consider him merely a silent partner.

This statement of the managers collectively is corroborated by a separate statement by Cibber in his *Apology,* in which he similarly insists in strong terms on Steele's obligation:

∴. if I don't mistake the Words of the Assignment [of the patent], there is a Clause in it that says, All Matters relating to the Government or Menagement of the Theatre shall be concluded by a Majority of Voices. Now I presume, Sir, there is no room left to alledge that Sir *Richard* was ever refused his Voice, though in above three Years [before 1725] he never desir'd to give it: And I believe there will be as little room to say, that he could have a Voice if he were not a Menager. But, Sir, his being a Menager is so self-evident, that it is amazing how he could conceive that he was to take the Profits and Advantages of a Menager without doing the Duty of it. And I will be bold to say, Sir, that his Assignment of the Patent to *Wilks, Booth,* and *Cibber,* in no one Part of it, by the severest Construction in the World, can be wrested to throw the heavy Burthen of the Menagement only upon their Shoulders. Nor does it appear, Sir, that either in his Bill, or in his Answer to our Cross-Bill, he has offer'd any Hint, or Glimpse of a Reason, for his withdrawing from the Menagement at all; or so much as pretend, *from the time complained of,*[9] that he ever took the least Part of his Share of it.[10]

---

[8] P.R.O., C11/2416/49.

[9] Italics mine.

[10] *Apology,* II, 200.

Cibber is thus unyielding in his insistence that Steele enjoyed no immunity from the work that fell to the managers. Though he overstates his case—Steele as a member of Parliament and man of affairs was obviously in a position different from that of the others, a fact that was certainly recognized when he entered the management—Cibber here establishes the actor-managers' attitude toward Steele. In asserting that he neglected his duties "from the time complained of," clearly Cibber implies that before that time he rendered the assistance they expected of him.

It is possible, to be sure, that Cibber, Wilks, and Booth overstated the amount of Steele's service to Drury Lane from 1714 until 1720 to provide a more forceful contrast to his neglect of the theater after 1720. Except about details, however, Steele himself concurred in what they said. He denied, as I have previously pointed out, that upon entering the partnership he had promised to attend meetings of the company or to instruct young actors. But he had agreed, he asserted in his deposition of June 23, 1726, "to write plays & other performances & to Sollicite persons of Quality & other persons of distinction to resort to the sd Theatre & to use his best endeavours to support the interest thereof all which this deft saith he hath accordingly done & performed as long as he was able & according to the utmost of his power of which the Complts. themselves have been soe far sensible that they have frequently acknowledged the great services done them by this deft. ...."[11] Steele denied ever having refused a request by the actor-managers that he be present on any important occasion for the service of the company; on the contrary, "whilst his health permitted him he gave all necessary attendance for their service and did his uttmost to promote and advance the interest and advantage of the Company."

In support of his assertion that the actor-managers acknowledged their gratitude for his service to Drury Lane, Steele cited Cibber's dedication to him of a play, *Ximena, or the Heroic Daughter* (in September, 1719, three months before Steele's suspension). After an association in the management of nearly five years, Cibber wrote in affectionate terms: "How much You have done for us was visible to all the world, what sense we have of it is yet known to few; I therefore take this occasion to make our ac-

[11] P.R.O., C11/2416/49.

knowledgments, if possible, as public as our obligations." This dedication, Steele maintained, was testimony to his substantial contribution to the theater. Though Cibber in rebuttal, in the heat of the legal controversy, insisted that he had referred to Steele's writing the *Tatlers* years before he entered the partnership, not to Steele's activities as patentee,[12] the timing of the dedication speaks for itself: Had Steele proved to be an unsatisfactory partner, Cibber would scarcely have looked back over an interval of ten years for a motive to pay him a compliment.

Cibber included in his *Apology*, moreover, an unequivocal statement about Steele's service to the company (obviously during the first five years of his governorship). "His Rank and Figure in the World," Cibber wrote, "while he gave us the Assistance of them, were of extraordinary Service to us: He had an easier Access, and a more regarded Audience at Court, than our low Station of Life could pretend to, when our Interest wanted (as it often did) a particular Solicitation there."[13] Writing years after the death of Steele had ended the animosity aroused by the protracted law suits, Cibber thus gratefully remembered what were doubtless many substantial services to Drury Lane.

From this group of statements made in retrospect emerges an intelligible if incomplete account of Steele's relation to the management. Neither Steele nor the actor-managers considered his position, during the first five years of the association, as a sinecure.[14]

---

[12] *Ibid.*

[13] *Apology*, II, 202.

[14] One contrary bit of evidence must be cited. In a letter written in October, 1715, to Lord Chief Justice Sir Thomas Parker requesting appointment to the mastership of the charterhouse, Steele mentioned his governorship of Drury Lane in a manner implying that his duties at the theater were slight: "The matter of being elsewhere Employed is nothing but that I have an income out of the Play house as Patentee, and am Surveyor of the Stables at Hampton-Court, where I have nothing to do but to give in an estimate in case they want being repaired. So that there is nothing in either of these cases that hinders my Residence at Charterhouse. . . ." (*Correspondence*, pp. 106–107).

It must be remembered that Steele was here applying for a remunerative position and hence would minimize his Drury Lane duties. I have already shown, moreover, that his obligations to the theater were not of a regularly recurring, time-consuming nature.

He was an active member of the partnership from whom aid was expected and received, particularly in matters demanding political or social influence. Though his responsibilities were not identical with those of the actor-managers (Cibber's statement to the contrary), they were acknowledged both by himself and his colleagues to be substantial. He was doubtless irregular in attending to the theater's affairs, but he did, it seems, probably in his own erratic fashion, attend to them.

Such are the outlines. It is fortunately possible to add a number of details.

The major threat to the prosperity of Drury Lane during the first year of Steele's governorship was, as previously noted, the competition provided by the recently opened, handsomely redecorated Lincoln's Inn Fields; under John Rich the rival theater attracted crowds at the expense of Drury Lane. This formidable competition, affecting his income, led Steele to direct action in Drury Lane's behalf.

His efforts are first apparent in a letter written to him from Paris on November 27, 1715, by the Earl of Stair, then minister plenipotentiary to that city. The letter is a reply to a request Steele had made earlier, but one about which nothing is known except what may be inferred from Stair's letter.

I received yr commands some time ago concerning Mr Baxter and his companion, they took some days to consider wt answer they should make, it is yt they are engaged to a woman here for ye fair of St Germain wch begins ye 2nd of February. Baxter has 5000 livres from her, so ye time being so short they are unwilling to make ye journey into England; when the fair is over you may command ym but I suppose yt wont answer to yr view wch was to have em for ye winter.

I'm sorry my negociation has no better success, but I hope yt wont rebut you from employing mee whenever you think I can be usefull to you. . . .[15]

Steele evidently had requested that Stair attempt to engage two actors then in France for an appearance in England, and the nobleman, unsuccessfully as it here appears, had made the attempt. That he should employ a man of Stair's rank for such a task suggests the prominence Steele enjoyed during the first years after the accession of George.

---

[15] *Correspondence*, p. 109.

It is possible to identify Baxter and his companion[16] and to determine positively that they were at Drury Lane during the spring of 1716, immediately after the winter of which Lord Stair writes. Steele, it appears, preferred to engage them late in the theatrical season rather than not at all.

Baxter was an Englishman, who at least since 1707 had acted on the French stage.[17] He was well known in the role of harlequin, appearing in such pieces as *Arlequin Invisible Chez le Roi de la Chine* (1713), *Arlequin Mahomet* (1714), *Arlequin Columbine* (1715), and *Arlequin Devin, ou le Lendemain de Noces* (acted at the fair of St. Germain in 1716). From 1712 until 1716 Baxter belonged to the troupe of Mme Baron, presumably the woman to whom Lord Stair refers as his employer. An actor by the name of Sorin appeared with Baxter and was doubtless the person mentioned as his "companion." A brief contemporary account of *Arlequin Devin*, presented in France soon after Stair's letter, suggests the type of entertainment for which Baxter was known when Steele engaged him:

... il a été représenté sur un théâtre orné de lustres et de decorations difreréntes, une pièce comique qui a pour titre: *Arlequin devin par hasard, ou le Lendemain de noces,* en trois actes et un prologue, et nous avons remarqué que les acteurs et actrices chantent et que pendant le cours de ladite pièce tous lesdits acteurs se parlent et se réspondent quelquefois sur le même sujet de la pièce qu'ils représentent par de courts dialogues et colloques en prose, et ce pendant toutes les scènes de ladite pièce et particuliérement ledit Baxter, qui fait le rôle d'Arlequin, ledit Sorin dans le prologue où se joue une critique de la Comedie-Italienne et deux autres acteurs qui dans le même prologue font le rôle, savoir, l'un d'un procureur et l'autre d'un abbé....[18]

Exigencies of competition with Lincoln's Inn Fields obviously had forced Steele to compromise, at least temporarily, his plans for reforming Drury Lane. In the *Town Talk* he apologized for such entertainments as these in which Baxter appeared, explaining that they were the result of business necessity.[19] Steele deplored the

[16] They have not previously been identified. Cf. Aitken, *Life,* II, 79–80; *Correspondence,* p. 109n.

[17] E. Campardon, *Les Spectacles de la Foire* (Paris, 1877), pp. 100–104.

[18] *Ibid.,* p. 103.

[19] The *Town Talk,* Nos. 2, 6.

taste of audiences who preferred "non-rational" entertainments to legitimate drama, but he insisted on the need for meeting the competition offered by the rival theater. John Rich drew large crowds with vaudeville-type entertainments; to compete successfully with him, Drury Lane was compelled to offer similar attractions.

On April 4, 1716, the usual Drury Lane advertisement in the *Daily Courant* announced a performance by Baxter and Sorin as an afterpiece for the play of the evening: "The Country Wife. . . . [and] an Italian Farce call'd The Whimsical Death of Harlequin. The Parts of Scaramouch and Harlequin to be perform'd by Mons. Sorin and Mr. Baxter, lately arriv'd from Paris. Who have variety of Entertainments of that Kind, and make but a short stay in England." For more than a month Baxter and Sorin appeared regularly at the theater about twice a week, performing in pantomimes and dances; they repeated *The Whimsical Death of Harlequin* several times and presented also a pantomime called *La Guinguette or Harlequin Turned Tapster,* a "new Italian scene," and "an Entertainment of Mimick Dancing, by Harlequin, call'd, La Caprice."[20] Never offering a full evening's entertainment, they appeared only in supplementary afterpieces, and, if we may judge by the frequency and prominence of the advertisements of their performances, they were highly popular and aided in the competitive struggle with Lincoln's Inn Fields.

As an even more substantial effort in behalf of Drury Lane than engaging these actors, Steele undertook during the winter of 1715–1716 a new periodical, published weekly, entitled the *Town Talk, In a Series of Letters to a Lady in the Country.* It was "particularly designed to be helpful to the stage," Steele wrote to John Hughes in January, 1716 (inquiring if Hughes wished a puff for a recently completed masque soon after presented at Drury Lane).[21] In inviting Steele to join them in the management, the actor-managers had anticipated just such direct journalistic assistance as he set

---

[20] The *Daily Courant,* April 4, 6, 11, 13, 18, 20, 23, 25, 27, 30; May 2, 7, 10, 1716.

[21] *Correspondence,* pp. 109–110. The masque was *Apollo and Daphne,* first presented at Drury Lane on January 12, 1716.

about to provide in the *Town Talk*.[22] He left no statement that in undertaking the journal he was moved by his obligation to his colleagues, but he conducted it as they would have wished—to give publicity to the theater.

The *Town Talk* is by no means exclusively concerned with the stage; it is what its title implies, a paper devoted to reporting what passed in the "town." Steele consistently followed the fictional device of the letter to a lady in the country, using it to justify the introduction of a number of different topics in a single paper. Whatever he wished to include could easily be explained in terms of the fiction of a letter reporting town gossip. The theater is nevertheless the most prominent subject in his letters, as he acknowledged to his correspondent: "You remember I told you in my first, that Covent-Garden is the heart of the Town, and by that rule, the Play-House is the Town-Hall. I must confess, my chief intelligence is in that neighborhood."[23] Politics, manners, philosophy, and science have their place, but the theater held the lion's share of the "town's" attention; and, if we may judge from the letters, the "town" was particularly interested in the change Steele's patent was to produce in the performances at Drury Lane.

Nowhere in Steele's writings does he assert more explicitly than in the *Town Talk* his intention to comply with the injunction in his patent that he reform the stage; his emphasis on his duty and on his intention to carry out the duty removes any doubt that he considered his governorship a mere sinecure. A "mighty amendment in theatrical entertainments" is anticipated, he declares; one that has been delayed by the competition offered by the rival theater. But Drury Lane having recovered from the effects of the competition (Steele mentions the "desertion" of the group of actors to Lincoln's Inn Fields), the new era of inoffensive performances will begin.[24] Drury Lane will initiate a policy of encouraging dramatists of ability to write inoffensively by performing their plays carefully and by paying them justly for the plays.[25] No longer,

---

[22] *Apology*, II, 205.

[23] No. 5. I quote from John Nichols's reprint of the *Town Talk* (London, 1789).

[24] Nos. 1, 2.

[25] No. 2.

according to Steele, are the characteristic themes of Restoration comedy to dominate the stage.[26]

To support his promise of a new theatrical era, Steele includes in the *Town Talk*, No. 6, the entire text of his theatrical patent, and in commenting on it, he makes one of his most informative statements of his theatrical ideals:

> This PATENT . . . is the LAW of the THEATRE; and by the rule of it, we are to expect that nothing new shall hereafter come upon the Stage, that may in the least offend decency or good-manners. The indulgence at present given to what is represented there, is a sufferance which it is to be hoped will be made up to the audience in future plays. If every thing that shall be represented is not virtuous, let it at least be innocent. This will bring a new audience to the house; and it is from the hope of entertaining those who at present are terrified at the Theatre, that the sharers must hope for their success hereafter. This will naturally have the desired effect, and Folly will be ridiculous without being at the same time so mixed with Vice, as to make it also terrible. The daughter may be agreeable and blooming, though the mother is at the same time discreet, careful, and anxious for her conduct. No necessary imperfections, such as old age, and misfortune, shall be the objects of derision and buffoonery. The fine gentleman is not absolutely obliged to wrong his friend in the most unpardonable instance, that of his bed; nor is the fine lady of course to like him best, who lavishes his youth among the abandoned of her sex.

With this statement at hand, it may be said emphatically that Steele received earnestly the part of his patent that echoed Jeremy Collier's *A Short View*. At the same time, it must be acknowledged that Steele was aware of the advertising value of such statements.

Within the context of declaration of intention to reform the stage, Steele described his academy or private theater in York Buildings, an enterprise to which he gave a name suggesting its didactic purpose—the Censorium. The *Town Talk*, No. 4, provides the most complete exposition of the plan for the Censorium that Steele ever wrote. But this project, in which he was interested for over ten years, must receive separate attention.[27]

Prominent though the theme of stage reform is in the *Town Talk*, it by no means monopolizes the theatrical portions of the

---

[26] Cf. No. 6.
[27] See below, pp. 98–118.

journal. As in the *Tatler*, Steele included news about the theater, news about the actors, and brief criticisms of and puffs for plays. The comments on specific plays followed the Drury Lane repertory: Steele wrote about plays that had just been performed or were about to be performed. Aware of his ability to attract the town's attention, he reassumed briefly the role of journalistic advocate for the players. And as earlier, he insisted on the dignity of acting as a profession, this time satirizing the prejudice against actors.[28] While it lasted, Steele's colleagues in the management must have found the journal a welcome contribution to their mutual efforts in support of Drury Lane.

The *Town Talk*, however, was short-lived: a bare two months—only nine issues—from December 17, 1715, to February 13, 1716. The reason for its abrupt and unannounced discontinuation is not known. As Steele's parliamentary affairs were then in a troubled state, it is likely that his preoccupation with politics caused its demise. Two weeks later another periodical appeared, advertised as "Chit-Chat, instead of Town-Talk, written to the same Lady in the Country, and concluding with an Argument, concerning the Executed Lords."[29] *Chit-Chat* was certainly the sequel to the *Town Talk* and was probably written by Steele;[30] but because it is concerned with political rather than theatrical matters, it has no relevance here.

A further indication of Steele's active concern for Drury Lane affairs during the winter of 1715–1716 is a letter he wrote to Sir John Stanley, secretary to the lord chamberlain. Stanley had communicated to Steele the lord chamberlain's order that Drury Lane should not hire any person "who has performed, or been entertained in the opera since May last."[31] The note of anger in Steele's reply reveals the persistence at Drury Lane of a defiant belief in the independence granted by the patent; Steele implies that the lord chamber-

---

[28] No. 2.

[29] The *Post-Man*, March 3 to March 6, 1716.

[30] See John Loftis, "The Blenheim Papers and Steele's Journalism, 1715–1718", *Publications of the Modern Language Association of America*, LXVI (1951), 197–210.

[31] *Correspondence*, p. 112.

lain has overstepped his authority in intervening in the affairs of a patent company:

> I delayed the acknowledgment of Yours of the 6th instant till I had Examined what grounds there were for such a signification as I had the Honour to receive from You.
>
> I cannot find that there has been any application made to gain any body from the Opera, and do not doubt but I shall receive as much favour as the other Patent,[82] against wch you know, My Lord Chamberlain denyed to protect the Late License, and sent me to the Lawyers. I speake this with all Humility, tho at the same time, I lay in my Claim to endeavour at pleasing the King, within the Powers He has given me, by representations of all Kinds as the Fashion, or Genius of the times, with regard to the true interest of the publick, shall present me with Opportunity.[83]

Steele's letter to Stanley implies that there was a rivalry between Drury Lane and the opera for performers, and within context his allusion to "representations of all Kinds" according to current fashion can be taken to mean that Drury Lane was presenting musical or operatic entertainments. It is obvious from contemporary newspaper notices and from published masques or operettas that Drury Lane was actually doing so. The patent (unlike the license that preceded it) authorized musical entertainments.

These musical afterpieces (they were merely supplementary performances, never replacing the play of the evening) were initiated on March 12, 1715, with Cibber's *Venus and Adonis,* in the published version of which Cibber included a preface containing criticism suggesting unmistakably the operatic criticism in Steele's major periodicals. Cibber announces that his masque was planned as a corrective to Italian opera.

---

[82] In the Blenheim MS of this letter, the phrase "the other Patent" is written as a replacement for "Mr. Rich," which is crossed out.

[83] *Correspondence,* pp. 112–113. It is barely possible that the bitterness expressed in this letter had origin in a personal rivalry. Several months earlier there had been a rumor that Steele was to succeed Stanley as the lord chamberlain's secretary. On July 16, 1715, James Greenshields wrote to Dr. Charlett: "Sr John Stanely is putt out from being my Ld Chamberlains Secretary, & is succeeded by Sr R. Steel." Quoted from Aitken, *Life,* II, 85n.

The following Entertainment is an Attempt to give the Town a little good Musick in a Language they understand: For no Theatrical Performance can be absolutely Good, that is not Proper; and how can we judge of its Propriety, when we know not one Word of the Voice's Meaning? But perhaps this is not all that the Italian Language has of late impos'd upon us, most of our Opera's being (if possible) as miserably void of Common Sense in their Original, as the Translation. . . .

It is therefore hoped, that this Undertaking, if Encourag'd, may in time reconcile Musick to the English Tongue. And, to make the Union more practicable, it is humbly moved, that it may be allow'd a less Inconvenience, to hear the Performer express his Meaning with an imperfect Accent, than in Words, that (to an English Audience) have no Meaning at all.

The statement has the ring of controversy—though the ideas expressed were widely held by literary critics.[34] Drury Lane, according to Cibber, was inaugurating a studied campaign against opera in which an attempt would be made to reconcile music with poetry. The campaign was prosecuted. *Venus and Adonis,* apparently popular (its mediocre verse notwithstanding), was performed repeatedly during the spring of 1715, whereas the following season Cibber brought out another similar entertainment, *Myrtillo,* as did John Hughes with *Apollo and Daphne* and Barton Booth with *The Death of Dido.*[35] It was about *Apollo and Daphne* that Steele wrote to Hughes in January, 1716, proposing to puff it in the *Town Talk.*

Such then is the immediate background for the rivalry with the opera suggested by Steele's letter to Stanley. Drury Lane was finding musical masques as afterpieces profitable—and justified them as counterblasts at the Italian opera. That Steele himself was concerned with them seems reasonably certain in view of the proprietary tone of the letter to Stanley, the marked similarity between Cibber's opinion expressed in his preface and Steele's known opinion of Italian opera, and Steele's direct reference to John Hughes's

[34] Cf. Siegmund A. E. Betz, "The Operatic Criticism of the *Tatler* and *Spectator," Musical Quarterly,* XXXI (1945), 318–330.

[35] The success of these highly rhetorical and serious masques at Drury Lane apparently gave rise to parodies of them at Lincoln's Inn Fields. Cf. the preface to *The Comick Masque of Pyramus and Thisbe* (London, 1716); and *Presumptuous Love: A Dramatic Masque* (London, 1716).

masque in his letter of January 8, 1716. Simultaneously with this
campaign against Italian opera at Drury Lane, moreover, Steele
was planning a similar campaign for his academy in York Buildings. His account of the Censorium included in the *Town Talk*
reveals, like Cibber's preface to *Venus and Adonis,* an animus
against the opera and a plan to oppose it by offering a competitive
entertainment incorporating with the appeal of music the rational
appeal of poetry. Both in the Censorium and at Drury Lane, it
appears then, Steele made an effort during 1715 and 1716 to translate his earlier theoretical objections to opera into the more effective
form of a rival entertainment.

One of the duties that fell to the managers of Drury Lane would
have been particularly attractive to Steele—that of selecting new
plays for performance. As a playwright and dramatic critic himself, his judgment about plays was much more than an amateur
one, though he was probably less sensitively aware than his colleagues of the financial problems posed by new plays. At any rate
there are several allusions during his active years in the management to his support of particular plays. Many of his literary friends
doubtless thought of him as an influential intermediary with the
actor-managers in arranging for the production of their plays[36]—
no easy task in those years.

It is not surprising to find Steele introducing to his colleagues
a play by his former collaborator and close friend Addison. In the
final number of the *Town Talk* (February 13, 1716) Steele related
that a new comedy had been delivered to him as governor of the
Royal Company of Comedians under a pledge of secrecy as to the
name of the author. The comedy was excellent, Steele explained,
yet it revealed a subtlety of design that made its reception uncertain, the debauched public taste requiring violence and extravagance. Hence the author's unwillingness to trust his reputation to
it. Steele promised, however, that he would himself insure it a fair
trial by a selected audience. The comedy was, of course, *The
Drummer,* acted at Drury Lane in March, 1716, where it met the
indifferent reception Steele had feared. The same month the play

---

[36] Cf. Steele's letter of January 30, 1722, to Henry Davenant. This letter
was, of course, written after Steele's alienation from the actor-managers.
Correspondence, p. 173.

was published anonymously with a laudatory preface by Steele, in which he mentioned the play reading. "My brother-sharers were of opinion, at the first reading of it, that it was like a picture in which the strokes were not strong enough to appear at a distance." The implication is that Steele had persuaded the actor-managers to accept the play. The importance of his support will be better understood when it is realized that *The Drummer* was the only new play acted at Drury Lane during the entire season of 1715–1716.[37]

The following season Steele aided his old friend Mrs. Manley in arranging for the production of her tragedy *Lucius*—or so it may be assumed from her dedicatory letter addressed to him, in which she thanked him for "the Zeal and Sollicitude which You shew'd for my private Interests in the Success of this PLAY." Steele, moreover, wrote a prologue for the tragedy, one which he later printed in the *Theatre* by way of a puff for a revival of the play.[38]

The next season Steele held in his own home a play reading of John Dennis's *The Invader of His Country*. Dennis himself later described the occasion in a letter to Steele (complaining about the managers' treatment of the play):

It was upon the 27th of February, 1717/8, that I receiv'd a Letter from Mr. *Booth* by your Direction, and the Direction of the Managers under you, desiring me to dine at your House on the 28th, and after Dinner to read the Tragedy of *Coriolanus* to you, which I had alter'd from *Shakespear*. You cannot but remember, Sir, that upon reading it, the Play with

[37] I base this statement upon an examination of the Frederick Latreille manuscript theatrical calendar in the British Museum: Add. MS 32249. The Latreille calendar, which is much more complete than the record of performances in John Genest, *Some Account of the English Stage, from 1660 to 1830* (Bath, 1832), is based chiefly upon the daily notices of performances printed in the *Daily Courant* and the *Daily Post.* Latreille also derived a small amount of information from the Burney Theatrical Register, similarly preserved in the British Museum. In extensive cross-checking between the Latreille calendar and the daily newspaper notices of performances, I have found Latreille thoroughly reliable. That *The Drummer* was the only new play presented at Drury Lane during the season of 1715–1716, I have varified in Genest, who, though he lists only representative performances, records the production of all new plays.

[38] The *Theatre*, No. 10.

the Alterations was approv'd of, nay and warmly approv'd of, by your self, Mr. *Cibber,* and Mr. *Booth,* (the other Manager was not there) and that Resolutions were taken for the acting it in the beginning of this Winter.[39]

Dennis reproaches Steele for the treatment the play received, assuming that much of the responsibility was his. To be sure, Dennis also charges Steele with neglecting his responsibility, but implicit in his charge is the assumption that Steele's obligations to the theater were substantial.

This instance of Steele's sharing the managerial burdens of Drury Lane has come to light only because it led to a dispute with Dennis. It is reasonable to assume that on a number of such occasions, of which no record remains, Steele joined with his colleagues in passing judgment on plays offered by hopeful playwrights.

Two of John Gay's farces acted at Drury Lane during the years of Steele's activity raise interesting questions about Steele's relations with the management. The first, *The What D'Ye Call It,* presented with success at Drury Lane in February, 1715, elicited a comment from Steele that has come down to us. According to Pope (in a letter to Caryll written in March, 1715), "Mr. Steele declares the farce should not have been acted if he had been in town. The new theatre in Lincoln's Inn Fields have thoughts of acting it without his consent."[40] The reason for Steele's objection may be deduced from the farce itself: merry though it is, it contains sharp satire directed at, among other plays, Addison's *Cato* and Philips's *The Distressed Mother* (which Steele had praised in the *Spectator* and for which he had written a prologue). Appearing at a time when Gay and Pope were separated by political feeling from Steele and his Whig friends at Button's—at a time, moreover, when rivalry over the competitive translations of Homer was acute—the farce necessarily assumed the character of a partisan document. Hence Steele's dissatisfaction that it was presented at Drury Lane. But presented it was many times; it won a permanent place, as an afterpiece, in the company's repertory. We may only

[39] Hooker, *Dennis,* II, 162.
[40] W. Elwin and W. J. Courthope, eds., *The Works of Alexander Pope* (London, 1871–1889), VI, 225–226.

assume that the managers were unwilling to sacrifice so successful a farce to Steele's prejudices.

Three Hours After Marriage, written by Gay in collaboration with Pope and Arbuthnot, raises similar problems concerning Steele's relations with his colleagues, though this time it appears likely that they shared his prejudices. Presented at Drury Lane in January, 1717, the farce was acted seven consecutive times (a good run); yet it was then dropped completely because, according to Professor Sherburn, "the prejudice of the wits at Button's made it impossible for them to enjoy the absurdities of the play, and . . . they drew many spectators to their contemptuous attitude."[41] In view of Steele's close association with Button's and his even closer association with Drury Lane, it is tempting to assume that he acted as an intermediary between the two groups. Evidence is insufficient, though not totally lacking. Pope implied that Steele was prominent in the opposition to the play. "Mr. Addison and his friends" complained so much about the obscenity in the farce, Pope told Spence, that Gay wrote a pamphlet on the subject in which he cited the passages in the farce that had aroused strongest criticism, opposing to them other passages in Addison's and Steele's plays.[42] When two years later Dr. Woodward, one of the chief butts of *Three Hours After Marriage,* was again satirized upon the stage (in *Harlequin Hydaspes* presented at Lincoln's Inn Fields), Steele came to his defense in print, deploring the poor taste that could make a public jest of a man admirable personally and professionally.[43] He did not mention *Three Hours* directly, but he could scarcely have been unaware of the parallel, so obviously does *Harlequin Hydaspes* suggest the earlier play.[44] We

---

[41] George Sherburn, "The Fortunes and Misfortunes of *Three Hours After Marriage, Modern Philology,* XXIV (1926–1927), 99. See this article for an excellent summary of the known facts about the production of the farce. I find it difficult, however, to accept Professor Sherburn's assumption (page 104) that Cibber would not have understood from the beginning that some of the satire was leveled at the actor-managers.

[42] Joseph Spence, *Anecdotes, Observations, and Characters, of Books and Men,* ed. Samuel Weller Singer (London, 1820), pp. 202–203.

[43] *The Antidote, In a Letter to the Freethinker,* Nos. 1, 2. In *Tracts and Pamphlets,* pp. 501–519. Woodward was Steele's personal physician.

[44] Cf. Lester M. Beattie, *John Arbuthnot: Mathematician and Satirist* (Cambridge, Mass., 1935), p. 257.

have only such indirect evidence, but it is enough to establish positively Steele's sympathies. Steele doubtless supported Cibber when the actor quarreled with Pope or Gay or both over some satirical lines directed at *Three Hours* inserted in *The Rehearsal*, revived soon after the farce's run.

Further glimpses of Steele's Drury Lane activities are provided by his letters to his wife written in 1717, when she was on a prolonged visit to Wales. His allusions to the theater in these letters reveal that he was following the fortunes of the company with a businesslike concern, as on June 11, 1717, when he observed that he was writing

from Richmond, where I have been since yesterday Morning at a Lodging near Wilks, who I beleive, will bring matters to bear so as that there will be no Play-House but Ours, allowing Rich, who is almost broke, a Sallary while there is but one House. I am in hopes one way or other let the Courtiers do as unthankfully as they please, I shall pick up a Comfortable fortune.[45]

So far had Drury Lane recovered from the depression into which the rivalry with Lincoln's Inn Fields drove it (Wilks's effort to silence Rich, however, was not successful). Two months later Steele wrote to his wife about a new plan for profiting from his theatrical association. "I am confident dayly intelligence of what passes at the Play House will be some Hundreds in my Way. And money is the main thing."[46] He was tentatively projecting a new periodical to be devoted, like the *Town Talk* earlier and the *Theatre* later, to news of the stage; indeed, his statement may record the inception of the plan for the *Theatre,* the first number of which, however, was not published until January 2, 1720. His active participation in Drury Lane affairs is further revealed by a statement in a letter to his wife written September 24, 1717: "My own studies at the Theatre, Gillmore [his partner in the scheme for importing fresh fish] &c will amply do anything I can form to my self, without Stooping to Servilities."[47] Resentful of the treatment he has received from the court, he resolves, as Lady Steele had advised him, to concentrate his activities more narrowly.

[45] *Correspondence*, p. 353.
[46] *Ibid.,* p. 367.
[47] *Ibid.,* pp. 374–375.

Whether the actor-managers saw him more frequently as a result of this resolution cannot be determined, but he did continue to follow their mutual fortunes. "The Theatre seems to be in a very prosperous way,"[48] he wrote the following month, in the last allusion to Drury Lane in this series of letters. We hear no more about the theater in his correspondence (until after 1720), not necessarily because he became less active there but because his principal correspondent—his wife—came home.

These brief remarks in his letters are supplemented by other similarly brief records from a variety of sources, which, fragmentary as they are, add to the total impression of his Drury Lane association. According to an early biography of Richard Savage, it was through the Drury Lane production of *Love in a Veil* (June, 1718) that Savage made Steele's acquaintance.[49] Steele's occasional presence at the theater is suggested by Theophilus Cibber's recollection of Steele's kindness to him when he entered the company about 1720:

'Twas about this Time Sir RICHARD STEEL, then *Governor* of his *Majesty's Company* of *Comedians*, took particular Notice of, and shewed a kind Regard for, me. Many pleasant and profitable Hours I enjoyed by his favouring me with a *Tete-à-tete*, and sometimes introducing me to Persons of Eminence, of whose Conversation (but for this Advantage) I could not hope to have been the humble and silent Admirer.—And as the Theatre was not an excluded Topic, from thence I frequently collected such Sentiments as gave me a better Chance for the Improvement of my Taste and Knowledge of the Theatre and World in general.[50]

Here is a glimpse of the companionship centered in the theater which Steele must certainly have relished. There has already been occasion to refer to several of the elder Cibber's statements about Steele, but one anecdote included in the *Apology* is appropriate here. Cibber describes the production of *Henry VIII* at Hampton Court in 1718, recalling Steele's reply to a nobleman who enquired how the king liked the play. "*So terribly well, my Lord, that I was*

[48] *Ibid.*, p. 377.

[49] *The Life of Mr. Richard Savage*, second edition (London, 1727), p. 10.

[50] Theophilus Cibber, *The Lives and Characters of the Most Eminent Actors and Actresses of Great Britain and Ireland* (London, 1753), pp. vi–vii.

afraid I should have lost all my Actors! For I was not sure the King would not keep them to fill the Posts at Court that he saw them so fit for in the Play.[51] According to another anecdote, reported anonymously in a newspaper many years later, about 1716 Steele registered his disapproval of the dancing master Weaver in a couplet he wrote on the back of one of the playbills at Button's:

> Weaver, corrupter of this present age,
> Who first taught silent sins upon the stage.[52]

A satire directed at Drury Lane in 1723 pictures Steele (Sir Harry Gubbin, Knt.) present at a policy-making meeting of the managers in the green room as they discuss means to outdo the extravagance of Lincoln's Inn Fields performances.[53] These several allusions are, to be sure, widely scattered, yet they suggest the contemporary association of Steele with Drury Lane.

Steele's dispute with the lord chamberlain during the winter of 1719–1720, which brought his suspension from the theater and which marked the end of his active association with the management, occasioned several informative statements about his activities as governor during the previous five years. It must be remembered, however, that these statements—whether sympathetic or hostile to Steele—were made in the course of a dispute; they express partisan views. Hence they must be used with caution.

Even when allowances are made for the bitterness of his opponents, Steele fared rather badly in this dispute; the charges that he neglected his duties at Drury Lane carry more conviction than his own vehement insistence that he performed them satisfactorily. Truth probably lies somewhat closer to his opponents than to himself. It is significant, however, that both he and his opponents assumed that his responsibilities at Drury Lane were real, not merely nominal.

Steele several times asserted (as later during the lawsuit with the managers) that he performed his duties at Drury Lane faith-

---

[51] II, 217.

[52] British Museum, Additional MS 25391. The anecdote is related in a clipping, dated 1763, from an unidentified newspaper.

[53] *To Diabebouloumenon: Or, The Proceedings At the Theatre-Royal in Drury Lane* (London, 1723), p. 15; cf. also p. 29.

fully. In a petition to the king, presented January 22, 1720, he declared "That Your Petr humbly Conceives that he has fully answered all the Designes of Your Matys Grant, to the Great Improvement of the Theatre,"[54] while in the *Theatre*, No. 8, he maintained that under his governorship Drury Lane flourished in an unprecedented degree. In the *Theatre*, No. 13, he insisted forcefully on his service:

THE INJURED KNIGHT [Steele himself] has his greatest complaint still to make, to wit, that he is represented as not having shewed zeal to his Majesty's service in this his Government, but been careless in that particular. . . . Our Knight has not omitted in the way of the Stage (over which he had the happiness, and has the right to preside) to do his duty to his Sovereign, any more than on better occasions.

But there were many to contradict him.

On the contrary side of the dispute, the strongest voice was that of John Dennis, who, moved partly by his personal animus against Steele and the actor-managers, insisted that under their government the drama had vilely degenerated, principally because Steele, his obligation to Drury Lane notwithstanding, left the management to the three actors. Steele was a "mere Nominal Sovereign," Dennis charged; the actual supervision of the stage was entrusted to his "Viceroy" (Cibber) and to the two other "Deputy Governors," none of whom was by ability, training, or interests qualified for such a responsibility.[55] In strongly vituperative terms Dennis described Steele's career at Drury Lane:

He had one while . . . obtain'd a Patent to be Governour of the *Beargarden;* tho that Patent was invalid and void, by vertue of a previous Statute. Yet when he thought himself establish'd in that Post, he chose a *Bear,* a *Baboon,* and a *Wolf* for his Deputy Governours; but partly growing Lazy, and being partly convinc'd, that the Deputies were fitter for Government than the Principal, he abandon'd all to them; who conducting themselves by their Bestial Appetites, play'd such Pranks, that both Governours and Deputies were all remov'd. . . .[56]

Dennis sacrificed accuracy to rhetoric, but he made his point.

[54] *Correspondence,* p. 532.
[55] *The Characters and Conduct of Sir John Edgar,* in Hooker, *Dennis,* II, 182–186.
[56] *Ibid.,* II, 216.

Corroboration of Dennis's indictment is to be found in several places. In a thinly disguised allegorical narrative included in the eighth number of the *Anti-Theatre* (an anonymous periodical written in answer to Steele's the *Theatre*), the author, writing in the person of a fictional actress, asserts that several years ago a "King" was put over her company, who, "being lazy and indolent, neglected his government; and, to throw all care off from himself, chose three Viceroys, in which he neither consulted merit nor dignity." In *The Crisis of Honesty* (published anonymously in the spring of 1720) Steele and his partners receive the title of "a Dean and his Chapter," Steele being denounced for "accepting of a profitable publick Employment, and refusing to act in it."[57] The most convincing support for Dennis's accusation, however, appears in *The State of the Case . . . Restated* (an anonymous answer to Steele's *The State of the Case*), in which Steele is vigorously reprimanded for failing to reform the stage. The author charges that Steele

has not at any time, during his administration, made one step towards those glorious ends proposed by his Majesty, for the service of religion and virtue, nor reformed the least abuse of either. The same lewd Plays being acted and revived without any material alteration, which gave occasion for that universal complaint against the English Stage, of lewdness and debauchery, from all the sober and religious part of the nation; the whole business of Comedy continuing all his time to be the criminal intrigues of fornication and adultery, ridiculing of marriage, virtue, and integrity, the giving a favourable turn to vicious characters, and instructing loose people how to carry on their lewd designs with plausibility and success; thus, among other Plays, they have revived "The Country Wife;" "Sir Fopling Flutter;" "The Rover;" "The Libertine destroyed;" and several others. . . .[58]

Steele must himself assume responsibility, the author continues, or he must, by blaming his partners for the Drury Lane offenses, admit that he has no authority in the playhouse—an uncomfortable dilemma.

---

[57] *The Crisis of Honesty, Being an Answer to the Crisis of Property* (London, 1720), pp. 27–28.

[58] *The State of the Case . . . Restated*, in John Nichols, ed., *The Theatre* (London, 1791), II, 511–512.

From the terms in which the author of *The State of the Case . . . Restated* poses his denunciation, a chief reason may be determined why he, Dennis, and the others believed that Steele had neglected his duties at Drury Lane. Steele's early promises to the contrary, the Drury Lane repertory continued largely unaltered. These journalistic opponents of Steele knew that he had been commanded to reform the stage and that he had publicly promised (in the *Town Talk*) to do so; that he had failed was demonstrated unequivocally by the plays appearing daily at Drury Lane. These writers were not interested specifically, as we are, in the biographical facts of Steele's relations with the management, if, indeed (apart from Dennis), they knew anything about the relations.

Their conclusion nevertheless seems in a measure justified. That Steele was somewhat slovenly in conducting his Drury Lane affairs—as he was in conducting almost all his affairs—is apparent. He was indisputably a less effective reformer as governor of the theater than as an essayist; certainly he did not supervise the day-to-day business of the theater as Dennis thought he should. If he had made a sustained effort to modify sharply Drury Lane managerial policies, a more positive record in the contemporary theatrical literature would remain. Yet there is no reason to doubt his own and his colleagues' assertions that from 1714 until 1720 he was active in support of the theater. Rather, on the evidence of Lord Stair's letter to Steele about engaging two harlequins popular in France and Steele's own letter to Sir John Stanley protesting his right to meet the taste of the town, there is a suspicion that Steele, convinced of the necessity of sacrificing stage reform to the exigencies of theatrical competition, aided his colleagues in providing popular entertainment.

2 | Drury Lane under Steele

THE CHARGE voiced by Dennis and the author of *The State of the Case . . . Restated* that Steele did not reform Drury Lane can scarcely be refuted. The author of *The State of the Case . . . Restated* provided evidence; he named specific plays—*The Country Wife* and *Sir Fopling Flutter* among others—that continued to appear at Drury Lane despite the long-standing complaints against them. Recalling the denunciation of *Sir Fopling Flutter* in the *Spectator,* this author charged Steele with either ineffectiveness or indifference[50]—the incongruity between Steele's publicly announced convictions and his action at Drury Lane was inescapable. All Steele's promises of stage reform rang false when confronted with the fact of the Drury Lane repertory.

The charge against Steele is most clearly and convincingly expressed by the author of *The State of the Case . . . Restated.* His indictment and those of Dennis and the authors of the *Anti-Theatre* and *The Crisis of Honesty* are, however, but representative of a legion of others. To be sure, in most of them Steele is not mentioned, the attacks concentrating on Cibber, Wilks, and Booth, but (as pointed out in *The State of the Case . . . Restated*) Steele was compelled to assume responsibility for Drury Lane or disavow his governorship. He was indubitably held responsible by the lord chamberlain when he was suspended in January, 1720, for, among other offenses, mismanagement of the theater.

Steele's dereliction of duty at Drury Lane may be loosely referred to as a failure to "reform" the stage, but the term must be qualified if it is to have much meaning. Certainly many of his contemporaries who found Drury Lane under his supervision unsatisfactory objected on other grounds than strictly moral ones, strong though the moral objections were. They complained most

---

[50] *Ibid.*

frequently of the inadequacies of the actor-managers as arbiters of drama, resenting Steele's grant of authority to them to super-intend the usual business of the theater. The actor-managers, their detractors charged, were mercenary, sacrificing drama to an in-satiable desire for profit; knowing that they could draw a full house with the established plays in their repertoire, they refused new plays to avoid the expense of the dramatist's benefit night; they frequently raised their prices, confident that they could draw a crowd anyway; they were tyrannical in their treatment of aspiring dramatists, capriciously refusing good plays, frequently for in-significant or personal reasons; they lacked judgment on dramatic questions; their personalities—notably Cibber's but to a lesser degree Wilks's—were objectionable. For all these grievances Steele, as governor of the theater, was held at least indirectly re-sponsible. He failed, not only to improve the moral tone of Drury Lane performances, but also to correct these alleged abuses in the theater's management.

Rather than diminishing, the chorus of complaints about the theater grew progressively louder and more insistent, reaching a climax with the suspension of Steele in January, 1720. Pope, Gay, and Arbuthnot's farce *Three Hours After Marriage* (January, 1717), itself containing pointed satire at the ineptitude and greed of the actor-managers and at the consequent difficulty in getting a new play accepted at Drury Lane, touched off a public review of Drury Lane's shortcomings.[60] A dedicatory letter written the same year contains a lament that reveals the tenor of many of the com-plaints. "The Masters of the Play-house have always used me very barbarously, in returning my Plays without giving me the least Hope or Encouragement to proceed in my Studies for the future."[61] There is a similar complaint expressed ironically in a preface writ-ten the following year. "This Play was design'd for the Stage, but it happen'd not to please the Directors, who are Men of too much

---

[60] *The Confederates: A Farce* (London, 1717); *A Letter to Mr. John Gay, Concerning His Late Farce, Entitled, a Comedy* (London, 1717); *A Complete Key to the New Farce, call'd Three Hours after Marriage* (London, 1717). See also Sherburn, *op. cit.*

[61] Edward Biddle, Dedication to *A Poem on the Birth of the Young Prince* (London, 1717).

Piety to countenance any thing that does not savour of Virtue and Religion, for whose Support they use their utmost Endeavours; which may be easily seen by any Body that frequents the Play-House. . . ."[62] The irony notwithstanding, it may be assumed that the managers were paying lip service to moral reform, but it may be similarly assumed, from this and other statements, that their accomplishment was unsatisfactory—witness the following denunciation provoked by Cibber's *The Non-Juror* (1718). " 'Tis possible, that by the Tenure of their Grant from the Crown, which entitles them to call their Nursery of Vice and Debauchery the *Theatre-Royal,* they may, with some colour of Justice, write themselves *His Majesty's Servants.* . . ."[63] The next year (November 17, 1719) the *Delphick Oracle* contained a powerful blast at stage immorality, though it was not directed specifically at Drury Lane. The preface to George Sewell's *Sir Walter Raleigh* (1719) included an explicit criticism of the actor-managers' treatment of playwrights. "Yet I hope a young Author may be excused if upon hearing their [Drury Lane's] *shocking Treatment* of the Best Writers, he trembled to think how a New Unexperienced one was to be used." A critical essay of the same year denounced the insipidity of the new plays at Drury Lane, the critic implying that the managers made their choices capriciously. ". . . the Author [of *The Masquerade,* one of the new plays] had indeed a great deal of Reason to mention his Obligation to Mr. *Wilks,* by whose Interest in the House, without doubt both this and his other Plays have obtain'd the Favour of being acted, when the Performances of Men, infinitely his Superiours in Merit, have been neglected or thrown by. . . ."[64] Substantially the same opinion is voiced by Lewis Theobald in an obvious allusion to Drury Lane in the preface to his adaptation of *Richard II* (1720). "The brightest Performance, if

[62] *The Match-Maker fitted: Or, the Fortune-Hunters rightly serv'd* (London, 1718).

[63] *The Theatre-Royal Turn'd into a Mountebank's Stage* (London, 1718), pp. 1–2. But see the strong defense of Drury Lane in *Some Cursory Remarks on the Play call'd the Non-Juror* (London, 1718).

[64] *Critical Remarks on the Four Taking Plays of this Season; Viz. Sir Walter Raleigh, The Masquerade, Chit-Chat, and Busiris King of Egypt* (London, 1719), pp. 50–51.

not forc'd upon the Stage by a high Hand, or creeping to it with a servile Submission, may be neglected, lost, or what is worse, the Writer abus'd, and his Reputation, as Such, lost, before he has tried it." Thus the critics in the chorus of complaints leading to the lord chamberlain's action of 1720.

What was the basis for these complaints? It is certain some of them were exaggerated or were provoked by personal malice or disappointment. The managers, frequently beset by aspiring playwrights possessing more ambition than talent, were forced in the interests of their own livelihood and of the public stage to refuse plays, often at the expense of arousing ill-will. In defense of the managers, moreover, the prosperous condition of the theater during these years may be cited. Drury Lane played consistently to crowded audiences, most of whom were probably satisfied with the entertainment they received. Plays were handsomely mounted, and the quality of acting was good. Nevertheless, the complaints about the theater were too frequent and too harsh to have been completely unprovoked. Their basis in fact may be revealed by a closer look at the company's repertory during the years 1714–1720.

The play notices provide abundant evidence that the "immoral" comedies, peopled by fine ladies and gentlemen motivated by loose desires, continued to appear prominently at Drury Lane.[65] The repertory of the theater underwent no remarkable change; Restoration plays formed, as previously, the staple commodity— but not to the exclusion of plays by Shakespeare, Jonson, Beaumont and Fletcher from the earlier period, and by Farquhar, Rowe, Cibber, Addison, and Steele from the later. No sudden omission of the reprehensible plays occurred, though the occasional appearance of the phrase "carefully revised" in the advertisements for some of them suggests that an attempt was made to remove the most objectionable portions of the action and dialogue.[66] Throughout

---

[65] I base the following analysis of the Drury Lane repertory chiefly upon the Latreille calendar (Brit. Mus., Add. MS 32249). The analysis may, in all essentials, be verified in Genest, *Some Account of the English Stage*, II, 545–647.

[66] *Greenwich Park* was so advertised on February 8, 1716; *The Country Wife* on September 29, 1716. Colley Cibber reported one such "revision": "In 1725 we were call'd upon, in a manner that could not be resisted, to

the six seasons such plays as *The Old Bachelor, Love for Love, The Way of the World, The Country Wife, The Man of Mode, The Relapse,* and *The Spanish Friar* were performed—good plays, to be sure, but ones possessing qualities Steele had condemned in the *Tatler,* the *Spectator,* and the *Guardian* (inconsistently he had also praised some of these plays in the periodicals). The charge of inconsistency—or of incompetence—advanced by the author of *The State of the Case ... Restated* is corroborated by the record of the theater's performances.

The entr'acte entertainments and afterpieces featured at Drury Lane during these seasons provide similar evidence of an incongruity between Steele's theory and practice. There has already been occasion to speak of his engaging two pantomimists from France for an appearance at Drury Lane during the spring of 1716, performers who specialized in "non-rational" entertainment of a kind Steele frequently deplored. To be sure, he apologized in the *Town Talk* for such performances, promising an amendment inasmuch as the company was emerging successfully from a competitive struggle with Lincoln's Inn Fields. But the amendment did not come. Pantomime, farcical afterpieces, dancing, tumbling, juggling, epilogues spoken from asses' backs—all such added attractions became increasingly prominent with the passing seasons, as the notices in the newspapers bear witness. From the bare announcements of the name of the play and an occasional afterpiece in the season of 1714–1715, the notices grew gradually to substantial proportions (though they remained consistently briefer than the full paragraphs itemizing the competitive attractions at Lincoln's Inn Fields). Typical of the emphasis on spectacle and novelty is the notice for October 12, 1717.

---

revive the *Provok'd Wife,* a Comedy which, while we found our Account in keeping the Stage clear of those loose Liberties it had formerly too justly been charg'd with, we had laid aside for some Years. The Author, Sir *John Vanbrugh,* who was conscious of what it had too much of, was prevail'd upon to substitute a new-written Scene in the Place of one in the fourth Act, where the Wantonness of his Wit and Humour had (originally) made a Rake talk like a Rake in the borrow'd Habit of a Clergyman. . . ." *Apology,* II, 233.

The Maid's Tragedy. With a new set of scenes after Le Brun's Battles of Alexander. And the dramatic entertainment of dancing called The Loves of Mars and Venus.[67]

And the notice for May 5, 1719.

. . . Love's Last Shift. With several entertainments of Dancing,—viz: a Flute Chacone by Mrs. Santlow,—The Strippers by Birkhead and Mrs. Bicknell,—a dance by Shaw and Miss Younger,—a Harlequin by Miss Lindar. With an Epilogue by Penkethman riding on an Ass.[68]

Singing and dancing (often "dramatic entertainments of dancing") are nearly always mentioned; the vaudeville-type entertainments provided a regular supplement to the evening's play. Steele did not, then, drive from Drury Lane the nonintellectual spectacles that consistently provoked the scorn of contemporary dramatic critics.[69]

Much more infuriating to critics and playwrights than the tolerance of spectacle at Drury Lane, however, was the company's reluctance to accept new plays. The company relied heavily— indeed, almost exclusively—on their stock plays, accepting only one, two, or three new plays a year. "The partiality of the Town," wrote John Dennis, "makes the Managers of the Theatre in Drury Lane stick to their old Plays, and reject all new ones unlesse those which are forcd upon them."[70] During the season of 1714–1715 Drury Lane presented only two new plays (exclusive of afterpieces),[71] one of them by the famous Nicholas Rowe. During the season of 1715–1716 they presented only one—by Joseph Addison. During 1716–1717, a better year for the dramatists, they presented four new plays, one of them, Lucius, evidently with Steele's support. During 1717–1718 they were back again to two, one of these being Cibber's

---

[67] The Daily Courant, as recorded in Latreille calendar (Brit. Mus. Add. MS 32249), fol. 267.

[68] Ibid., fol. 303.

[69] For a discussion of the contemporary criticism of these spectacles, see Emmett L. Avery, "The Defense and Criticism of Pantomimic Entertainments in the Eighteenth Century," ELH, A Journal of English Literary History, V (1938), 127–145.

[70] The Causes of the Decay and Defects of Dramatick Poetry, and of the Degeneracy of the Publick Tast [1725?], in Hooker, Dennis, II, 278.

[71] I base these figures on the Latreille calendar (Brit. Mus., Add. MS 32249), though I have verified them in Genest, op. cit., II, 545–647.

The Non-Juror. During 1718–1719 the number was up to three, but from the dedication of one of them (Edward Young's *Busiris*) it would appear that the lord chamberlain forced the managers to accept it.[72] We see the point to the couplet in the epilogue to *Sir Walter Raleigh* (Lincoln's Inn Fields, 1719):

> What! Two New Plays! and those at once appear!
> Sure, Authors fancy this a thriving Year!

The frustrating results of this niggardly treatment of new plays may easily be surmised. Ambitious and sometimes capable dramatists often could not get their plays staged—to their own and to dramatic literature's disadvantage. Drury Lane and Lincoln's Inn Fields enjoyed jointly a virtual monopoly on drama in London. Of the two houses, Drury Lane during most of the seasons of Steele's active governorship was decidedly the more popular and hence the more attractive to hopeful playwrights; Lincoln's Inn Fields remained an alternative but an unattractive and often, of course, an unwilling one. We can understand then why so many prefaces and dedications to published plays express bitterness toward the Drury Lane managers.

Steele recognized the error of the company's failure to encourage dramatists, and in that testament to his good intentions, the *Town Talk*, he promised a change in policy. "I have been credibly informed," he wrote in No. 2, "that the sharers in ... DRURY-LANE had formed a design of reforming the present taste of it, by giving due encouragement to men of abilities, as well by a careful performance of what they should act, as a just recompence for the purchase of their works, to engage them steadily and heartily in their interests." The opening of Lincoln's Inn Fields, Steele explained, delayed the inauguration of this design, but Drury Lane, having emerged successfully from the competition, would put it into effect. Nothing of the kind happened; that promise went the way of Steele's other good resolutions.

In view of this series of broken promises, Steele's multitudinous

[72] Young dedicated the play to the lord chamberlain, Newcastle, remarking that "by its good Fortune in a Season of some Danger to it, [it] received its Life and Success on the Stage." Young, Dedication, *Busiris, King of Egypt* (London, 1719).

pleas for a more carefully regulated stage are open to a charge of insincerity. Why, if he were sincere, does the record of Drury Lane performances not show more signs of amendment?

Steele in his writings, I would hazard, habitually overstated his concern for reform. Having discovered in the *Tatler* a vein of writing that was immensely popular (the moralizing of an old eccentric), he exploited it in his subsequent periodicals—witness the consistency of tone throughout at least all the nonpolitical ones. He learned early the journalistic appeal of humorous moral instruction and made the most of it thereafter. This is not to deny altogether sincerity to his writings; his record as a practical reformer is impressive, and he was without any doubt deeply interested in the reform of, among other things, the stage. But in much of his moralizing, Steele was probably motivated more by habit and by knowledge of what would be popular than by conviction.

There were, moreover, compelling practical reasons why Steele could not easily "reform" Drury Lane, not the least of which were the stubborn personalities of the veteran actors with whom he was associated. Wilks, Booth, and Cibber would not have accepted lightly any major change in their manner of conducting the theater—one that, with all its shortcomings, had brought them substantial prosperity. They were acutely aware, if Steele seemed sometimes not to be, of the precarious nature of their hold on the public favor, and they were not ready to endanger their popularity in a quixotic attempt at public improvement. The contemporary allusions to their greed are too numerous to be without foundation. Cibber, dominant in business affairs, was renowned for his ability to meet successfully the changing whims of public taste. Steele had little chance of gaining his wholehearted coöperation in altering the company's repertoire according to a design that might meet public resistance.

The force of inertia would also have resisted any sudden and substantial change in the company's policies. It must be remembered that Drury Lane was a repertory theater and that the repertory system made heavy demands on the actors of the company. During the season of 1715–1716, as an illustration, the company presented sixty-four *different* plays (exclusive of afterpieces), the principal actors appearing in most of them. It was not uncommon for an actor to appear in a different role every night of the week. With such demands made on the company's personnel, there could be no wholesale change in the plays presented, because the actors could learn only a limited number of new parts a year. Any substantial change in the repertory had thus to come about gradually, though it doubtless could have come about much faster than it did in fact. The managers had no alternative but to present their stock plays—those the actors knew—if they were to offer the variety of plays demanded by the town.

It is doubtful also whether many new "innocent" plays of a quality to merit production were being written. Much of the dramatic criticism written in the name of reform came from people ignorant of playwriting, and was often irresponsible and futile; most of the advice given to playwrights was negative. When in his periodicals and in *The Conscious Lovers* Steele set about to provide a pattern that other dramatists might follow, he implied that a satisfactory pattern was lacking. Though the formula he evolved was less original than he believed, his self-conscious campaign in support of it suggests the lack of direction that marked many of the earlier attempts at writing reformed comedy. There were then, it seems, few suitable comedies available to the Drury Lane managers as replacements for their Restoration plays. A few plays, such as *The Drummer,* appeared from time to time with indifferent success, but many plays that could draw crowds were needed if the managers were to make any substantial change in their repertoire.

Another force in preventing any marked change in the policies of Drury Lane was the acute and continuing rivalry with Lincoln's Inn Fields. The immediate effect on Drury Lane profits of the opening of the rival theater in December, 1714, has already been noted. Under John Rich, a specialist in novelties and spectacles who felt no compulsion to "improve" the drama, Lincoln's Inn Fields proved to be a debilitating rival that forced Drury Lane to adopt its tactics in order to survive. The play notices of Lincoln's Inn Fields appearing in the newspapers consistently outdo those of Drury Lane for novelty and variety, as a few examples will make evident. The theater advertised the following attractions for March 22, 1715.

The Jew of Venice. And the Walking Statue. Singing by the new Boy. A dialogue between Leveridge and Pack and a piece of musick to be performed on the flute by Mr. John Bastion. With several entertinments of dancing. . . .[73]

For October 24, 1715:

Two new Farces, never Acted before. The Lucky Prodigal or, Wit at a Pinch. . . . And Woman's Revenge or a Match in Newgate. . . . With several new entertainments of dancing, both serious and comic . . . particularly an Italian Night Scene between a Scaramouch, a Harlequin and a Punchinello.[74]

And for May 6, 1718:

Love Makes a Man. With singing in Italian and English by Mrs. Barbier. A mad Dialogue by Leveridge and Mrs. Thurmond. And several entertainments of dancing,—particularly a grand dance composed by Thurmond Jr. A Scaramouch by a Gentleman for his own diversion. A French Peasant by Moreau and Mrs. Bullock.[75]

Such attractions at the rival house compelled Drury Lane to enlarge its own offerings of music, dancing, spectacle, and farce, in spite of Steele's good resolutions. Commenting on his own toleration of such entertainments at Drury Lane (specifically the dramatic dances), Cibber later asserted that he assented against his conscience, lacking the virtue to starve opposing the multitude.[76]

Drury Lane, as I have already said, fared well in the competitive struggle with Lincoln's Inn Fields. After the first two seasons of Steele's governorship, the theater gained a clear ascendancy over the "new house," which it maintained until the season of 1723–1724, forcing Lincoln's Inn Fields at times to the verge of closing.[77] There are repeated allusions in the theatrical literature to the town's prejudice against Lincoln's Inn Fields, a theater that in 1719, according to one critic, was "the Contempt of the Town."[78] Writing in 1723 or 1724, another recalled its miserable state a year or so

[73] The Daily Courant, as recorded in Latreille calendar (Brit. Mus., Add. MS 32249), fol. 202.
[74] Ibid., fol. 225.
[75] Ibid., fol. 290.
[76] Apology, II, 181–182.
[77] Cf. Correspondence, p. 353.
[78] Critical Remarks on the Four Taking Plays of the Season, p. 6.

before, when bailiffs chiefly made up the audience, arresting players while they strutted on the stage[79]—rhetorical overstatement perhaps, but testimony to Drury Lane's success in winning the town.

As a curious correlation of the acute rivalry between Drury Lane and Lincoln's Inn Fields, the two theaters became identified with the rival political parties: Drury Lane becoming known as the Whig house, and Lincoln's Inn Fields, somewhat reluctantly, as the Tory house. Even before Steele's time there had been Whig feeling at Drury Lane (the Tory partner William Collier notwithstanding) as may be surmised from the subsequent ostentatious displays of devotion to the house of Hanover by two of the partners. To Doggett's devotion the annual waterman's race on the Thames remains a singularly tenacious memorial; to Cibber's, *The Non-Juror,* if less long-lived, is equally conspicuous. But after—and no doubt partly because—Steele became governor of the theater, the association of Drury Lane with the Whig party became stronger and more open, the managers encouraging it from the stage with frequent declarations of loyalty to the Protestant succession.[80] John Rich, of course, found it unprofitable to be assocated with the losing side politically;[81] but Steele and the actor-managers, recognizing the profit to be derived from the popular identification of Drury Lane with the victorious Whigs, were not inclined to let their advantage slip away.[82]

Emphasis on Drury Lane's rivalry with Lincoln's Inn Fields must not obscure the fact that competition came also from the

---

[79] Gabriel Rennel, *Tragi-Comical Reflections, Of A Moral and Political Tendency, Occasioned By the Present State of the two Rival Theatres in Drury-Lane and Lincoln's-Inn-Fields* (London, [1723?]), p. 8.

[80] Cf. the *Flying Post,* No. 3619, February 26–March 1, 1715; the *Original Weekly Journal,* March 17–23, 1716; the *Weekly Journal, or British Gazeteer,* November 24, 1716, January 5, 1717.

[81] Cf. preface to *Wit at a Pinch: Or, The Lucky Prodigal* (London, 1715); epilogue printed in the *Weekly Journal, or British Gazeteer,* April 7, 1716.

[82] In a letter to the lord chamberlain written September 21, 1721, Steele suggested that, in view of Lincoln's Inn Fields' demonstrated disaffection to the king, the term "Theatre-Royal" as applied to that theater might be open to an ambiguous interpretation. *Correspondence,* pp. 165–166.

Haymarket; not so consistently, to be sure, but frequently and with noticeable effect on the company's profits. Operas were performed there during the season on an average of about once a week. They were popular and enjoyed the support of wealthy noblemen as well as of the royal family; many of the operas were performed at the command of the Prince of Wales. Particularly after 1719, when the Royal Academy of Music was founded (an organization supported by a series of munificent subscriptions including a grant of £1,000 a year from the king), the opera assumed a formidable aspect as a competitor to Drury Lane.[83] Between 1719 and 1722, moreover, companies of French actors appeared occasionally at the Haymarket, though seldom performing more than two or three times a week.[84] All these attractions were, to be sure, irregular, but they provided an undercurrent of concern at Drury Lane supplementary to that regularly provided by Lincoln's Inn Fields.

Theatrical competition is nearly as old as theaters. There was nothing outrageous, as Steele and Cibber sometimes implied, in other companies' vying with Drury Lane for the favor of the town—at least when the other companies could do so without violating the loosely formulated tradition of theatrical monopoly, as Lincoln's Inn Fields certainly could. Nevertheless, competition seems to have been a decisive force in preventing Steele from making any substantial change in the Drury Lane repertory.

Despite the theater's shortcomings, it is easy to underestimate Drury Lane's positive accomplishment. We must remember that the actor-managers and many of their subordinates were skillful actors and that they presented consistently plays of high literary quality. Most of the plays that formed their repertoire are still read by students of the drama. Though they did not produce many good new plays, night after night they acted plays by Shakespeare, Jonson, Fletcher, Beaumont and Fletcher, Crowne, Etherege, Dryden, Otway, Wycherley, Congreve, Farquhar, Vanbrugh, and Addison. In the season of 1715–1716—to illustrate the wealth of their offerings—they presented ten different plays by Shakespeare in a total of twenty-seven performances.[85] *Hamlet* alone was performed

---

[83] Cf. the *Theatre*, No. 18.

[84] Barker, *Cibber*, pp. 133–134.

[85] These figures are based on the Latreille calendar (Brit. Mus., Add. MS 32249).

five times (once, as evidence of its popularity, for Cibber's benefit). No single play by any dramatist was performed during the season more than seven times—only Addison's *Cato* reaching that number—but a number were performed four or five times. Most of these are still familiar, as the following—each performed at least four times—will show: *The Country Wife, The Old Bachelor, The Beaux' Strategem, The Constant Couple, Sir Courtly Nice, The Careless Husband, Love for Love, The Maid's Tragedy, The Tender Husband, Timon of Athens, The Tempest, The Rover, The Relapse, Love's Last Shift, Hamlet,* and *Cato.* In a season when these plays were the company's favorites, it is obvious that Drury Lane was not grossly degenerate; but it is obvious also that the company was not doing much to encourage new dramatists, nor was it acting on the precepts of the moralistic reformers—beyond the possible omission of especially licentious dialogue and scenes.

3 | Mortgages

"Sɪʀ *Richard,* though no Man alive can write better of Oeconomy than himself," Cibber remarked, "yet, perhaps, he is above the Drudgery of practising it. . . ."[86] Certainly in their Drury ·Lane association Cibber had opportunity enough to observe Steele's shortcomings in the conduct of his personal business; the records of Steele's financial relations with the theater tell a story so complex as frequently to appear absurd. Though some of the details of his negotiations defy explanation, the outlines are clear enough and they point inescapably to a naïveté and ineptitude for practical business. Of the large sums that were Steele's share of the Drury Lane profits he received only a fraction, so thoroughly did he entangle his title to the patent.

Steele's income from the theater, before deductions were made for his creditors, was consistently large, though it varied sub-

[86] *Apology,* II, 201.

stantially from year to year. When he entered the management, it will be recalled, he received a fixed stipend of £700 a year; but when Lincoln's Inn Fields cut into Drury Lane profits, he exchanged, at his colleagues' request, the stipend for an equal share of the profits. This exchange, made generously to help the actor-managers, may have turned to Steele's advantage, his equal share amounting, according to Cibber, to £1,000 a year on an average.[87] However, Cibber's figure seems high. In 1720, in estimating his losses resulting from his suspension, Steele valued his annual income from the playhouse at only £600 a year;[88] in 1724 he valued it at £700, noting, however, that the figure would be higher if it were not for the managers' deduction from the profits of their "salaries."[89] In 1720, though not in 1724, Steele may have purposely underestimated the figure for politic reasons; yet the extant financial records seem more consistent with his estimates than with Cibber's. To be sure, records are lacking for the seasons when his income was no doubt largest—1716–1717 through the first half of 1719–1720—but for several other seasons he received much less than £1,000. During the second half of the season 1714–1715 (after he exchanged his stipend for an equal share) he received, the sole available records indicate, around £100; and for the entire season 1715–1716 he received only between £200 and £300.[90] A gap in the records follows, unfortuantely coinciding with the period of increased prosperity at Drury Lane, when Steele probably did receive about £1,000 a year. The next set of reliable figures extant pertain to several seasons following his suspension and subsequent reinstatement, after the actor-managers had begun their deduction of £5 a day exclusive of him. Even with this deduction his share was large: £700/18/2 for 1721–1722;[91] £868/10/0 for 1722–23;[92]

---

[87] Ibid., II, 175.

[88] The State of the Case, in Tracts and Pamphlets, p. 607.

[89] British Museum, Additional MS 5145C, fols. 132–133. Aitken, Life, II, 298–299.

[90] I base these estimates on a computation of a fifth share of the company's clear profits as recorded in P.R.O., C33/335 (master's report terminating the dispute with Doggett). The estimates may be regarded as only rough approximations.

[91] British Museum, Additional MS 5145C, fol. 138.

[92] Ibid., fol. 109.

and £617/4/11 for 1723–1724.[93] For all seasons after 1715–1716, however, most of his playhouse income went to his creditors.[94]

A memorandum in Steele's handwriting, written some time after the summer of 1723, records the major stages in his complex series of negotiations affecting his patent. Since the memorandum was a personal document Steele wrote hastily for his own use, it is elliptical in expression and puzzling in certain details, but it is informative in that it provides Steele's own summary of the tangled affairs otherwise recorded only in court records.

The deed for Sale of the patent to Minshull for £4000 is dated Jan: 31st, 1716 [1717]—

Edward Minshull set over the said patent and shares for £4000 to Charles Gery on the 24 of July 1716.

Charles Gerey set over by deed, on the 4th of April 1721, the said patent and shares to William Woolley for £1947, the said Gerey becoming Bankrupt, Wooley and his Assignees agreed with Sr R.S. to disengage him from all Mortgages of the said premises to Gerey & Minshull upon payment of £1200 in manner following viz. £300 upon delivery of the deed of mortgage and two hundred pounds yearly out of the profits of the play House till the whole £1200 be discharged, the £200 to be paid on the 23 of Jan. Every year, and as a Security Sr R.S. was to make an Assignment of his Interest in the Stock—[95]

Fortunately we can supplement this summary with additional information from chancery records.[96]

As Steele uses the old-style calendar in this memorandum, the earliest date he mentions is July 24, 1716, when Minshull transferred the assignment of the patent to Gery in exchange for £4,000. The date is right, but Steele's statement is misleading. On that date Steele gave a mortgage of his fifth part in the patent and in the stage properties to Minshull in consideration for a loan of

---

[93] *Ibid.,* fol. 140.

[94] Though there is no record that Steele and the actor-managers quarreled over the division of profits before 1721, a possible source of disagreement arose during the springs of 1716 and 1717 when the actor-managers gave themselves benefits. Cf. Latreille calendar (Brit. Mus., Add. MS 32249), fols. 218, 247.

[95] British Museum, Additional MS 5145C, fol. 134.

[96] P.R.O., C11/1424/35. Aitken prints abstracts of these records: *Life,* II, 95–106.

£1,500; he also gave a note to Castleman, the treasurer of Drury Lane, directing him to pay his (Steele's) share of the profits to Minshull; Minshull in return signed a defeasance to become effective when the debt with interest should be discharged from the sums he received from Castleman. About the same time, unknown to Steele, Minshull assigned the mortgage to one of his own creditors, Gery (it is this transfer to which Steele refers in the memorandum quoted above, which he, of course, wrote much later).

That Steele in the summer of 1716 found it necessary to mortgage his patent can perhaps be explained by the reverses Drury Lane had experienced during the two preceding seasons; no doubt he had received from the theater much less than he had anticipated.

It is significant that in 1716 Steele held and thus could mortgage only a fifth share of the patent and stage properties; Doggett's claim to a fifth share had not yet been settled. When the following year Doggett was by court order deprived of his share, and Steele's was consequently increased to a fourth, Steele found himself in clear possession of the difference between a fourth and a fifth share—in other words, of a twentieth part of the patent (an amount referred to in some of the records as "the fourth of the fifth").[97] For several seasons it was only from this twentieth part that he personally received any return.

In Steele's memorandum quoted above, the next date cited is January 31, 1716 (1717), the date he gave a deed of sale of the patent to Minshull in consideration for £4,000. The word "sale" is ominous, and it is only slightly misleading. Minshull and Gery wished to buy Steele's share of the patent outright for £4,000, but Steele refused to sell; he did agree, however, to increase his loan from Minshull to £4,000, as collateral for which he gave an absolute bill of sale, receiving in return a defeasance to be effective if he repaid the debt with interest within two years. It was agreed that the bill of sale was not to be used within the two-year period, during which time it was to remain for safekeeping in the custody of Ralph Wilbraham, Minshull's attorney. That Steele later perceived the uncertainty of the position in which he had placed himself is implied by an undated memorandum in his handwriting.

---

[97] This point has previously been ambiguous: cf. *Correspondence*, p. 170.

Whereas Sr R:S: has made a Sale of His income and interest in a Patent of the . . . [an illegible word] an Absolute sale in Words yet it was never intended nor should be ever insisted upon as a sale in fact, but that when the money lent by Mr. Wm. Minshull should be repaid to him, the Instrument of Sale or all other deeds or securities should be rescinded and made void or ineffectual in what soever [wd.?] Manner Sr. Richard Steele should require either before or after the time limited in the said instruments.[98]

Such at least was Steele's understanding of the negotiation. He appears to have received not cash but only Minshull's promissory note for the additional £2,500 pounds (above the original £1,500), in consideration for which he gave the bill of sale, though he did receive later some small sums from Minshull.

Gery, Minshull's creditor, continued to receive Steele's share of the Drury Lane profits by authority of the note to Castleman dated July 24, 1716, the money received being applied, Steele believed, to discharging the debt. In October, 1717, Steele paid Minshull an additional £400 and requested that they state accounts; after preliminary disagreement they decided that a balance of £1,211 was due Minshull. Gery, who was a party to this stating of accounts, continued to draw Steele's share of the profits until January 24, 1719, when the total debt, interest and principal, was reduced to £886/16/6. At that time Steele offered Minshull £900 as payment in full, demanding his bill of sale of January 31, 1717, as well as the earlier assignment of July 24, 1716, which Minshull, contrary to his promises, had not yet delivered to him. It will be noted that Steele offered to redeem the mortgage on January 24, 1719, exactly one week before the expiration of the two years allowed. Minshull asserted, however, that he was not able to deliver the assignment because Wilbraham, the custodian of it, was not at home; he requested that final settlement be postponed. Meanwhile he wished to receive, as before, Steele's theatrical profits, the sums he received to be deducted from the remainder of the debt. Steele agreed, and the debt was extended beyond the originally stipulated two-year period.

From time to time Minshull advanced additional sums to Steele, and Steele on one occasion paid £400 to Minshull. When

<hr/>

[98] Blenheim MSS. Aitken, *Life*, II, 98n.

they again stated accounts on December 11, 1719, the amount of the debt stood at £596/2/9, and on this occasion Minshull gave Steele a written statement that full payment had been tendered before the expiration of two years from January 31, 1717, though it had been impossible to deliver the bill of sale to him; Minshull requested that Wilbraham deliver it upon receipt of £596/2/9. Steele sent the statement together with the money to Wilbraham, hoping to receive the bill of sale from him, and also, from Minshull himself, the assignment of 1716 and the note to the Drury Lane treasurer. But he was sharply disappointed.

Wilbraham refused to deliver the bill of sale to him, threatening instead to deliver it to Gery, whose role in the dispute Steele discovered for the first time. Gery told Steele that the mortgage had been assigned by him to still another individual, a creditor of Gery himself, William Woolley. This introduction of still another person into the negotiations made it even more difficult for Steele to obtain an accurate statement of accounts. He believed that only about £220 remained of the debt, but his creditors insisted that he owed the entire £4,000 plus interest from January 31, 1717—an incredible discrepancy! To obtain a true statement of accounts, Steele in 1722 entered suit against Wilbraham (who was custodian of the bill of sale), requesting that the court issue writs of subpoena to Minshull, Gery, Wilbraham, and Woolley to force them to explain their parts in the negotiations.[99]

The enormous difference between the size of the debt as reported by Steele, on the one hand, and his creditors, on the other, apparently grew out of the transfers, unknown to Steele, among the creditors. Steele had erroneously considered Minshull his creditor; he had believed that sums paid to Minshull were deducted from his debt and that the part of the original loan to him that Minshull had never paid except by an unredeemed promissory note was likewise deducted. However, Gery and Woolley refused to acknowledge these credits. It seems, in short, that Steele was the victim of a group of unscrupulous men who attempted to make use of his ineptitude for business to defraud him of his in-

[99] It is from the court records of this suit that most of our information about the mortgages comes. P.R.O., C11/1424/35. See Aitken, *Life*, II, 95–106, for abstracts of the records.

terest in the theatrical patent. This impression is strengthened by what is known of the later career of Minshull, who in 1722 was found guilty of defrauding a goldsmith.[100]

Steele, however, was not without responsibility in the affair. Since the available information comes mainly from records prepared by him, this version of the dispute is probably unfairly prejudiced in his favor.[101] He was grossly irresponsible in financial affairs—the multitudinous contemporary allusions to his prodigality and incapacity for practical business leave no doubt that he was a trying man to his creditors. But in this episode he seems to have encountered creditors who maliciously schemed to take advantage of his irresponsibility.

The case was apparently settled out of court—no record of a hearing remains. Though the precise terms of the settlement are unknown, its major conditions may be surmised from Steele's memorandum summarizing the affair and from later court records. Woolley, who received from Gery the mortgage for the patent on April 4, 1721 (before Steele entered suit), agreed with Steele on June 17, 1723, "to disengage him from all Mortgages of the said premises to Gery & Minshull upon payment of £1200 in manner following viz £300 upon delivery of the deed of mortgage and two hundred pounds yearly out of the profits of the play House till the whole £1200 be discharged," Steele providing an assignment of his interest in the stage properties as a security.[102] The troublesome affair was thus prolonged into Steele's later years at Drury Lane, continuing to plague him and, so Cibber wrote,[103] his colleagues, the actor-managers.

Without any doubt the mortgages and resulting disputes and lawsuits adversely affected Steele's governorship of Drury Lane. Preoccupied as he frequently must have been with his disagreements with his creditors, he could scarcely have given wholehearted attention to his responsibilities to the theater. It is

---

[100] Aitken, *Life*, II, 106.

[101] Wilbraham's bill also survives, but it is much less detailed than Steele's. Though it differs from Steele's in several details, it does not alter fundamentally the impression conveyed by the negotiations.

[102] British Museum, Additional MS 5145C, fol. 134. P.R.O., Cɪɪ/66/22.

[103] *Apology*, II, 201.

significant that he was most active at Drury Lane during the first two seasons of his governorship—before the first mortgage. The mere fact, moreover, of his employment of the patent as a security in borrowing money—with the danger that he might not be able to repay the money and consequently might lose the patent—implied a lack of earnestness toward his obligation to Drury Lane. He narrowly averted a complete loss of his share in the patent to Gery or Woolley, whom the actor-managers might have been compelled to accept into the management—an unattractive prospect that gave concern to the lord chamberlain as well as to the actor-managers.[104] Steele's mortgages were a major cause of his subsequent disputes with both the lord chamberlain and with his colleagues.

4 | The Censorium

DURING the years of his activity at Drury Lane, Steele devoted much attention to an enterprise that, at least in his own mind, was closely associated with the theater. "When I Petitioned for the direction of the Theatre," he wrote in 1716 by way of an introduction to an essay on his "Censorium," "I had hopes of being Serviceable to the Town, and the Publick, by a method which I flattered my self I could make conducive to the purposes mentioned in the . . . Patent."[105] From about 1712 until 1722 or 1723 Steele invested freely of his time and money in this enterprise, which he variously described as a little theater and as an academy. For a time at least he seems to have considered his work in support of the

[104] In October, 1718, the lord chamberlain addressed a query to the attorney general concerning Steele's right to sell or alienate his interest in the patent. P.R.O., L.C. 5/157, fols. 142–144.

[105] Manuscript draft of the *Town Talk*, No. 4, preserved among the Blenheim papers. The statement does not appear in the published version of the essay.

Censorium as complementary to his work at Drury Lane: "This Project will be to the Stage," he wrote, "what an Under-plot is to a play."[106] He further asserted that he intended to employ the Censorium as an auxiliary agent in fulfilling the obligation to reform the stage imposed on him in the patent granting him the governorship of Drury Lane. Conversely, he made use of the resources of Drury Lane in the Censorium. In the single performance there of which a detailed account is preserved, two Drury Lane actors appeared—Robert Wilks and Miss Younger—neither or them receiving any compensation. Probably there were other such occasions; it was undoubtedly useful for Steele in conducting a concert room or an academy to be also at the head of one of the chief theatrical companies of London.

The surviving records convey the impression that the Censorium was planned on the model of the Continental academies, notably Italian and French, of the Renaissance, and perhaps more immediately on the adaptations of these academies introduced into England in the middle of the seventeenth century by Sir Balthazar Gerbier and Sir William D'Avenant.[107] Though Steele left no statement that he was working in an established tradition—that is, beyond the use of the word "academy" to describe his project— his plan for the Censorium bears more similarities of detail to the earlier academies than can be accounted for merely by coincidence. To Steele and his contemporaries the relationship was perhaps sufficiently obvious to require no elucidation.

That the derivation of the Censorium from the Continental academies may become apparent, consider it for a moment in association with the most famous of the French academies—that of Baïf, which flourished in Paris in the 1570's and 1580's.[108] Steele envisaged an aristocratic society of friends who would meet together periodically in his great room in York Buildings to be enter-

---

[106] The *Town Talk*, No. 4 (the published version).

[107] I am indebted to my colleague Professor Hugh G. Dick for pointing out to me the similarity between the Censorium and the Continental academies.

[108] On the entire subject of the Continental academies, I am heavily indebted to Frances A. Yates, *The French Academies of the Sixteenth Century* (The Warburg Institute, University of London, 1947).

tained and improved by a variety of activities ranging from recitals of poetry with a musical background to scientific experiments and lectures. "All Works of Invention, All the Sciences, as well as mechanick Arts will have their turn,"[109] he asserted, and contemporary newspaper announcements show that scientific lectures and experiments were conducted in the room he maintained for the Censorium; but he explained that he intended to give greatest attention to music, eloquence, and poetry—the arts he believed affected most powerfully the passions and hence the conduct of men. Emphasis on these arts suggests opera, and probably Steele planned the Censorium with an eye on the huge success of the Italian opera, critical of that success as he was. (Suggestive of the close relationship between opera and the academies is the fact that opera had arisen in Renaissance Italy from the "academic" interest in the interrelations between poetry, music, and the passions.)[110] Steele planned also dramatic representations of events from classical antiquity, historical authenticity to be attained by careful research. The deference to the ancient Greek and Roman civilizations is indeed abundantly evident in the program of the Censorium; George Berkeley, in fact, remarked in 1713 that the entertainments were "chiefly to consist of the finest pieces of eloquence translated from the Greek and Latin authors."[111] All these activities were to be supported by the members of the society sponsoring the Censorium, though Steele had hopes also of governmental assistance for the project.

Now the essential features of the program and several features of the projected organization of the Censorium have parallels in Baïf's academy of almost a century and a half before. The parallels indeed extend even to such a small matter as the use of a specially coined medal as a permanent admission ticket. Jean Antoine de Baïf's Academy of Poetry and Music, established by royal patent in 1570, was a society of aristocratic friends who met regularly for the avowed purpose of recovering "both the kind of poetry and the measure and rule of music anciently used by the Greeks and

---

[109] The *Town Talk*, No. 4 (Blenheim MSS).

[110] Yates, *op. cit.*, p. 10.

[111] Rand, *Berkeley and Percival*, p. 110.

Romans."[112] Baïf and a collaborator, Joachim Thibault de Courville, established an organization consisting of a membership of two classes—"musicians" and "auditors"—devoted to the exploration of the effects of music in varying modes and poetry in combination with music on the passions. Like Steele later, Baïf and Courville were especially interested in the psychological effects of poetry and music, in isolation and in combination; and as with Steele, their interest in these effects led them to experiments with classical rhetoric. The program of the Academy, moreover, like that of the Censorium later, included activities in all the arts and sciences, not merely in poetry and music as we understand the words. The word "music" was used in an encyclopedic sense that embraced all the arts and sciences[113]—recalling Steele's statement that in the Censorium the sciences as well as the arts would receive attention.

Steele need not have taken his plan for the Censorium directly from Baïf's Academy of Music and Poetry, which was, of course, only one of many such Continental enterprises. The tradition of the academies, deriving, if not directly from the Continent, at least from Gerbier and D'Avenant, no doubt persisted in England to Steele's time. Sir Balthazar Gerbier had in 1649 set up an academy near London in which rhetorical, musical, and scientific activities were pursued;[114] and Sir William D'Avenant presented in 1656 an entertainment, described in detail in his pamphlet *The First Days Entertainment at Rutland-House, by Declamations and Musick: after the Manner of the Ancients,* resembling in many particulars the programs of the earlier academies and the later Censorium.[115] Evidently D'Avenant did not plan a society or academy, but he did entertain his paying guests, as Steele was to do later, in an especially decorated room with, as is apparent from the title of his pamphlet, recitations and music in imitation of classical models. Perhaps there were still other English academies

---

[112] The royal patent, quoted from Yates, *op. cit.,* p. 21.

[113] *Ibid.,* p. 25.

[114] Leslie Hotson, *The Commonwealth and Restoration Stage,* pp. 134–136.

[115] *Ibid.,* pp. 149–151; Alfred Harbage, *Sir William Davenant, Poet Venturer 1606–1668* (Philadelphia, 1935), p. 121; Arthur H. Nethercot, *Sir William D'Avenant* (Chicago, 1938), pp. 299, 302–308.

or English entertainments adapted from those of the Continental academies. There certainly was a widespread interest in the effects of music and poetry on the passions, that chief preoccupation of the academies—witness Dryden's "Alexander's Feast." "Alexander's Feast" was at one time "performed" in the room that became the Censorium, and Pope's "Ode for Music on St. Cecilia's Day" may have been expressly written for use there.

There is no specific reference to the Censorium until 1713, but Steele's plan for it originated in the days of the *Tatler* and the *Spectator,* when he was associated with Thomas Clayton, a musician who played an important role in introducing Italian opera into England.[116] Steele seems to have been interested in his work as early as 1710, when an advertisement for a concert by Clayton appeared in the *Tatler,* No. 163, followed soon after by a studied puff in No. 166. Clayton had "introduced" Italian opera in *Arsinoe* (1705), an English opera "after the Italian manner," but by 1710 he had joined the champions of English words for English music— a fact that probably accounts for Steele's interest. As is well known, Steele and Addison urged the absurdity of presenting Italian opera (in either Italian or English) to an English audience, and could thus welcome Clayton as an ally.

Not until after the *Spectator* was established, however, did Steele become directly associated with Clayton. Beginning in May, 1711, Clayton and two colleagues, Nicola Francesco Haym and Charles Dieupart, with Steele's assistance, presented a series of concerts featuring poems in English recited to a musical background in the great room in York Buildings (a group of houses on the corner of Villars Street in the Strand), where Clayton's concert was performed the year before. The first of these concerts, advertised in the *Spectator,* No. 73, was presented on the evening of May 24, 1711, being repeated a few days later. The advertisement in the *Spectator* for this second performance suggests the type of entertainment provided:

An Entertainment of Musick, consisting of a Poem, called, the Passion of Sappho: Written by Mr. Harison. And the Feast of Alexander: Written by Mr. Dryden; as they are set to Musick by Mr. Thomas Clayton

---

[116] Professor Blanchard includes a note on Clayton's activities in *Correspondence,* p. 47.

(Author of Arsinoe) will be performed at his House in York-Buildings, to Morrow the 29th Instant: Beginning at 8 in the Evening. Tickets, at 5s. each.[117]

Dryden's "Alexander's Feast" obviously lends itself to dramatic presentation with a musical background; William Harrison's "Passion of Sappho," an adaptation of the epistle in Ovid's *Heroides*, reveals an effort to imitate Dryden's virtuosity in suggesting a series of different emotions.[118] Steele is not mentioned in the advertisements, but that he was assisting Clayton is indicated by his correspondence.

Two or three months before the first of these concerts Steele wrote to his friend John Hughes, already experienced in adapting poetry for music,[119] requesting his assistance:

Mr. Clayton and I desire you, as soon as you can conveniently, to alter this poem for music, preserving as many of Dryden's words and verses as you can. It is to be performed by a voice well skilled in recitative, but you understand all these matters much better than . . . R. Steele.[120]

Steele specifies "recitative," evidence of the influence of Italian opera on the concerts.[121] Hughes complied with the request, supplying the version of "Alexander's Feast" that was used, and later he supplied Steele also with a sharp criticism of Clayton's music.[122] Nor was Hughes alone in his low estimate of Clayton as a composer.[123] Whatever the merit of the aesthetic theory responsible for

[117] No. 76. I quote from Lawrence Lewis, *The Advertisements of the Spectator* (London, 1909), p. 251.

[118] For a discussion of the poem see Robert C. Elliott, "Swift's 'Little' Harrison, Poet and Continuator of the *Tatler*," *Studies in Philology*, XLVI(1949), 544-559.

[119] Hughes had previously written six cantatas that were set to music by Dr. Pepusch. See John Hughes, *Poems on Several Occasions, With Some Select Essays in Prose*, ed. William Duncombe (London, 1735), p. xv.

[120] *Correspondence*, p. 44.

[121] For the identification of "recitative" with Italy, see Cecil Forsyth, *Music and Nationalism* (London, 1911), p. 115 (cited in Siegmund A. E. Betz, "The Operatic Criticism of the *Tatler* and *Spectator*," *Musical Quarterly*, XXXI [1945], 324).

[122] *Correspondence*, pp. 45-47.

[123] See *Dict. Nat. Biog.*, article "Clayton."

the concerts, Steele seems to have been unfortunate in the musician with whom he was associated.

Steele, however, did not at once lose interest in Clayton. Another concert, much like the earlier ones, was presented on July 16, 1711.[124] Ten days later Steele wrote to Alexander Pope, whom he had only recently met, asking him "to help Mr. Clayton, that is Me to some Words for Musick against Winter,"[125] a request that Pope mentioned in a letter to John Caryll, asserting that he had consented in order to please Steele, though he did not like the task.[126] That he sent Steele an ode, possibly his "Ode for Music on St. Cecilia's Day," is suggested by a remark in a letter to Steele written the following year.[127] Steele evidently wanted to use the poem in another series of concerts by Clayton, Haym, and Dieupart, to be presented by subscription in the early months of 1712, a series announced in letters signed jointly by the three musicians and printed in the *Spectator*, Nos. 258 and 278. Whether more than one concert (on January 18, 1712) in this series was given, however, is not clear—probably not, as no more advertisements appeared; Clayton drops out of view, to be heard from no more.

Upon the collapse of the series of concerts with which he merely assisted, Steele conceived the more ambitious plan for the Censorium, a project that was wholly his own. Its beginnings are uncertain. Presumably Steele rented sometime in 1712 the house in York Buildings in which the great room was located. It appears significant that the notices of entertainments of various kinds in the great room—notices that had appeared at irregular intervals in the newspapers since late in the seventeenth century—cease abruptly with the advertisement of Clayton's concert on January 18, 1712 (before that date, apparently, the room was sometimes engaged for single evenings). At any rate the notices concerning the great room that appear in the newspapers from January, 1712, until

---

[124] The *Daily Courant*, July 16, 1711.

[125] *Correspondence*, p. 49.

[126] Pope, *Works*, VI, 155.

[127] Steele, *Correspondence*, p. 66. See also Rae Blanchard, "Pope's 'Ode for Music on St. Cecilia's Day,'" *ELH, A Journal of English Literary History*, VIII (1941), 143–145.

June, 1717, are associated with Steele's activities.[128] The inference is obvious: when Steele engaged the room, the public concerts stopped.[129]

Correspondence between Steele and Pope in November and December, 1712, suggests that Steele solicited aid from Pope for the Censorium, as he had previously for Clayton's concerts. Steele concluded a letter to Pope on November 12, 1712, with a remark that, though long interpreted as a reference to the *Guardian,* has been more plausibly explained by Professor Rae Blanchard as a reference to the Censorium:

I desire you would let me know whether you are at leisure or not? I have a design which I shall open a month or two hence, with the assistance of the few like yourself. If your thoughts are unengaged, I shall explain myself further.[130]

If Professor Blanchard's interpretation is correct, then Pope referred to the Censorium when in February, 1713, he complained to Caryll of his many obligations including "an affair with Mr. Steele, that takes up much consultation daily."[131]

The first definite news of the Censorium itself appears in a letter written by George Berkeley on March 7, 1713:

He [Steele] is likewise proposing a noble entertainment for persons of a refined taste. It is chiefly to consist of the finest pieces of eloquence translated from the Greek and Latin authors. They will be accompanied with the best music suited to raise those passions that are proper to the occasion. Pieces of poetry will be there recited. These informations I have from Mr. Steele himself. I have seen the place designed for these performances: it is in York Buildings, and he has been at no small expense to embellish with all imaginable decorations. It is by much the finest chamber I have seen, and will contain seats for a select company of 200 persons of the best quality and taste, who are to be subscribers.[132]

---

[128] I base this statement in part upon an examination of Professor Emmett L. Avery's unpublished calendar of theatrical performances in London during the eighteenth century.

[129] Clayton seems to have had the house before Steele: the advertisement in the *Spectator,* No. 76, refers to Clayton's house in York Buildings.

[130] *Correspondence,* pp. 63–64. Cf. also pp. 65–66.

[131] Pope, *Works,* VI, 182–183. Cf. also VI, 397–398.

[132] Rand, *Berkeley and Percival,* p. 110.

Another letter of Berkeley's, dated March 27, 1713, provides further information:

Mr. Steele's entertainment at York Buildings only waits the finishing of two pictures, the one of truth, the other of eloquence, which are designed as part of the ornaments of the place where it is to be. He tells me he has had some discourse with the Lord Treasurer relating to it, and talks as if he would engage my Lord Treasurer in his project, designing that it shall comprehend both Whigs and Tories.[133]

Obviously by this time the plan for the Censorium was mature; from its small beginnings in the concerts of Clayton, Steele's project had become ambitious indeed.

Berkeley's assertion that Steele had attempted to interest the lord treasurer, Harley, in the Censorium suggests, of course, that Steele and Harley were on good terms during the early months of 1713: it is not unlikely, as I have pointed out, that at about the same time the Tory ministry led by Harley offered Steele the governorship of one of the public theaters. An undated, unaddressed draft of a letter in Steele's handwriting, containing a request that the addressee speak to the lord treasurer in Steele's behalf to procure for him £250 due from his pension—needed because the Censorium has cost him £1,000 and thus has stripped him of money—may refer to this attempt in 1713 to interest Harley in the project. Professor Blanchard has, with reservations, suggested March, 1716, as an approximate date for the letter, but several allusions in it, particularly one to the queen and one to Steele's activities during the previous four years, seem more consistent with 1713.[134] But whatever the date of the letter, it establishes the high

---

[133] *Ibid.*, p. 112.

[134] *Correspondence*, pp. 113–115. Cf. Aitken, *Life*, II, 62. What has apparently led to the assumption that the letter was written after the accession of George is its implication that Steele at the time of writing was on good relations with and had access to the lord treasurer, a state of affairs that has seemed more likely after the Whig party came into power in 1714. Berkeley's letter establishes positively, however, that Steele was on good terms with Harley in March, 1713, and, more specifically, was trying to interest Harley in the Censorium.

Consider, moreover, the significance of the following sentence in dating the letter: "And when I consider what admirable things by my procure-

cost of the Censorium. Nothing further is known of Steele's attempt to gain Tory support for it.

It is evident from Berkeley's letters that the Censorium was almost ready in March, 1713. Yet no record exists of a performance there until May 28, 1715—a curious delay in view of the money and time that must have gone into the Censorium. Steele's activities during those two years, however, provide an explanation: the fall of 1713 through the spring of 1715 was the period of his most intense participation in political controversy, not only as a journalist but also as a member of Parliament—expelled early in 1714 for "seditious" writings.[185] His plan for the Censorium to "comprehend both Whigs and Tories" became submerged in the intense party rivalry into which he was drawn after June, 1713, when he resigned his post in the Stamp-Office in order to be eligible for election to the House of Commons. After he began publishing late in 1713 his series of violently Whig pamphlets, there was little

---

ment or sollicitation have been produced to the learned world within this four years last past, I cannot but think any pertinaciousnesse in private opinion ought to be over-looked, and I, if not received in particular favour, ought at least [to be] distinguished from the Crowd of those who partake the Queen's Bounty by a prompt payment of it." Now four years before 1713 was 1709, the year when Steele began his distinguished series of periodicals with the *Tatler,* writing some of the essays himself and obtaining others by "sollicitation"; certainly he made his greatest contribution "to the learned world" during these years, which saw the *Spectator* and the *Guardian* in addition to the *Tatler.* Note also his allusion to "the Crowd of those who partake the Queen's Bounty." The tense is present, not past; nor is the phrasing of his allusion to the queen appropriate if he were writing two years after her death.

In this letter Steele evidently requests that, by virtue of his literary work, his disagreement with the lord treasurer not be held against him and made the occasion for delaying his pension (which he received as gentleman-waiter to the late Prince George of Denmark). The amount of money to which he refers is large, but he suggests a reason why it is so—the pension has been held up because of his "pertinaciousnesse in private opinion," a circumstance not unlikely in 1713, when for three years a Tory ministry had been in power.

[185] Professor Blanchard assumes that "absorption in politics in 1713–14 caused him to defer the opening." *Correspondence,* p. 114n.

chance that he could interest Harley in the Censorium. One of his contemporaries may have referred to this interruption of Steele's plans when he wrote, just after Steele's death, that "His Proposals for an *Academy* of *Music*" would have been more successful if party prejudice had not aroused opposition.[136]

Prevented by his political activity from opening the Censorium, Steele nevertheless kept his lease on the house in York Buildings in which the "great room" was located,[137] suspending his plans for the project until his political and, quite likely, financial affairs provided him with the needed freedom for the undertaking.

His time came in May, 1715. On the evening of May 28 Steele entertained handsomely a company of more than two hundred gentlemen and ladies in the Censorium in celebration of the king's birthday and possibly also of his knighthood, bestowed only a few days before. The event was reported immediately in the *Weekly Packet*, May 28 to June 4, 1715, and later, enthusiastically, by Steele himself in the *Town Talk*, No. 4. The entertainment was designed to appeal to the eye as well as to the ear, Steele explains; the walls were adorned with paintings of architectural designs and of human figures, the lights were skillfully placed, and the seats for the audience were arranged in the manner of an amphitheater, with the ladies and gentlemen seated on opposite sides. George Berkeley had observed two years earlier that the room was much the finest he had seen. On the evening of May 28 a rostrum for the speaker was provided, as well as a throne upon which sat a person dressed symbolically to represent Liberty.

The entertainment itself was introduced by a prologue spoken by Miss Younger of Drury Lane, in which the purpose of the Censorium was announced to the audience, the carefully chosen "Cabinet of Wit":

> To please you here shall different ages strive,
> New Arts shall flourish, and the Old revive.
> To the raw tribe of Templars shall be shown
> The Grecian Gesture, and the Roman Tone:
> VIRGIL shall be the talk of every Beau,
> And Ladies lisp the charms of CICERO.

---

[136] *The New Political State of Great Britain*, January, 1731.
[137] Cf. *Correspondence*, p. 300.

The land shall grow polite from You, who sit
In chosen ranks, the CABINET OF WIT:
To You shall Bards their Virgin-works reveal,
And hoarse contending Orators appeal;
And your applause the rival Arts shall sue,
And Musick take its melody from You.[138]

Next, an ode honoring the king and the royal family was addressed to Liberty on her throne—perhaps recited to the music of
the orchestra provided for the occasion. The remainder of the formal entertainment consisted of an ode of Horace set to music and
sung, and of several other songs and instrumental numbers, not
identified in the accounts of the evening. All this was concluded
with an epilogue, probably written by Addison, remarkable for
a number of jovial allusions to Steele's failings and to incidents in
his past life: his youthful quest for the "Chemic Stone," his en-
deavors at reform in his periodicals, his personal campaign for the
destruction of Dunkirk, and his efforts "to convert the Pope."
Robert Wilks recited this epilogue, boldly pointing to Steele as he
spoke the critical lines, arousing the company's laughter at his
expense. Steele relates this with relish in the *Town Talk,* taking
pleasure even in the good-humored ridicule of himself. After the
entertainment the company enjoyed a handsome feast and concluded the evening with country dances.

Steele's lavishness in conducting this entertainment extended,
it appears, to coining a medal, which probably was distributed to
his guests beforehand as an admission ticket. At any rate, among
the curiosities found in Alexander Pope's Twickenham home
when it was put up for auction in 1802 was a medal bearing on the
obverse a picture of the sun, surrounded by the inscription "Sen-
sorium. Anno Primo. Georgii. 1715," and on the reverse two human
figures and the Latin word "suadere." An engraving of the medal
appeared in the *Gentleman's Magazine* for August, 1802, a correspondent explaining in the issue for the following month that
the medal was used as an admission ticket to the Censorium. He
does not cite his authority, but his explanation is plausible enough.
The presence of the medal at Pope's home suggests that he attended the entertainment on the evening of May 28, 1715, or was
at least invited.

[138] Steele printed the prologue in the *Town Talk,* No. 7.

After the celebration of the king's birthday, the Censorium seems to have remained dormant for several months, probably because Steele, lacking financial assistance with it, could not afford other entertainments. In describing the entertainment in the *Town Talk*, No. 4, he insists, to be sure, that the expense "was much below what some with a kind, and others with a malicious design, reported it," everything the audience saw before them costing no more than £16. But he protests too much; having a reputation as a spendthrift, he had reason to be sensitive to charges of prodigality. His assertion that the evening's entertainment cost only £16 can hardly be questioned, but certainly the impression of economy conveyed is misleading. He made a statement in an undated letter that he had spent £1,000 on the Censorium. Doubtless it was a costly venture, which he could not for long conduct without assistance.

Early in 1716 he included a series of puffs for the project in the *Town Talk*, presumably attempting to arouse public interest and support. Here for the first time in print (so far as I have been able to determine) the word "Censorium" is used,[139] though it appeared on the medal coined the year before. The most extended discussion of the project occurs in the *Town Talk*, No. 4 (January 6, 1716), in which, with the account of the celebration of the king's birthday, there appears an announcement of future plans. The project, Steele writes,

has nothing in it more chemerical than to suppose that there are two hundred persons in this town, who will be glad to meet, when they are summoned, to be entertained for two hours and a half, at a lower expence than seeing an OPERA, with all the pleasures which the liberal and mechanic Arts in conjunction, and in their turn, can produce—Musick, Eloquence, and Poetry, are the powers which do most strongly affect the imagination, and influence the passions of men. The greatest Masters in these sciences will find their account, in turning their thoughts towards

---

[139] Steele offers an explanation for the word in the *Town Talk*, No. 4: "The CENSORIUM, every body knows, is the organ of sense, as the eye is of sight; and it seems more proper to use a word, which implies the *Sentio tantum*, the bare conception of what is presented to the spectator, rather than any name which in a didactic manner pronounces what ought to be received or rejected."

the entertainment of this select assembly, which is to consist of a hundred gentlemen and as many ladies, of leading taste in politeness, wit, and learning.

The type of entertainment described here corresponds to that actually provided on the king's birthday: chiefly poetry recited to a musical background. However, he planned other activities as well, including, he explains, dramatizations of ancient historical events based on research among classical remains. A cancelled passage of a manuscript draft of the essay, moreover, provides evidence that he, as I have previously suggested, intended to encompass also scientific lectures and experiments. The manuscript concludes thus:

All Works of Invention, All the Sciences, as well as mechanick Arts will have their turn in entertaining this Society. But since Musick [here the draft breaks off].[140]

Long interested in experimental science (indeed, once a sponsor of experiments in alchemy), Steele evidently planned to intersperse with the musical and dramatic entertainments educational, scientific lectures, probably by such men of his acquaintance as John Theophilus Desaguliers, mentioned in the *Town Talk,* and William Whiston, mentioned in *Chit-Chat,* the sequel to the *Town Talk.*[141]

Several statements in the *Town Talk* and *Chit-Chat* show Steele's intention that the Censorium should be supported by an organized group or academy. In the *Town Talk,* No. 4, he refers several times to "subscribers" and once, more definitely, to a group who will direct the activities of the project:

... we who are promoters of the design, do expect more from the joint endeavours of a sett of learned and well-bred gentlemen, who take upon them, with the most excellent performers in their friendship and direction, to exhibit much more entertaining scenes, than ever were produced by the Italian theatre, or any company of actors that have ever appeared.

"The most excellent performers in their friendship and direction" may well have been members of the Drury Lane company. In

[140] Blenheim MSS.
[141] Whiston delivered a lecture on an astronomical phenomenon in Steele's great room on March 16, 1716. Cf. the *Daily Courant* for that day.

Chit-Chat, No. 3, appears the tentative suggestion that the organization supporting the Censorium will be incorporated, the fictional author observing enthusiastically:

... we are all contriving, as well as the Knight, and forming Subjects and Decorations for that little theatre, which may be incorporated, for ought I know, at last, and the Masters and Members be allowed to Meet in habits, suitably distinguished, for the honor of them set a-part to Improve those Noble Arts of Eloquence, Poetry, and Music.

The distinction here made between "Masters" and "Members" suggests the distinction made in Baïf's scheme of organization between "musicians" and "auditors." In the *Town Talk*, No. 7, the Censorium is called specifically an "academy."

After the series of puffs for the Censorium early in 1716 in the *Town Talk* and *Chit-Chat*,[142] references to it become scarce and fragmentary. They are sufficiently informative, however, to indicate that, although the project may have undergone some modifications, it was not abandoned. Steele's plan to establish an academy was apparently not successful, but the Censorium nevertheless survived, with long periods of inactivity, until at least a year or so before he retired from London.

For more than a year after the reference to the Censorium in *Chit-Chat*, No. 3 (March 16, 1716), I have been able to discover nothing about the great room in York Buildings. The lack of notices suggests that the plan announced by Steele in the *Town Talk* was, for an unknown reason, unsuccessful.

Then, beginning in June, 1717, the advertisements for musical concerts reappear—the type of advertisements printed at semi-regular intervals before January 18, 1712, when the last of the notices for Clayton's concerts was published. The *Daily Courant* records

---

[142] Though *Chit-Chat* was long considered Steele's work, G. A. Aitken presented arguments against his authorship (*Life*, II, 91). There are, nevertheless, elements of continuity between the *Town Talk* and *Chit-Chat* (not recognized by Aitken) which indicate that the later periodical was intended as the sequel of the earlier, whether or not it was written by Steele. For example, a fictional character, a Mr. Johnson, appears in both periodicals. See John Loftis, "The Blenheim Papers and Steele's Journalism, 1715–1718," *Publications of the Modern Language Association of America*, LXVI (1951), 197–210.

that on June 14, 1717, a concert was sung by Signor Bernacchi and Signor Berenstatt at the great room in York Buildings for the benefit of Mr. Roseengrave. No more notices appear in 1717, but five were published in 1718, none of them suggesting that Steele was in any way concerned with the concerts.[143] The notices sometimes specified songs in Italian, which would, of course, have been inconsistent with the aesthetic theory expounded in his periodicals. Probably Steele, beginning in June, 1717, occasionally rented out his concert room for single evenings while retaining the lease.

After the death of his wife in December, 1718, Steele took up residence in his house in York Buildings,[144] an event that apparently led him to use his great room more frequently. At any rate, beginning in 1719 there are again evidences of his activity in the room, in spite of the continued appearance from time to time of advertisements for public concerts in it.

In November, 1719, a series of scientific lectures was presented there by, among others, Steele's friend Dr. Desaguliers. Steele's support of the series is implied by the dedication to him of the published lectures by Paul Dawson, a young man whom Steele had befriended. Through the generosity of Steele, Dawson asserts, he was enabled to attend the lectures, an assertion confirmed by Desaguliers, who in a second edition of the published lectures describes Dawson as a young man placed under his care by Steele.[145]

Much more informative than the scant records of these lectures, however, is a series of satirical discussions of the Censorium appearing in the *Original Weekly Journal* from April 2, 1720, until July 9, 1720, which suggest that there was more activity in the room during these later years than has hitherto been known.[146] Because Steele understandably did not advertise in the newspapers for his own entertainments in the Censorium, chance reports, such as

[143] It might be objected that these advertisements may refer to some room other than Steele's. At no time, however, is there any suggestion that there was more than one "great room" in York Buildings.

[144] He was in residence in York Buildings at least by February 19, 1719; cf. Aitken, *Life*, II, 195–196.

[145] Cf. *Correspondence*, p. 218n.

[146] So far as I am aware, these satirical discussions appearing in the *Original Weekly Journal* have not previously been identified with the Censorium by modern scholars.

these in the *Original Weekly Journal,* supply the only available information. These reports occur among a series of thinly disguised satirical attacks on Steele and the actor-managers, probably precipitated by their dispute with the lord chamberlain (Steele was then under suspension from Drury Lane). The allegory in which this, the first of the accounts of the Censorium, is presented, will offer no obstacles; the editor writes that he has received a report from a foreign land of

an Oration, or Speech, spoken at the Opening of a sort of Meeting, or Assembly, call'd the Capricioso, set up by the Chevalier of the brazen Countenance [Steele], an eminent Member of the Family of the Wrong Heads, and a great Projector, of whom I shall have Occasion to speak more hereafter. In the Capricioso there are Orations spoken pro and con on several Subjects, from a certain Desk, or Rosteram, not very unlike our Pulpits, and in the intervals of these Speeches, the Company are entertain'd with Musick, Vocal and Instrumental. The first Speech that was made was to prove the Excellence of human Nature, by a young Bonzi, or Philosopher; the next that mounted was a middle aged Man, and one of the Cacafuogos, which is the Name of the establish'd Teachers of that Country, who being mounted, and having adjusted all Preliminaries, thus began.

His speech is reported in this and in the following issue of the paper, April 9, 1720, the speech concluding with another allusion to Steele:

I had some thoughts of showing likewise that the worthy Chevalier of the Brazen Countenance, under whose Roof I make this Discourse, tho' a Wit and a Celebrated Author, is, however, no Animal Rationale; but I fear I have been too tedious upon these Heads already. . . .

Thus, four years after the account of the project in the *Town Talk,* there appears a description, albeit a satirical one, of a meeting in the Censorium that coincides closely with Steele's announced plans—the plans that owe much to the Continental academies. (Orations on ethical subjects such as the one here parodied on "the Excellence of Human Nature" had indeed been a common feature of the academies.)[147]

The identification of the Capricioso with the Censorium is virtually certain in view of the similarity of the names, the direct

---

[147] See Yates, *op. cit.,* chap. vi.

statement that the assembly met under Steele's roof, and the close approximation of the activities described with those Steele planned. In the *Town Talk*, No. 4, a speaker's rostrum is specifically mentioned; on the king's birthday in 1715 the entertainment included vocal and instrumental music; the speeches on ethical subjects, parodied in the newspaper, are completely consistent with Steele's objectives. Hence, since the newspaper was satirizing Steele's current activities, it may be concluded that the Censorium was in operation early in 1720. There were unquestionably meetings in the great room, probably many of them, of which no record remains.

These satirical accounts of the Censorium are the last extended contemporary reports of the project available, but brief allusions to the great room appear in several other newspapers. The *London Journal* for January 7, 1721, reports in considerable detail a meeting of the proprietors of the "fish pool" (the project, of which Steele was a leader, for importing fresh fish into England) in Steele's "Oratory in York Buildings." Though this meeting obviously was in no way related to the Censorium, the use of the word "Oratory" suggests that the great room was known for forensic activities. More informative is an announcement in the *London Journal* of May 27, 1721: "We hear that Sir Richard Steele is preparing a magnificent Entertainment of Musick at his House in Villars-street, York Buildings, for the Nobility and Gentry, on Monday next." The same paper reported on June 7, 1721, however, that the entertainment had been put off until "the Beginning of next Week." In the *Freeholder's Journal* of December 5, 1722, more than a year later, appears a brief satirical jibe at Steele, suggesting that, until at least a short time before that date, he continued his efforts to establish some kind of organization in support of the Censorium. "The Philosopher's Stone having been once a Spirit, he would have overtaken, as the *Fish-Pool* and the Musick-Room are two other Spirits that have lately haunted him in a very disagreeable manner." Within context this allusion implies that the "Musick-Room" was an ambitious scheme in which Steele had failed; presumably he persisted in his efforts to establish an academy.

Late in the eighteenth century John Nichols recorded a tradition that Eugene Steele, Steele's son, was taken home to York

Buildings from the Charterhouse about 1721, where he was "indulged (as his genius lay that way) in acting plays in the great
room there, called the Censorium,"[148] a tradition confirmed by the
presence among the papers at Blenheim Palace of an unfinished
work draft of a prologue in Steele's handwriting obviously intended to be recited by his son in the Censorium. Incomplete and
rough as it is, the fragment is informative:

> A cunning Cripple rais'd
> This Little Theatre, This Nations [wd.?] gawdy Dome
> To bring at one [several words illegible] can rome
> Were at one an Apartment Never Glame [?] assembled be
> What 'twere worth travelling ye World to See,
> My Sire sent me the Company to Greet
> And since his Rent that He made you meet
> [line omitted except for rhyme word "weather"]
> It is by Him contriv'd you are together
> His Knews [?] you're Generous or Candid [?] all
> Or Would not Venture what from Me can fall
> No: prejudiciall favour 'tis He fears
> And trembles only that He you sinceres [?]
> Tis this that does with greatest terror Strike
> And fears to offer because you're apt to like.

From the personal nature of this prologue it may be assumed that
it was intended to be recited to a group of Steele's friends; those
present were to be his guests—paying guests. The allusion to their
paying his rent is not clear; presumably they were to pay for the
entertainment, perhaps as Steele formerly intended that the two
hundred subscribers to the Censorium should pay. In calling himself a cripple, Steele refers to the gout that plagued his later years.
Whether the prologue was completed and used is not known, nor
can it be dated exactly, but an approximate date is made possible
by the facts of Eugene Steele's life: he died in 1723 at the age of
eleven. One limiting date is thus established, and the other is implied by the fact that for not more than a few years before his
death would he have been old enough to recite a prologue in
public. According to John Nichols, he acted in theatricals at the
Censorium after 1721.

[148] John Nichols, ed., *The Epistolary Correspondence of Richard Steele*
(London, 1787), I, 222n.

Though it leaves a number of unanswered questions, the fragmentary draft of the prologue, together with the newspaper notices, suggests Steele's interest in the Censorium in the early 1720's. Ten years after the inception of the project, he still conducted elaborately planned entertainments, and evidently he persisted in his attempt to gain financial support. Steele did not give up the great room until he retired permanently from London in the summer of 1724; it was advertised for rent in the *Daily Post* on August 17, 1724.

Steele's name nevertheless continued to be associated with the room for a number of years, a fact that in itself indicates his activities there were widely known in London. In the *Daily Courant* of March 8, 1728, a concert of music was advertised to be performed "At SIR RICHARD STEELE's Great-Room in YORK-BUILDINGS," and as late as 1735 Aaron Hill wrote in the *Prompter,* No. 60, about a performance of the tragedy *Zara* "at Sir Richard Steele's Great Musick Room, in Villars-street, York Buildings." Hill and his contemporaries undoubtedly remembered entertainments in Steele's Censorium of which we know nothing.

It nevertheless appears that, persistent as were Steele's attempts to establish the Censorium, he did not succeed in a measure approaching his sanguine expectations. The mere paucity of allusions to the project, the fact that to gain a knowledge of it we must piece together chance allusions scattered over many years, is sufficient evidence, negative though it be, of its relative failure. However, its failure was not complete. Certainly there were many more entertainments there than the thoroughly documented one on May 28, 1715—the one early in June, 1721, for example.

Conceived originally as an academy when Steele was at the height of his success and reputation as an essayist, the Censorium became associated in a distant and informal way with Drury Lane after Steele became governor of the theater. Though the relevant evidence is scant indeed, I surmise that Steele's plans for the Censorium were altered and perhaps emboldened by his appointment to Drury Lane, where he found himself in intimate association with actors who could be of great value in the Censorium. Only after his appointment to Drury Lane did he speak of the project as a "little theatre"; before, his references to it imply that he thought of it merely as an academy. Whatever the ambitious plans he conceived of theatrical scenes in the great room, they do not seem to have been realized. So far as the extant records permit us to judge, the activities of the Censorium remained largely those traditionally associated with the Continental academies.

Part Three | The DISPUTE with the LORD CHAMBERLAIN

1 | Beginnings

THE MUTUAL distrust and resentment between the lord chamberlain and his subordinates, on the one hand, and the managers of Drury Lane, on the other, reached during the winter of 1719–1720 an intensity that at last brought them into open conflict. From the time Steele's patent was granted, there had been misunderstandings, Steele and his colleagues assuming that the patent assured them of a large measure of independence, whereas the lord chamberlain had several times made it clear that he considered Drury Lane within his jurisdiction. Steele and his colleagues, motivated by their belief in their independence, had defied the lord chamberlain. They had refused to obey the lord chamberlain's order to pay Vanbrugh rent on his stage properties; they had refused to submit their plays to the master of the revels for licensing; Steele had written sharply to the lord chamberlain's secretary protesting an order that they not employ actors from the opera. The ambiguous relationship between patentee and lord chamberlain was, to be sure, older than the grant to Steele, but since no patentee before Steele had with determination insisted on his rights,[1] the legal issues implicit in the overlapping authorities remained unsettled.

The dispute, which came to a climax during the winter of 1719–1720, was essentially a legal, jurisdictional one. However, in its development it became associated with a series of other issues—theatrical, political, and personal—that frequently obscured the legal problems.

One of the chief precipitating agents in the dispute was certainly the battery of complaints, from 1716 to 1719 growing increas-

---

[1] Cf. Nicholson, *The Struggle for a Free Stage in London*, p. 18.

ingly louder, about the Drury Lane management—complaints about the managers' treatment of playwrights, their failure to present new plays, their frequent raising of prices, their (particularly Cibber's) tyrannical and undiplomatic behavior. The theater was flourishing financially, enjoying crowded houses, and probably many Londoners were grateful for the consistently well-acted plays of literary quality they saw night after night at Drury Lane. The many highly articulate critics of the theater who were deeply dissatisfied, however, raised a clamor that the lord chamberlain could not choose but hear.

As the years passed, it became increasingly clear that Steele's promises to "reform" Drury Lane would come to nothing. The Drury Lane repertory remained unchanged—the same plays continued to be performed, and the afterpieces grew more offensive to serious dramatic critics. Steele's mortgages of his patent, moreover (the later one amounting almost to a direct sale), implied an indifference to the theater's affairs; after insisting on his personal responsibility to improve the stage, he exposed Drury Lane to the grave risk that Minshull or Gery would replace him as governor of the company. It is understandable that the lord chamberlain should have been dissatisfied.

Although direct action was not taken against Steele and his colleagues until the Duke of Newcastle came to be chamberlain, Newcastle's predecessor, the Duke of Bolton, contemplated intervention at Drury Lane—at any rate, so much may be assumed from the draft of a letter (dated March, 1716/17, one month before Newcastle took office) preserved in the Public Record Office. The letter presumably was addressed to the attorney and solicitor-general by Sir John Stanley, Bolton's secretary (the extant draft bears neither signature nor endorsement):

My Ld Chamberln has directed me by his maties command to send yu the inclosed copy of Sr Richard Steels patent for erecting a Company of Comedians, in order to yr giving yr opinions upon ye following Querys for his Maties information.

Q Whether his Matie may not by his Ld Chamberln give orders from time to time for ye better regulation & govermt of ye Playhouse as formerly notwithstanding ye present grant to Sr Richard Steel ye Patentee & of ye players under him

Q In case of refusal to obey or comply with such orders of ye Ld Cha-
berln what may be done to compell ym.[2]

Obviously Bolton, uncertain of the prerogatives of his office,
wished to assume a more direct supervision of the theater. But
nothing came of his queries, so far as is known, and Newcastle
soon inherited his responsibility.

Steele's estrangement from and ultimate break with Newcastle
was the more bitter because it followed several years of personal
association.[3] The two men had probably become acquainted as
early as 1713, when they were both members of the Hanover Club;
and in the years immediately after the accession of George they
were closely associated in Whig politics. Steele, in fact, was elected
to Parliament in February, 1715, upon Newcastle's nomination.
That their relations were cordial during the first years after
George's accession is implied by Steele's letters. In March, 1715, he
wrote to his wife from Claremont, Newcastle's seat: "My Lord
Clare (who you will own to have some pretence to command Me)
will not let me come away from Hence this night. Pray forgive . . .";[4] and as late as 1717 he was still making the same kind of
apologies: "The omission of last post was occasioned by my attendance on the Duke of Newcastle who was in the chair at the
Kitt Katt. Be so good as to forgive me."[5] Newcastle was a powerful
patron whose support Steele desired; it was Newcastle who presented him to the king in April, 1715, on the occasion when he was
knighted, and again introduced him to the king in August, 1715,
when he delivered an address expressing the loyalty of his con-
stituency in Boroughbridge. In a letter to Newcastle, on May 25,
1715, Steele made an open demand for money in exchange for his
journalistic support of the ministry in terms that indicate familiar-
ity as well as dissatisfaction.[6] His dissatisfaction was with the Whig
ministry itself, however, rather than with Newcastle. Eight days
later Steele published a volume of his collected political writings—
the tracts he had written in support of the Protestant succession—

---

[2] P.R.O., L.C. 7/3.

[3] Cf. *Correspondence*, pp. 98–101: 498–499n.

[4] *Ibid.*, p. 310.

[5] *Ibid.*, p. 336.

[6] *Ibid.*, pp. 101–103.

with an eloquent dedication to Newcastle.[7] Yet after this tribute in June there is another letter, dated July 19, 1715, to Newcastle expressing his resentment at the failure of the ministry to reward him for his political journalism.[8] He and Newcastle were on close terms, but Steele was not satisfied with the rewards his patron secured for him.

Still, there is no indication of hostility between the two until Newcastle became lord chamberlain on April 13, 1717. Then, almost immediately, trouble began.

At this time, though a man of considerable ability, Newcastle was an ambitious and inexperienced young nobleman, not yet twenty-three years old. He was later to become secretary of state and eventually prime minister—impressive attainments even for one so fortunate in his family connections as himself; and the personal qualities that equipped him for those high positions could not have been lacking when, as chamberlain, he supervised—somewhat too diligently according to Steele—the affairs of the theater. There was an incompatibility between the young nobleman, insisting on the prerogatives of his office, and the managers, complacent in their many years of experience and in the authority granted them by the patent; and the incompatibility became apparent at once.

Upon assuming the office of lord chamberlain, Newcastle sent for Steele and the three actor-managers and demanded that they resign their patent and accept a license in its place. Steele tells of the episode in an open letter he wrote to Newcastle three years later:

When your Grace came to be Chamberlain, from a generous design of making every office and authority the better for your wearing, your Grace was induced to send for me and the other Sharers, and in an absolute manner offered us a Licence, and demanded a resignation of the Patent, which I presumed as absolutely to refuse. This refusal I made in writing, and petitioned the King for his protection in the grant which he had given me. This matter rested thus for many months. . . .[9]

---

[7] *The Political Writings of Sir Richard Steele* (London, 1715).

[8] *Correspondence*, pp. 105–106.

[9] Steele printed the open letter in the *Theatre*, No. 8 (January 25, 1720). Neither his original reply to Newcastle nor his petition to the king is extant.

Newcastle took no action against the managers, as Steele observed, for many months after this initial skirmish—not until the end of 1719. However, in the fall of 1718 there was further friction when the Theatre-Royal presented a series of seven plays before the king in the great hall at Hampton Court, reviving the old custom of court performances. The first play produced was Farquhar's *Beaux' Stratagem,* for which Steele as governor of the company wrote a prologue; but unknown to him, Newcastle some time earlier had commanded Thomas Tickell to supply the prologue.[10] On September 21, 1718, two days before the *Beaux' Stratagem* appeared, Steele, having just learned of Tickell's prologue, wrote to Newcastle suggesting that Tickell's poem be used as an epilogue and that his own be used as he had intended.[11] Though carefully phrased in the most obsequious terms, Steele's letter failed to accomplish its purpose: his prologue was not used. That the episode, undeniably a minor one, gave offense to Steele is implied by his reference to it in the *Theatre,* No. 13, where, amidst sharp criticism of Newcastle, he prints his prologue and explains how it came to be written. He cannot assert that it was rejected, he writes, "because it was not vouchsafed to be read."

The month after this episode—in October, 1718—Newcastle took steps to clarify his relationship with Steele and his colleagues—as had the Duke of Bolton before him in a disputed situation—requesting legal advice. He addressed two queries to Nicholas Lechmere, the attorney general, with a preamble describing the company's insubordination:

His Majesty being inform'd that the Managers of the playhouse at Drury Lane refuse to receive or Obey any Ordrs: or regulations for their Govermt. from the Lord Chamberlain of his Majts. Household which all other playhouses acting by Authority of the Crowne have been Subject to, time out of mind, under pretence that by a patent granted by his Majesty to Sr. Richd. Steele, they are Subject to no Authority but his, as their Sole Governe.[12]

---

[10] Tickell had painstakingly prepared his prologue, consulting, among others, Addison. Cf. Richard Eustace Tickell, *Thomas Tickell and the Eighteenth Century Poets 1685–1740* (London, 1931), pp. 70–71; 231–232.

[11] *Correspondence,* pp. 129–130.

[12] P.R.O., L.C. 5/157, fols. 142–144. Aitken, *Life,* II, 189.

Newcastle first asked what Bolton had asked: whether as lord chamberlain he could regulate the affairs of Drury Lane in spite of Steele's patent; companies acting under the Killigrew and D'Avenant patents, Newcastle observed, had been subject to the authority of previous lord chamberlains.

His second query to Lechmere is more specific, and it reveals his dissatisfaction with Steele's mortgages:

Q Whether Sr. Richd. Steele has power to Sell, Alienat or dispose of his Interest in the Said patent, or any part or Share of the profitts thereof and whether he may Appoint and impower any person to be Managers and Governes. of the Said Company, and assigne over and vest in them the Authority and power granted to him by the Said patent, and in Case he has no Such power, how far his patent may be Affected by it.

Here Newcastle questions Steele's right to regard the patent as a piece of property, as a freehold he can mortgage or sell and the authority of which he can assign to other persons. Steele was granted his patent in part at least, as has been noted, because it was believed that he was capable of supervising judiciously the Drury Lane stage; and he insisted vigorously that his personal authority in the theater be recognized. Yet he assigned four-fifths of the patent to his colleagues and encumbered his remaining fifth share with mortgages. Newcastle, apparently interested in discharging faithfully his duties as chamberlain, had reason to be concerned about the fate of Drury Lane when there was a chance that Minshull or Gery would gain a voice in the management; indeed, he was dissatisfied, it would appear from the phrasing of his query, with Steele's transfer of authority to the actor-managers.

Lechmere's answer to Newcastle's queries is not extant. It may be assumed from Newcastle's failure to take action against Steele and the actor-managers until the end of the following year—though other explanations cannot be ruled out—that the opinion he received was more favorable to them than he desired.

A record of some further questions submitted by Newcastle in 1718 (a more precise dating is impossible) about Steele's patent has survived, this time submitted to Thomas Pengelly, serjeant-at-law. The questions reveal Newcastle again attempting to determine the status of the patent, now questioning its very legality:

1. Whether a patent granted for erecting and forming a company of comedians or stage players to act in any part of the kingdom be not against

law? 2. Whether the patent to Sir R. Steele be not against law? 3. Whether the King may not by the Lord Chamberlain make orders for the government of the players under Steele, notwithstanding the patent? 4. In case of disobedience, whether the Lord Chamberlain may not silence the company?[18]

Pengelly's reply to these queries is not known.

2 | Suspension

THE FRICTION between Steele and the Duke of Newcastle in the fall of 1718, of which these legal documents preserve an imperfect record, proved to be merely preliminary to the conflict that developed during 1719. In 1718 the differences between them were primarily matters immediately relevant to Drury Lane, directly concerning the patent itself; but in 1719 political differences completely irrelevant to the theater intensified the animosity. Steele, elected to Parliament through the patronage of Newcastle, directly opposed him on a major political issue of personal importance to the duke—the Peerage Bill. Newcastle and other even more prominent Whigs resented Steele's action, his seeming desertion of his party allies, and their resentment found an outlet in the theatrical dispute.

The Peerage Bill, first introduced into Parliament in February, 1719, was a measure to limit the king's prerogative in creating new

<hr>

[18] H.M.C., *Seventh Report* (London, 1879), p. 684b. This report mentions a "Draft of an Opinion on the above case," but it gives no indication of the contents of the opinion. In the Public Record Office (S.P. 35, vol. lxxiv, No. 43) the same queries are recorded (though without date), but there is no reference to an opinion. I have been unable to find any further reference to the questions or to the advice Pengelly gave. A later opinion on Steele's patent written by Pengelly (with J. Cheshire) is available, however, which answers, either directly or implicitly, all the questions posed in 1718. See below, pp. 246–247.

peers.[14] The Whig ministry remembered bitterly Anne's creation of twelve peers overnight in 1712 to insure a Tory majority, and sought to make repetition of such an act impossible. Little was feared from George I, but the prospect of the accession of the Prince of Wales caused anxiety to the Whig ministers. The king openly disliked his son; he distrusted him and several times publicly humiliated him. The prince resented such treatment, and his resentment extended to his father's ministers, some of whom he knew to be partly responsible for his humiliations. It was then also to protect themselves against retaliation by the Prince of Wales when he should become king that the Whig ministry presented and supported the Peerage Bill, conceived apparently by Sunderland, the lord treasurer, whom the prince particularly disliked. But the bill had the support of many other prominent members of the party, including Joseph Addison and Newcastle. In the fall of 1717 the prince had made a public demonstration of the violence of his feeling against Newcastle, amounting, as the duke erroneously thought at the time, to an actual challenge to a duel.[15]

Steele's objections to the Peerage Bill were clearly ones of principle: the changes proposed, he believed, would upset the balance of power between the House of Lords, the House of Commons, and the king, the balance on which English liberty depended.[16] Ostensibly the bill was designed to safeguard the people from abusive use of the royal prerogative; actually it would have the effect of strengthening dangerously the power of the lords. These objections Steele presented on the floor of the House of Commons and—perhaps more tellingly—in printed pamphlets. On March

[14] For a discussion of the Peerage Bill, see A. S. Turberville, *The House of Lords in the Eighteenth Century* (Oxford, 1927), pp. 169–185.

[15] S. H. Nulle, *Thomas Pelham Holles, Duke of Newcastle: His Early Political Career* (Philadelphia, 1931), pp. 102–105.

[16] Cf. the *Plebeian*, No. 1 (March 14, 1719). In this essay Steele summarizes the provisions of the bill: "It is affirm'd by some People, that a bill will be offer'd to the House of Commons, in which the present Sixteen Peers of *Scotland* are to be made Hereditary, to the Exclusion of their Electors, and Nine more added upon the same foot; and Six more are to be added to the number of *English* Peers; and then the Crown is to be restrain'd from making any new Lords, but upon the Extinction of Families."

14, 1719, the day when the Peerage Bill was first read in Commons, Steele published the *Plebeian*, No. 1, summarizing the objections to the bill. Addison replied with *The Old Whig*, published anonymously on March 19, in which he put forth the ministry's arguments. Steele answered with the *Plebeian*, No. 2, on March 23, and No. 3, on March 30, before Addison replied with his final paper on April 2; Steele terminated the debate with his final *Plebeian* on April 6. Some bitterness is apparent in these later numbers, a bitterness unfortunate in view of the death of Addison in June. The opposition to the bill, led by Robert Walpole but strengthened in no small measure by Steele, proved to be so strong that the ministry considered it prudent not to let the measure come to a vote in the first session of Parliament, adjourned in May. At the time of adjournment Steele published another tract, *The Joint and Humble Address of the Tories and Whigs Concerning the Bill of Peerage*, in which he insisted tactfully that opposition to the measure was not disloyalty, although the king had graciously consented to it.

When the second session of Parliament convened in November, the ministry reintroduced the bill, and again Steele was prominent in the opposition. The fate of the bill was finally determined on December 8, when it was read the second time and decisively defeated by the opposition under Walpole, Steele himself speaking in the eight-hour debate. In the forenoon of that day there appeared his last tract directed against the measure, *A Letter to the Earl of O[xfor]d, Concerning the Bill of Peerage*, in which he paid his compliments to his former political enemy, the nobleman responsible for his expulsion from Commons in 1714 but now his ally in the fight against the Peerage Bill. Steele repeated and expanded the basic arguments he had used before, eloquently relating the principles at stake to the theory of government by which England had been ruled since the expulsion of James II. His arguments were strong[17]—and they were resented by his patron and the Whig ministry.

[17] That the pamphlet was effective is indicated by the journalistic attention it received. Portions of it were reprinted in the *Orphan Revived: Or, Powell's Weekly Journal* (December 26, 1719, to January 2, 1720) and in *The Political State of Great Britain* (December, 1719).

Such then is the immediate political background for the action against Steele at Drury Lane. His suspension was not merely an act of political retaliation—the seeds of the trouble existed before the Peerage Bill was introduced—but the political dispute brought the stage dispute to a crisis, hastening and intensifying if not occasioning the reprisals taken against him. Steele, to be sure, considered himself a political martyr: the feeling of self-righteousness that his conviction of martyrdom gave him is evident throughout his writings on the theatrical dispute,[18] and that it was sincere even if not entirely justified is suggested by an entry (not intended for publication) he made in his personal journal more than a year after his suspension:

I have this morning resolved [he wrote on April 9, 1721] to pursue very Warmly my being restor'd in my Government of the Theatre Royall which is my right, under the Title of the Governor of the Royall Company of Comedians & from which I have been violently dispossessed by the Duke of Newcastle Lord Chamberlain of his Majesty's Household, upon a frivolous pretence of Jurisdiction in His office which He has been persuaded to assert against the Force of the King's Patent to me. This Violation of Property I take to have been instigated by the late Secretaryes Stanhope and Craggs for my opposition to the *Peerage* Bill by Speeches in the House and Printed Pamphlets.[19]

Steele's allusion to Stanhope and Craggs, the two secretaries of state, as the individuals ultimately responsible for his expulsion

[18] Cf. the *Theatre*, No. 14; *The State of the Case*, in *Tracts and Pamphlets*, p. 607. The anonymous author of *The State of the Case ... Restated* counters: "He [Steele] first would insinuate, that all this evil is come upon him for the freedom of his conduct in Parliament; and very gratefully tells the Duke [of Newcastle], that others who were chosen Members of Parliament by his Grace's interests have voted as they thought fit, and yet that his Grace has not entered upon their estates, as he has done upon his; but we shall plainly presently see that there is no need of having recourse to this vain, this groundless, this ingrateful, this imaginary cause of what has happened to the KNIGHT; and therefore that Sir RICHARD has only trumpt up this, to throw an odium upon the Duke." In the *Theatre*, ed. John Nichols (London, 1791), II, 531–532.

[19] *Correspondence*, p. 541.

provides the only known evidence that they were concerned in the matter; and from his phrase, "I take to have been instigated," it appears that he was himself uncertain of their part in the action. About Newcastle's part, however, there was no question.

As their antagonism with Newcastle mounted during the fall of 1719, Steele and the actor-managers appear to have been firmly united. Cibber, at any rate, even before any drastic action was taken against Steele, deplored the ill-treatment Steele had received from his political superiors in terms so outspoken that what was intended as a eulogy to him very likely contributed to his loss of the theater. This misguided effort was the dedicatory epistle to Steele (dated September 29, 1719) prefixed by Cibber to the published version of his tragedy *Ximena, or the Heroic Daughter* which contained extravagant praise of Steele's independence of spirit, of his unwillingness to sacrifice his principles, and of his refusal to follow his leaders in a bad cause. Coming as it did during the dispute over the Peerage Bill, before the measure was finally defeated, the application Cibber intended was unmistakable. He did not refer to Newcastle by name, but the circumstances of the duke's former patronage of Steele and of his current dissatisfaction with him were sufficiently well known for it to be unnecessary; Cibber repeated the complaint that Steele had not received the rewards he earned by his service to the Protestant succession, directing this familiar charge at Newcastle. It was doubtless not merely coincidence that the first formal action taken by the lord chamberlain against the managers of Drury Lane was an order of silence to Cibber. The anonymous author of *The State of the Case . . . Restated* observed that he was not certain this dedication caused the silencing of Cibber but that it was a sufficient provocation.[20]

Ill-advised as was the open criticism of Newcastle and the Whig ministry, there was in the dedication of *Ximena* a passage even more reprehensible. Cibber referred slightingly to Addison, dead only a few months, deploring Steele's admission of him into literary partnership only to have him gain the major share of fame; and in a moment of evil inspiration Cibber applied to Steele the lines of Dryden.

[20] In the *Theatre,* ed. Nichols, II, 532.

> Fool that I was! upon my Eagle's Wings
> I bore this Wren, 'till I was tired with soaring,
> And now, he mounts above me. . . .

Such a lapse of taste provoked a storm of derision.[21]

Steele was embarrassed by his inept apologist, whose anonymity in addition left Steele himself open to attack as the real author.[22] His enemies, wishing to make the most of the opportunity provided by the dedication, assumed that he had been a party to it. He was subjected to malicious allusions and limericks for some time to come, though he soon publicly disavowed the slighting reference to Addison—in the *Theatre*, No. 12.

Whether or not Newcastle believed Steele a party to the dedication, the abuse of the ministry and of himself in it, as well as the clumsy allusion to Addison, would have increased his dissatisfaction with Drury Lane.

That fall Steele and his colleagues, on their side, had discovered an additional reason for resentment of Newcastle—one immediately associated with Drury Lane's prosperity. Along with an impressive group of peers, headed by the king himself, Newcastle offered support to the newly formed Royal Academy of Music, the organization that was preparing to present operas on a grand scale at the Haymarket (the first season began in April, 1720). As lord chamberlain, Newcastle himself became governor of the academy; he personally subscribed £1,000 to it, an amount equaled only by the subscription of two other peers and exceeded only by the king's grant of £1,000 a year.[23] Finding themselves confronted with the prospect of competition from an organization with such extensive resources, the managers must have grown apprehensive; and they would have resented Newcastle's strong support of what was, after all, a rival company. In the *Theatre*, No. 18, Steele satirizes opera as often before, but this time he directs his ridicule specifically at the Royal Academy. There can be little doubt that

---

[21] Cf. the *Weekly Journal* (Mist's), October 31, 1719; *The Characters and Conduct of Sir John Edgar* in Hooker, *Dennis*, II, 182. See also Steele's own remarks in the *Theatre*, No. 12.

[22] Cf. the *Theatre*, No. 12.

[23] "List of Subscribers to the Royal Academy of Musick." In P.R.O., L.C. 7/3.

he and the actor-managers found in the organization additional grounds for believing themselves mistreated.

By November, 1719, the antagonism between Steele and New-castle had advanced to the point that Steele anticipated the action to be taken against him, though he underestimated the severity of it. Probably there had been clashes of which no record remains. Newcastle, it would seem from Steele's letter in reply to him, early in November demanded the account books of the theater, as a preliminary, Steele thought, to removing him from his governor-ship. Steele's letter provides our only information about the episode:

I understand, by Mr Booth, that your Grace has demanded an Account of the Charge of the Play-House. He, accordingly, will lay before You the Grosse Sum of Our last Year's Charge, and Give Yr Grace the reasons which I humbly Offer to convince Yr Grace how impracticable it is to lay open the Severall particulars of the Sallaries.

If your Grace desires this only to know what might be an Equivalent to dispose of me out of the Way, and put the direction of the Theatre into more acceptable hands I take this occasion to acquaint Your Grace that after the Actors, who are Partners with Me in the income, are Satis-fyed, You will have but very little trouble with Me, and find that I shall rejoice in an Opportunity of Showing with how disinterested a zeal I am, My Lord. . . .

Novbr 8th 1719[24]

Steele's quite surprising show of complaisance apparently grew out of his assumption that he would receive an "Equivalent" for his governorship; it was possibly because he did not receive this com-pensation that he accepted his suspension much less passively than he here promises.[25]

If Newcastle needed to be reminded of the shortcomings of Drury Lane under Steele, that service was performed for him by John Dennis, who on November 20, 1719, published his *The In-vader of His Country* with a dedication to Newcastle in which he resoundingly denounced the three actor-managers. *The Invader* had been produced at Drury Lane on November 11–13 with little

---

[24] *Correspondence,* p. 145.
[25] The anonymous author of the *Anti-Theatre* hinted (in No. 8) that if Steele were "allotted a sort of recompence for his damage," he would lose his anger.

success. Dennis, deeply disappointed, attributed the near failure of the play to the incompetency and malice of Cibber, Wilks, and Booth; and in his dedication he related all the slights, real and imaginary, he and the play had received from them. Aware of the estrangement between Newcastle and the managers, Dennis cleverly associated his own grievances with those of the nobleman: he wrote bitterly of the "separate Ministry" governing the theater in defiance of the chamberlain, and he appealed to Newcastle, for the sake of British drama and letters, to assert his legitimate control over the rebellious players. His remarks make it apparent that the break between Newcastle and the managers of Drury Lane was already an open one:

> My LORD, when I tell the World that *Coriolanus* has been unjustly ban-ish'd from our Theatre by two or three Insolent Players, I am sure all those will be apt to believe me, who will reflect with Indignation and Disdain, that that *Roman* is not the first Nobleman whom they have audaciously dar'd to exclude from thence.[26]

Since Newcastle gave Dennis a present, presumably he received the dedication sympathetically.[27]

Dennis in this dedication singled out Cibber from the other two actor-managers for particular abuse; Cibber alone is mentioned by name and accorded individual treatment. He had, of course, already made himself conspicuous in the developing struggle between Newcastle and Steele by his dedication of *Ximena;* and not long after the offensive dedication he offered an even more direct affront to Newcastle. When in October, 1719, the duke directed that Tom Elrington, an Irish actor, be given the part Torrismond in *The Spanish Friar,*[28] Cibber replied,

> "that it could not be done, because the part belonged to one of the Man-agers"; and when my Lord urged his authority, to enforce his commands, CIBBER, visibly slighting his authority, in half a laugh, said, "that they were a sort of separate Ministry," and so absolutely refused to obey my Lord Chamberlain. . . .[29]

---

[26] Hooker, *Dennis*, II, 176.

[27] *Ibid.*, II, 474.

[28] Thomas Davies, *Dramatic Miscellanies* (Dublin, 1784), II, 472. *The Spanish Friar* was presented at Drury Lane on October 21, 1719.

[29] *The State of the Case . . . Restated*, in the *Theatre*, ed. Nichols, II, 532.

The episode preceded Newcastle's demand to see the accounts of the theater and Dennis's dedication of *The Invader* and perhaps was a contributing cause of both events.

Not until about two months after Cibber's act of insubordination did Newcastle move to retaliate. Then, on December 19, 1719, he wrote to Steele, Wilks, and Booth in peremptory terms, directing them to dismiss Cibber from acting or from participating in any way in the management of the theater.[30] Steele recognized this first decisive step by Newcastle for what it was—an assertion of his authority over the patent. Moreover, Newcastle's move seems publicly so to have been recognized: the *Orphan Revived* (December 19 to December 26), after reporting the action against Cibber, adds significantly: " 'Tis also reported, that Sir Richard Steel, since his Writing and Speaking against the Peerage Bill, has met with some Displeasure from some persons that were in his Interest before." Steele replied to Newcastle immediately, protesting the invasion of his "Estate." Despite his courtly protestations of humility, he obviously felt himself deeply injured:

Your Grace has obliged me, this Evening, with an opportunity, I have long wished for, of showing How devoted I am to your Service; but I wish for Your sake, rather than my own, that you had given me any other occasion for manifesting this unreserv'd inclination for your Person and Character, than that of bearing Oppression from you.

Your Grace's Order has as many Exceptions against it, as so many words can carry.

Your Grace, in this instance, invades my Estate as a Parliament man, but this Honour I owe to you and I consider, if it had not been for that Great Generosity, I had not either provok'd or been liable to, this your Great Cruelty.

I leave it to your Grace's own reflection how consistent it is with bestowing such a Bounty to Hurt me for my Conscientious behavior in the Use of it.

Mr Cibber is a Principall Actor, and many Familyes (as well as my Property) are concern'd in His Appearance on the Stage. . . .[31]

Newcastle, resolved to bring the managers into subordination, took further offense at this letter of remonstrance, and through his

[30] *Correspondence*, p. 146.

[31] *Ibid.*, pp. 146–147. See also Professor Blanchard's long note on this letter, pp. 147–149.

brother, Henry Pelham (who acted as his secretary), forbade Steele to communicate with him, informing him that the patent would be legally prosecuted. Steele later reported that he was deeply grieved by the message but that he received it submissively and with humility;[32] though sorry to have lost so powerful a friend, he felt confident that in a court of law the invulnerability of the patent would be recognized.

Newcastle's next step, however, upset his plan of defense. The duke sent for Barton Booth and threatened to silence the theater with a sign manual—that is, he threatened a direct royal order rather than court proceedings. This threat alarmed Steele, for, as he explained, he would have no alternative but to submit to a sign manual, just or not.[33] His feeling of assurance leaving him, he initiated a campaign to arouse support for himself.

As several times before when he was deeply aroused, Steele began a periodical to present his arguments to the public, this time calling his paper (which proved to be his last) the *Theatre,* and adopting as his final pseudonym, "Sir John Edgar," the name then assigned to the "Sir John Bevil" of the still unfinished *The Conscious Lovers.*[34] The *Theatre* is marred by the purpose for which it was written, an argumentative and bellicose purpose alien to the genial spirit of the *Tatler,* the *Spectator,* and the *Guardian.* Steele admittedly undertook the periodical to enlist support for himself and the actor-managers against the lord chamberlain,[35] and his sense of outraged justice is abundantly evident (in the last number [No. 28], he apologized for the controversial spirit in which much of the paper is written). Of controversial bitterness there is enough in the *Theatre,* though it is relieved from time to time by moral essays, political and theatrical news, and dramatic criticism.

The periodical began harmlessly enough on January 2 with a paper in which "Sir John Edgar" introduced himself and his circle of friends in the conventional manner; in fact, not until the seventh number, January 23, did Steele mention the theatrical dispute. With that number, however, he plunged into it with fury, de-

[32] The *Theatre,* No. 8.
[33] *Ibid.*
[34] See below, pp. 191–192.
[35] The *Theatre,* No. 28.

nouncing Newcastle's action in bold terms. But by January 23 the dispute had progressed very far.[36]

Several details of Steele's attempt to block Newcastle's action in the period just before the appearance of this seventh *Theatre* are not clear; there is apparently an inconsistency in Steele's reports of his activities. In *The State of the Case,* which did not appear until March 29, he describes the circumstances attending Cibber's silencing and asserts that he, Steele, was threatened with a sign manual "When this lawless Will and Pleasure was chang'd," meaning, it would seem, when the order of silence imposed on Cibber was lifted. Exactly when this revocation came is not known, but a comment in the *Theatre,* No. 7, of January 23, shows that Cibber had not yet been reinstated; and on that date (which was a Saturday) the Drury Lane license was rescinded. Yet in a letter to Newcastle, dated the following Monday (January 25) and printed in the *Theatre,* No. 8 (January 26), before Cibber could possibly have been reinstated, because the theater was silenced, Steele mentioned Newcastle's summoning Booth and threatening the sign manual. There seems to be another error of detail. In *The State of the Case* Steele asserts that upon learning of Newcastle's threatened use of the sign manual, he wrote to two "great Ministers" requesting their protection; actually, drafts of letters from Steele to four (not two) "great Ministers" are preserved, all protesting the threatened use of the sign manual and all bearing the date January 17, before Cibber was reinstated. When Steele wrote *The State of the Case* late in March, either he did not remember the precise sequence of events or he purposely misrepresented for his own purposes. The other account, that in the open letter to Newcastle printed in the *Theatre,* No. 8, appears more trustworthy; it was, of course, written when the events were still fresh in Steele's mind.[37]

[36] That Drury Lane's trouble with the lord chamberlain was by January 11, 1720, a subject of current interest is implied by a reference to it in the epilogue to *The Half-Pay Officers,* first acted at Lincoln's Inn Fields on that date.

[37] Aitken implies that Newcastle did not threaten the sign manual until he revoked the license. Cf. *Life,* II, 224. This conception must be erroneous, because the use made of the sign manual was the revocation of the license. The theater was silenced by Newcastle's order alone.

It was then on January 17 that Steele wrote to the ministers of state, four members of the privy council, Stanhope, Craggs, Jr., Parker, and Argyle. The four letters are similar.[38] He described his predicament—his inability to communicate with Newcastle—and implored their intervention to prevent Newcastle's use of a sign manual, which, he asserted, would rob him of the means to protect himself in court; if Newcastle employed a royal order against him, he insisted, he would be dispossessed of his property in a summary and arbitrary way. There is no indication that these four letters produced any effect whatsoever; it is certain that they did not have the effect Steele desired. It may be significant that two of them are addressed to the men whom he, in his journal entry of April 9, 1721, held responsible for his expulsion from Drury Lane, Stanhope and Craggs. He had earlier been closely associated with both of them—Stanhope had assisted with his defense when he was tried by the Commons in 1714—and from both of them he had recently become estranged by his opposition to the Peerage Bill.

While Steele was requesting the assistance of the privy councillors, Newcastle again made inquiries about what action he could legally take against the patent.[39] Fortunately we know the advice

---

[38] *Correspondence,* pp. 149–152.

[39] The Historical Manuscript Commission, *Seventh Report,* p. 684b, records two letters that reveal glimpses of the behind-the-scenes action against Steele's patent. The first is headed "17 1/2 [sic], January 14, Cockpit, J. Pelham to Pengelly"; probably the actual date was January 14, 1720, and the writer of the letter, Newcastle's brother, Henry Pelham. "The Lord Chamberlain having desired Sir John Stanley and Serjeant Cheshire to meet him at your Chambers tomorrow at 6 p.m., to consult about the affair of Drury Lane Playhouse, his Grace has desired me to acquaint you therewith." Sir John Stanley had been the secretary of the Duke of Bolton, Newcastle's predecessor as lord chamberlain.

The second letter, from Lord Chancellor Parker to Serjeant Pengelly, is dated only "Thursday night." Since the royal warrant that Parker mentions was presumably the one by which Steele's license was revoked on Saturday, January 23, we may conjecture that this letter was written on Thursday, January 21, 1720. "It is necessary in point of form and decency that you should kiss the King's hand on this occasion. If you will go tomorrow to St. James's when I do, I will carry you into the room at the back-stairs next the King's closet, and go in and get the warrant signed, and then call you in to kiss his Majesty's hand."

he received on this occasion, because a copy of the formal opinion, dated January 20 and signed by Thomas Pengelly and Jo Cheshire, is extant in a French translation.[40] Because of its importance in determining the nature of the action taken against Steele, the opinion deserves close attention; much of the seeming ambiguity of the legal action can be understood in terms of it. Newcastle revoked the Drury Lane license, not the patent. It has not been clearly understood why he ignored the patent.[41] But the explanation is here in the legal opinion on which he acted. Pengelly and Cheshire advised him to leave the patent intact—to ignore it, but to render it impotent by removing from its jurisdiction the company of actors led by Cibber, Wilks, and Booth. The license to act, in which Steele's name appeared with those of the three actor-managers, was to be revoked and another issued in its place, in which Steele's name would be omitted. Pengelly and Cheshire believed that the powers conveyed in the patent were illegal; but they did not recommend that Newcastle contest the patent openly, rather, that he rob it of value by this stratagem. The legal subtleties of the maneuver were not generally understood at the time—Steele's writings show that he did not completely understand them—but in outline at least, they are intelligible to us, who can read the opinion.

Steele, of course, did not know of the advice given Newcastle by Pengelly and Cheshire,[42] but he knew that strong action was impending. Consequently on January 22 he resorted to the last step possible to protect himself: he petitioned the king. The ineffectiveness of his appeal may be accounted for by the fact that it was presented to the king in the presence of Newcastle himself. Helpless before such power, Steele merely outlined his grievances and begged for protection.[43]

Only one statement in the petition adds measurably to our knowledge of the dispute: Steele charges that Newcastle "by

[40] P.R.O., S.P. 35, vol. lxxiv, No. 43 (5). See below, pp. 246–247.

[41] Cf. R. W. Lowe's note, Cibber, *Apology*, II, 195n.

[42] Not until the *Theatre*, No. 9 (January 30, 1720), did Steele make any allusion to Pengelly; in the *Theatre*, No. 8, he asked Newcastle who was his legal adviser.

[43] *Correspondence*, p. 532.

promises does encourage . . . Actors to disturb Your Petrs said Government . . .," suggesting that even before he revoked the license, the duke intervened in the company's internal affairs. If we may believe Steele, Newcastle attempted to undermine his authority by alienating the actors. The members of the company, including perhaps Wilks and Booth (Cibber was still silenced), were probably torn between loyalty to Steele and a desire to choose the stronger side in the struggle.

On January 23, 1720, the day after Steele presented the petition to the king, the dispute reached its climax—the king issued a warrant, signed by Newcastle, revoking the license granted in October, 1714. The patent itself was not mentioned directly: Newcastle had followed Pengelly's advice. One portion of the revocation, however, might be interpreted as applying to the patent:

And Wee doe further (as much as in Us lies and as by Law Wee may) Revoke and make void all other Licences Powers and Authoritys whatsoever, at any time heretofore Given by Us to the said Richd. Steele, Robt. Wilks, Colley Cibber, Thomas Doggett, and Barton Booth, or to any of them Severally, for the Care and managemt of Our Company of Comedians Acting at the Theatre in Drury Lane, or for Acting and Representing any Comedies, Tragedies or other Theatricall performances, or to that or the like purpose or Effect. And We doe hereby Accordingly Declare Our Royall Pleasure that all such Licenses, powers, and Authorities shall be and are hereby Revok'd and made void."[44]

As the lawyers had recommended, the patent was ignored and the license only was revoked, but the status of the patent was left, perhaps purposely, in ambiguity. Steele himself observed in *The State of the Case* that the patent seems to be hinted at in this warrant:

The Reader will observe, that the Order mentions Licences, Powers and Authorities, to the Persons nam'd therein, and then obliquely aims at the Patentee in the Words, *or to any of them severally,* but not a Word of Grant or Patent, which was vested only in *Steele,* and would not have agreed well with the just and gracious Words, *as much as in us lies, and as by Law we may.*[45]

[44] P.R.O., L.C. 5/157, fols. 415–416. Aitken, *Life,* II, 226.
[45] In *Tracts and Pamphlets,* p. 606.

In spite of this ambiguity, the warrant in effect deprived Steele of any benefit from the patent—he was excluded from Drury Lane—and it was on this blunt fact that he based his journalistic campaign to force Newcastle to relent. Except for this one time in *The State of the Case,* he did not acknowledge the distinction made between the revocation of the license and that of the patent; he assumed that the patent had been illegally violated and attempted to force Newcastle to reinstate him.

Newcastle's maneuver was not without precedent: a similar though not identical action was taken by an earlier lord chamberlain against Christopher Rich in 1709. Rich, who then operated Drury Lane under the authority of the combined D'Avenant-Killigrew patents, was silenced by a royal order, whereupon a theatrical license was issued to William Collier, notwithstanding the complaints of Rich and his fellow sharers in the patent about the alleged unlawful invasion of their property.[46] Collier was informed that to be effective a patent required royal support.[47] Impotent for the remainder of Anne's reign, the patent was not annulled, for it was again recognized when George succeeded.[48]

[46] Cf. British Museum, Additional MS 20727.

[47] Nicholson, *The Struggle for a Free Stage in London,* pp. 13–14.

[48] The elusive nature of the property inhering in a theatrical patent is described in a legal opinion rendered late in the century on the question of whether or not the Killigrew patent could be sold separately from the D'Avenant one with which it had long been merged. Although this question had nothing directly to do with Steele's trouble, the opinion illuminates, where light is dim, the legal complexities of Newcastle's action against him. The opinion was written by Francis Hargrave in 1793: "In the first place it strikes me as deserving Consideration, whether it will not be Convenient to relieve the Counsel for the intended Purchasers of the Patent to Killigrew, And also myself . . ., from investigating what advantages in strictness of Law the Crown might take against the Patent in question or of any Property of the same kind, if there was a hostile disposition towards those interested—Such an investigation might carry the mind of a Lawyer into the discussion of nice points, upon which, from the want of any judicial decision to guide opinion, it might be found impossible to write without some degree of doubt; and thus this delicate and peculiar species of property might be universally wounded.—If speculation was to be let loose upon every possible disturbance, which may be

The uncertain status in which Steele's patent was left by the lord chamberlain's action is reflected in several contemporary discussions of the theatrical dispute. The anonymous author of *The State of the Case . . . Restated* insisted, apparently accurately, that the patent had not been molested, that it was still in effect. He declared that if Steele could hire a company of actors, he would be free to present plays.[49] Such a view perhaps was responsible for a curious though evidently unfounded report that appeared on August 6, 1720, in *Applebee's Original Weekly Journal:*

Two Executions having seiz'd the New Play-House in Lincolns-Inn-Fields, on violent Presumptions of Debt, the Company is dissolv'd, and the Playing is suspended till they have compos'd the Matter; after which they talk that Sir Richard Steele will be put at the Head of their Affairs.

The event certainly proved otherwise. A view of Newcastle's action similar to that expressed in *The State of the Case . . . Restated* appears in a letter written February 18, 1720, by Sir John Vanbrugh, a close friend of Newcastle who doubtless heard of the affair from the duke himself: ". . . a New Licence has been granted to Wilks, Cibber & Booth which they accepting of, and acting under; have Left him [Steele] with his Patent but not one Player. . . ."[50] John Dennis, on the contrary, declared that the "Patent was invalid and void, by vertue of a previous Statute"[51] (he failed to identify the statute). The anonymous author of *The Battle of the Authors* was

---

attempted against the enjoyment of theatrical monopoly, various other Objections might demand attention as well as the particular objection from long dormancy of the Patent in question. Hence, as I conceive, it is that heretofore professional Gentlemen, when consulted upon titles of this particular kind, have not considered themselves as called upon to enquire rigidly, either into the right of the Crown to create such property, or into the means, by which, being created, it may be merged, suspended, lost, disturbed or endangered. . ." (British Museum, Additional MS 12201). This is, to be sure, a hedging opinion. But it explains, in the words of an eighteenth-century lawyer who had made a special study of the general problem, why the action against Steele was necessarily inconclusive.

[49] In the *Theatre*, ed. Nichols, II, 523.

[50] Bonamy Dobree and Geoffrey Webb, eds., *The Complete Works of Sir John Vanbrugh* (London, 1928), IV, 125.

[51] Hooker, *Dennis*, II, 216.

more specific, asserting that the patent was invalid because the powers it conveyed were counter to the time-honored tradition of stage supervision by the lord chamberlain.[52] He and Dennis were evidently mistaken; their statements, however, reveal the confusion caused by Newcastle's legal strategy.

On the day that Newcastle revoked the Drury Lane license (Saturday, January 23), the *Theatre,* No. 7, appeared, in which Steele for the first time in the periodical mentioned the quarrel openly. Where before in his relations with Newcastle he had shown himself submissive and guarded, he now wrote venomously, denouncing his noble opponent in but slightly concealed allegory. As an introduction to the paper, he elaborated an idea he had originally employed in the *Town Talk,* No. 2: Colley Cibber suffered persecution because he was identified with the villainous roles he played so well on the stage; he was seen so often as Richard III, Iago, and Cardinal Wolsey that people had come to rejoice in his misfortunes. "It must certainly be for some such deep cause as this," Steele adds slyly, "that we do not see CIBBER on the Stage: for it were a most unreasonable thing to imagine, as many do, that it is done to mortify somebody behind the curtain. . . ." And having mentioned Cardinal Wolsey, Steele presses the attack even more directly. Wolsey was particularly reprehensible, he points out, in assuming credit for a benevolent deed performed by the king himself, in placing himself as a barrier between the king and his people.[53] With an obvious application intended, Steele continues boldly:

. . . but it very often happens, that in mixed Governments, with a Sovereign at the head of it, that Sovereign is the most injured person in the whole nation, by a misrepresentation of his friends by those about him.

[52] *The Battle of the Authors Lately Fought in Covent Garden* (London, 1720), pp. 37–38.

[53] There is a passage in Cibber's *Apology* that was perhaps suggested by this comment in the *Theatre,* No. 7. In describing the performances presented by the Theatre-Royal at Hampton Court in the fall of 1718, Cibber recalls that the king was particularly pleased, in a production of *Henry VIII,* by Cardinal Wolsey's whispered directions to his secretary to spread a rumor that an abatement in taxes was brought about by the cardinal's intercession. Thereupon Cibber quotes the lines spoken by the

This is the greatest of all injustice; and a person who should use the King's name in order to gratify his own humour or resentment, does a much greater injury to his Prince than the merit of any servant who is guilty of it can repair.

Coming as it did on the day that Steele's license was revoked by an officer of the household employing royal authority, no one could fail to understand what Steele meant. Only in this indirect way could Steele denounce the use of the royal warrant: to denounce the royal authority itself would have been treasonable; to declare that a king's minister had interfered with royal justice was another and less serious matter and a common device in eighteenth-century political controversy.

Steele's bitterness, however, did not halt the progress of the action against him. On Saturday, the twenty-third, according to a notice that appeared a week later in the *Weekly Journal, or Satur-*

---

cardinal, the very lines included in the *Theatre*, No. 7. Then a few paragraphs later Cibber tells that he received from the lord chamberlain as payment for the court performances, in addition to the company's expenses, £200 to be distributed among the managers. He adds, apparently recalling Steele's remarks in the *Theatre*, No. 7: "And I confess, when I receiv'd the Order for the Money from his Grace the Duke of *Newcastle*, then Lord-Chamberlain, I was so surpris'd, that I imagin'd his Grace's Favour, or Recommendation of our Readiness or Diligence, must have contributed to so high a Consideration of it, and was offering my Acknowledgments as I thought them due; but was soon stopt short by his Grace's Declaration, That we had no Obligations for it but to the King himself, who had given it from no other Motive than his own Bounty. Now whether we may suppose that Cardinal *Wolsey* (as you see *Shakespear* has drawn him) would silently have taken such low Acknowledgments to himself, perhaps may be as little worth consideration as my mentioning this Circumstance has been necessary: But if it is due to the Honour and Integrity of the (then) Lord-Chamberlain, I cannot think it wholly impertinent" (*Apology*, II, 214–219). This possible allusion, not previously recognized, is the only one in the entire *Apology* to Steele's dispute with Newcastle: cf. note by R. W. Lowe in *Apology*, II, 193–196. When Cibber wrote the *Apology*, though Steele had long been dead, Newcastle was still a very powerful nobleman whom it would not have been politic to antagonize. The *Apology* was indeed dedicated to Henry Pelham, Newcastle's brother.

day's Post, further performances at Drury Lane were suspended by a proclamation read from the stage; and two days later a written order of silence was issued. Steele himself mentioned receiving the order on the later day. "The Revocation came on the Saturday, your Grace was so good as not to break the Sabbath upon me; but the sufficient evil of this day, being Monday, is an order of silence."[54]

Newcastle was continuing in the course of action suggested by Pengelly and Cheshire. Pengelly in fact drafted the order of silence, as we learn from a letter (preserved in the Public Record Office) that Pengelly evidently wrote to the duke on January 22, the day before the license was revoked:

I have sent your Grace a Draught of an Order for Silencing the Players at Drury Lane which I humbly Submit to your Grace's Consideration and Judgment; It will be proper to direct that His Majesty's Revocation be served tomorrow Morning, according to the Method mentioned in the opinion. The Misbehaviours and Neglect of Submission may, amongst other Instances be assigned, in the Acting any new plays without the Leave and approbation of Your Grace, as Lord Chamberlain, and the frequent raising the Price of Boxes and Pitt, without just Reason and Permission. It may be very convenient to prepare some new Orders and Directions for their Behavior at the Theatre in support of your Grace's Authority and in Conformity to the Order for Silence and when a new Licence is given, the Managers admitted should be sworn before your Grace, as formerly was done, and at the same time the New Directions may be given 'em in writing. . . .[55]

In the order of silence itself, the offenses specifically mentioned were insubordination and frequent advancing of prices. Steele and his colleagues were forbidden to present plays until granted a new license "or other proper Order and Direction."[56] For three days, January 25 through 27, the playhouse was silent; the lord chamberlain had positively reasserted his authority over the company.

Steele meanwhile continued his futile journalistic campaign. In the *Theatre,* No. 8 (January 26), he printed a long letter, signed openly with his own name, to Newcastle in which, after courteous preliminaries, he recited uncompromisingly what he believed to

[54] The *Theatre,* No. 8.
[55] P.R.O., S.P. 35, vol. lxxiv, No. 43 (9).
[56] P.R.O., L.C. 5/157, fols. 280–281. Aitken, *Life,* II, 227–228.

be the injuries the duke had done him.[57] He described the nature of the patent and the powers granted to him by it, insisting that it made him sole governor of the company for life; he recounted his assignment of shares in the patent to the actor-managers, asserting that under their mutual direction the theater had flourished in an unprecedented fashion. Turning to Newcastle's action, he virtually charged the duke with obtaining the sign manual through deception. "My Patent cannot be hurt, except it can be proved it was obtained *per deceptionem,* as according to my duty I am to believe this order was. . . ." Since the charge was a bold one to hurl at a powerful nobleman, Steele did not allow it to go unmodified. Who was the lawyer, he asked, who had so far imposed on the duke as to have advised the course of action he had taken? Not Newcastle himself but his legal adviser was responsible—a note of caution appended to a bold charge.

Heedless of Steele's impotent raging, Newcastle moved on to the next step suggested by Pengelly and Cheshire. On January 27 he issued a new license to Cibber, Wilks, and Booth, signed not only by himself but by the king, authorizing them to act plays during the royal pleasure. The license contains another statement of revocation of "all former Licenses and Powers."[58]

On January 28, the day after receiving this new license, the three managers resumed acting in spite of an angry letter (delivered by an attorney) from Steele. Making no allusion to Newcastle's action, Steele in quite formal terms reminded them that he was governor of the company under the authority of the patent and commanded them to refrain from acting until they received orders from him.[59] But the actor-managers apparently saw the hopelessness of his position.

Steele had reason to feel strongly the participation of Cibber in the new license, because much of what he had undergone was

---

[57] According to Aitken, Steele had actually sent this letter to Newcastle the preceding day, i.e., the day the letter was dated (*Life,* II, 228). I know of no reason for assuming this. On the contrary, Steele stated that he had no way of conveying his letter to the duke except through the pages of "Sir John Edgar's" paper; Newcastle had forbidden him to write directly. Cf. the *Theatre,* No. 8.

[58] P.R.O., L.C. 5/157, fol. 282.

[59] *Correspondence,* pp. 152–153.

precipitated by his defense of Cibber; indeed, in the *Theatre,* No. 12, he mentions him in terms that reveal a touch of irony:

But, after all that has been said, I think Sir RICHARD extremely obliged to Mr. CIBBER; but would not have him own it at present, lest CIBBER too should be turned off the *Begging Bridge* (to which he is but just restored) as well as his Patron; for whose sake, as it is shamelessly declared, he was banished.[60]

The new license probably had the effect of lifting the order of silence against Cibber, and Steele would have seen the irony implicit in the circumstance. He had initiated the quarrel that led to his own dismissal by defending Cibber; he was finally excluded from the theater by the act that apparently had the effect of restoring Cibber.

When Wilks, Booth, and Cibber received Steele's letter ordering them to refrain from acting, they turned to Newcastle for instructions—or so it appears from a letter Newcastle addressed to Pengelly. The letter is not dated, but the circumstances leave little doubt that it was written at this stage in the controversy.

The enclosed was by Sr Rd Steel's Attorney served last night upon ye players. He seems very fully to insist upon His Sole Power, and has also told them He will prosecute them by law. I begg you will be so good as to consider wt further steps are necessary. I am going out of town, and shall not return till Monday, when I will receive ye Kings order for the Attorney Genl. . . .

Friday morning [January 29, 1720][61]

Pengelly's letter in reply is dated the following Monday morning, February 1, 1719 {20}:

I had the Honor of a Gracious Letter, with the Governor's Order of Silence inclosed; the Managers very justly slighted it so it met the

---

[60] In the *Reader,* No. 2, Steele tells a story about the "Begging Bridge." A man, having lost all his possessions in the defense of his country, was given the meager recompense of permission to beg.

[61] *Correspondence,* p. 153n. Professor Blanchard quotes this letter in her note on Steele's letter to the managers, remarking that "This letter [Steele's] may be that referred to in the following from Newcastle to Serjeant Pengelly. . . ." Pengelly's reply (not cited by Professor Blanchard) makes this interpretation of Newcastle's letter all but certain.

same reception as the other papers subscribed with his best hand. There is nothing further to be said, but that the managers stand upon their Defense and take care to secure the Lease or quit rent of the House, thereby to preserve the Possession of it; and also that they promise Sir Richard's part of the Cloathes and Scenery to be at their own Disposal, which I believe may be obtained upon moderate Terms from Mr. Gry [Gery] the mortgager, and this will deprive Sir Richard of the power & opportunity of giving them any inconvenient Disturbance. I am apt to think that Sir Richard's process, his artillery upon which he chiefly depended, has been discharged, not only without Direction, but without Terrors, and I Do not apprehend anything more terrible even from the Thunderer Himselfe, as he is pleased to call his Director. It will not be proper to ask any new order or Direction from His Majesty to defend the Players, until Sir Richard has Commenced some Prosecution, that it may be known in what method he intends to proceed against them; His Tuesday and Saturday's Process did not attack the managers in Drury Lane—I intend to pay my Duty to yr Grace tomorrow morning at 11 if it may be convenient. . . .[62]

This remarkably explicit letter offers few obstacles to comprehension. Gery was, of course, the mortgager from whom the managers were to obtain Steele's share of the clothes and scenery. In the latter part of the letter Pengelly apparently refers playfully to the *Theatre,* Steele's "artillery" and "His Tuesday and Saturday's Process." The tone of Pengelly's letter reveals the confidence he felt in Newcastle's case against Steele.

By the time the ninth number of the *Theatre* appeared on January 30 (two days before Pengelly wrote this reassuring letter to Newcastle), Steele had discovered the identity of Newcastle's legal adviser, and in perhaps the most bitter essay of the series he berated Pengelly, making a series of puns on his vulnerable name. Steele had doubtless learned how closely Newcastle's campaign against him was controlled by Pengelly's advice.

Pengelly had not overestimated the strength of Newcastle's position. For the time Steele could do nothing—except carry on a strenuous journalistic debate with the literary supporters of Newcastle. In April he discontinued even that, acknowledging

---

[62] P.R.O., S.P. 35, vol. lxxiv, No. 43 (10).

publicly the futility of continuing the controversy.[83] His fortunes had come to a low point. He had lost his wife, he had lost his major source of income, he was alienated from the leaders of his party, and his health was wretched. The note of self-pity prominent in the *Theatre* may be objectionable, but it is understandable.

3 | Reinstatement

STEELE'S political activity during 1720 confirmed the Whig party leaders in their ill-opinion of him and in their conviction that he deserved suspension from the theater. As in the preceding year, he strongly opposed the ministry on an important issue— this time, the South Sea Bill. In 1720 the South Sea Scheme and the financial transactions accompanying it held the interest of the nation: public and private finance were preoccupied with the insane popularity of stock jobbing to which the scheme gave rise; Parliament was sharply and bitterly divided by the proposal to support the South Sea Company; and when the crash came it shattered the ministry. Steele, as an active member of Parliament and a man with a sensitive public conscience, had strong convictions about the company which brought him into further conflict with many of the leading Whigs and which indirectly affected his chances of regaining his governorship of Drury Lane.

The South Sea Bill was introduced into Parliament to relieve the government of the burden of a large national debt contracted

---

[83] The *Theatre*, No. 28. This paper, the last of the series, appeared on April 5. On April 22 (according to an advertisement in the *Daily Post*) there was acted at Lincoln's Inn Fields "... a new Farce of two Acts, call'd, *The Theatre*. All in the Characters of the Italian Theatre. With a new Prologue to the Town by Sir Richard Steele. ..." I have not been able to trace this prologue. The question necessarily arises of whether or not Steele's prologue or the farce called *The Theatre* contained comment on Steele's trouble with Newcastle.

during the wars of Queen Anne's reign. The company offered to assume the entire burden of these obligations, to increase its capital by the total amount of both the redeemable and irredeemable annuities, the form in which the debts existed. Though ultimately accepted, the proposal met strong opposition from, among others, Robert Walpole, himself an advocate of a competitive scheme. When, after the violent explosion of the South Sea Bubble, public resentment turned with fury against the men responsible for it, Walpole found himself in a strong position; and it later proved to Steele's advantage that in the parliamentary debates occasioned by the South Sea Bill he was an ally of Walpole's. He was associated with that statesman as he had been the preceding year in the debates over the Peerage Bill. However, the immediate effect of his opposition to the ministry on both of the measures was damaging.

As in the previous year with the Peerage Bill, Steele's opposition to the proposal of the South Sea Company extended to pamphleteering. On February 1, 1720, the day a committee of the entire House of Commons resolved that the proposal should be accepted, Steele issued his *The Crisis of Property*, bearing on the title page his name followed boldly by the titles of his two major employments, "Member of Parliament, and Governor of the Royal Company of Comedians."[64] The one had been taken from him already, and there was danger that the other soon would be. In the pamphlet he denounced the South Sea Bill as an unjust and even immoral proposal: Parliament had no right, he insisted, to violate its agreement with the annuitants merely because it would be profitable to do so. His arguments were direct, and they were reinforced three and a half weeks later when he issued a second pamphlet, *A Nation a Family*, even more outspoken in criticism of the South Sea Bill. Here he actually questioned the company's motives: why were the directors so eager, he asked, to gain possession, even at high costs, of the annuities?[65]

[64] Steele's defiant inclusion of his titles provoked comment. Cf. *The Political State of Great Britain*, February, 1720.

[65] In *A Nation a Family*, Steele presents a counterproposal of his own for funding the national debt—a lottery scheme.

Not unnaturally his opposition to the ministry aroused strong resentment. A letter of Sir John Vanbrugh, written on February 18, 1720, to Jacob Tonson in Paris, reveals the grave light in which Steele's conduct was regarded by many:

Our South Sea, is become a Sort of a Young Mississipy, by the stocks rising so vastly.... People in general are much pleas'd with the Parlementary Scheme lately started. But Sir R. Steel is grown such a Malecontent, That he now takes the Ministry directly for his Mark; and treats them (in the House) for some days past in so very frank a manner that they grow quite angry; and 'tis talked as if it would not be impossible, to see him very soon expel'd the House. I don't know whether you have heard, he has a month ago work'd a Quarrel So high with my Lord Chamberlain, That a New Licence has been granted to Wilks, Cibber & Booth which they accepting of, and acting under; have Left him with his Patent, but not one Player, and so the Lord Chamberlain's Authority over the Playhouse is restor'd, and the Patent ends in a joke. I take hold of this Turn, to call upon those three Gentlemen about the Stock they had of mine, and think they will be willing to come to some tollerable Composition.[66]

Steele clearly had no chance of regaining his governorship until a major change in the ministry occurred. Nothing came of the rumor that he would again be expelled from Commons, nor is anything more known of Vanbrugh's renewed effort to force the managers to pay him for the stage properties removed from the Haymarket.

The South Sea Scheme is an increasingly important subject in the later numbers of the *Theatre;* Steele interspersed denunciations of the scheme with complaints of unjust treatment from the lord chamberlain. He first mentioned the proposal of the company in the *Theatre,* No. 17 (February 27, 1720), thereafter turning to it frequently—Nos. 20, 22, 23, 24, 25, and 27 are devoted almost entirely to the subject. The ideas are for the most part those he presented in the two pamphlets, though they are given new dress and emphasis by the pen of "Sir John Edgar." However, Steele's opposition to the proposal of the South Sea Company was as futile as was for the moment his fight to regain the governorship of Drury Lane. In April, the month in which he discontinued the *Theatre,* the South Sea Bill was made law.

_____
[66] Vanbrugh, *Works,* IV, 125.

Meanwhile Newcastle regulated the affairs of Drury Lane. On March 4, 1720, the company of actors, including Cibber, Wilks, and Booth, were administered an oath of obedience, in the lord chamberlain's office at Whitehall, not only to the chamberlain himself but to his subordinates, the vice-chamberlain and the gentleman usher-in-waiting.[67] Again the step was one Pengelly had advised.

A few days before he took the oath, but after he had received notice that he must do so, Robert Wilks wrote a letter to Newcastle which, though it is obsequiously phrased, suggests that the managers found the new supervision irksome.[68] The letter is indeed merely confirmation of what can be assumed from the circumstances. Though he had no fear of unjust treatment from Newcastle himself, Wilks wrote diplomatically, he feared oppression from the duke's subordinates. However, Wilks and his colleagues could not help themselves; in order to continue acting, they had to submit, Steele's wishes to the contrary. Whether or not Steele persisted in his resentment of their submission to the lord chamberlain, it is impossible to say; but he seems at least to have been in communication with Wilks and Cibber during his suspension.[69]

Even before the actors were sworn to obedience, Newcastle began a close supervision of Drury Lane. There were probably many instances of his intervention in the theater's affairs of which no record is extant, but there are records enough to indicate that he controlled the company's policies, even to the choice of plays for presentation. Early in February he issued instructions concerning matters the managers had previously considered within their own province.

---

[67] The *London Journal*, March 5, 1720 (quoted in the *Theatre*, ed. Nichols, I, 156n). Cf. the *Anti-Theatre*, No. 7.

[68] George A. Aitken, "Sir Richard Steele," the *Athenaeum*, 1890 (July to December), p. 890.

[69] In memoranda dating from August, 1720, Steele, then in Scotland, recorded that he had written to, among other people, Wilks and Cibber (Brit. Mus., Add. MS. 5145C, fols. 156, 157). Steele bought fifteen shares in the "fishpool" from Wilks on April 29, 1721 (*Correspondence*, pp. 541–542). It is significant that when Cibber reprinted *Ximena* in his collected works in 1721 he omitted the dedication to Steele.

Whereas I have thought fit for the better Regulation and Government of his Majts Theatre in Drury Lane, to Require you the Manager or Managers of the Sd Company Acting under his Majts Licence to take care that no benefit might be Allowed for the future to any Actor before Mrs Oldfield and Mrs Porters benefitt Night and that the prizes [sic] of the House be never raised without my leave first had. Given under my hand this 2nd day of February 1719 [1720] in the 6th Year of his Majts.

To the Managers of the   Holles Newcastle
Company of Comedians in
Drury Lane.[70]

Benefit nights and admission prices had become subject to the orders of the lord chamberlain. The frequent advances of prices at Drury Lane had, of course, been one of the most common causes of public complaint; and probably there had been complaints from the actors themselves about the apportioning of benefits. The same month Newcastle appears to have commanded the managers to present John Hughes's tragedy, *The Siege of Damascus* (acted at Drury Lane from February 17, 1720, through February 26). Such a command at least seems implied in a letter of thanks, dated February 4, addressed to the duke by Hughes: ". . . I cannot forbear returning you my most humble thanks for your protection and recommendation of my play to the care of the actors, and your zealous encouragement of it. . . ."[71] A "recommendation" of a play from Newcastle at that time could have had the aspect of little less than an absolute order.

Newcastle named also a play to follow *The Siege of Damascus,* though for an unknown reason his command was not obeyed. "I do hereby Order and direct," he wrote to the managers on February 16, "that Mr. Gays Pastoral Tragedy be immediately Acted after Mr. Hugh's",[72] presumably referring to Gay's *Dione,* which was not acted by any contemporary company. By forcing the managers to present two new plays successively, Newcastle perhaps wished to forestall objections that Drury Lane failed to encourage

[70] P.R.O., L.C. 5/157, fol. 284.

[71] John Duncombe, ed., *Letters by Several Eminent Persons Deceased* (Dublin, 1773), I, 150–151. Steele puffed *The Siege of Damascus* in the *Theatre,* No. 15.

[72] P.R.O., L.C. 5/157, fol. 287.

playwrights.[73] He underestimated the strain, I suspect, that staging two new plays successively would inflict on the company.

The managers' problems were now, however, none of Steele's; his was a separate course. When in the spring of 1720 he saw that his journalistic campaign had come to nothing, he gave up his effort to gain popular support and turned his hopes to the law. His writings had unquestionably gained him adherents,[74] but not in sufficient numbers or of sufficient influence to compel Newcastle to alter his course. Steele hoped for more from the courts. First he threatened Newcastle, through his brother Henry Pelham, with an announcement that if Newcastle persisted in barring him from the theater, he would enter a petition against him. Steele wrote to Pelham on two successive days, May 27 and May 28, 1720,[75] his second letter containing the ultimatum that if Steele did not hear from Newcastle by the following Monday noon, he would assume the duke intended to persist in his course of action, and consequently he, Steele, would take appropriate legal action. Steele's threats could scarcely have frightened the duke, who had acted on competent legal advice. Indeed, the ultimatum in the second letter appears ridiculous in view of Newcastle's high station and Steele's long and thus far futile attempt to regain control of Drury Lane. Steele had lost his temper and was shaking his fist in a defiant but impotent show of strength.[76]

Although Newcastle failed to comply with the terms of his ultimatum, Steele did not, so far as is known, initiate a petition for several months. Before he did so, moreover, he again wrote to the duke informing him of his intention.[77] Finally, on February 6, 1721,

[73] In March, 1719, as I have already said, Newcastle may have forced the managers to produce Edward Young's *Busiris*. See above, p. 85.

[74] Cf. James Dallaway, ed., *Letters of the Late Thomas Rundle, L.L.D., to Mrs. Barbara Sandys* (Gloucester, 1789), pp. 11–12; 18–19.

[75] *Correspondence*, pp. 153–154.

[76] A brief, undated note from Steele to Newcastle may belong to this same time—May, 1720. Steele wrote: "You have injur'd a man that cannot bear it longer and you may depend upon it that when you meet conveniently the dispute between you will soon be at end." *Correspondence*, p. 154.

[77] *Correspondence*, pp. 159–160. The letter is undated, but in all likelihood belongs to this stage of the dispute. Cf. Professor Blanchard's note, p. 160n.

Steele enclosed in a letter to Viscount Townshend (then president of the privy council) a petition to the king, requesting that the king in council hear his case.[78] The duke had dispossessed him of the government of the theater, he complained, although the king's order of revocation mentioned only such powers as were legally subject to recall. Steele did not concern himself in the petition with the niceties of the question—whether or not the patent was still in effect—but based his appeal on the blunt fact that he had been dispossessed of his governorship,

Although there is no indication that Steele's petition produced any direct results, the course of events was at last moving in his favor. Action against Steele was inspired in part at least by the ministry led by Stanhope in retaliation for his opposition to the Peerage Bill and the South Sea Bill; now action to reinstate him commenced when, as a result of the South Sea disaster, that ministry was replaced. Steele's position on the two bills, as I have said, coincided with Robert Walpole's; it is understandable that after Walpole came into power, following the South Sea panic, Steele found his own fortunes improved. One month after Walpole was made first lord of the treasury and chancellor of the exchequer, Steele, on May 2, 1721, was restored to the governorship of Drury Lane.

Steele understood immediately the significance to himself of the change in the ministry. In his journal there is an entry that reveals him, one week after the cabinet shift, resuming his attempts to regain the theater. He recorded his conviction (in a passage previously quoted) that Stanhope and Craggs were the instigators of his suspension, and he recorded also the steps he had taken to gain reinstatement:

The Duke of Newcastle brought Me into this present Parliament for the Town of Burrough Bridge upon which consideration I attempt all manner of Fair methods to bring his Grace to reason without a Public Tryall in a Court of Justice, and therefore after applying to my Lord Sunderland and Mr. Walpole for their Good offices I writ the following letter to His Grace's Brother, Mr. Henry Pelham lately appointed one of the Lords of the Treasury.

---

[78] *Correspondence*, pp. 159, 532–533.

Sir

I presume to address myself to you for your favour and Patronage with your Brother the Duke of Newcastle; the Matter is too publick and necessarily made so even in print by a command to Me from his Grace to apply to Him neither by Friends Speech or letter and consequently Leaving Me no other Way to represent my Condition. It is my Misfortune to do exactly as the Question lyes before Me in a certain House where I am glad to See you are growing Eminent.

By this means Good Will towards Me is tossed from one interest into another, as the point which I vote for is respectively acceptable or ungratefull. At present I am wholly Friendless for no one is obliged to one (who will do nothing but what he thinks just) because His Suffrage never attends persons or Partyes. However, Sr, your Quality and time of Life make me hope you have the disinterested Magnanimity to espouse an Unhappy man to the dissuasion even of yr Brother from prolonging a mortification, which unhappy incidents (without any particular provocation from Me, or personall resentment in His Grace) brought upon Me, to the Suffering for a long series of time all the evils and Sorrows that this life can afford.[79]

More than a little self-righteousness appears here. Steele's expressions of humility are too intense to be convincing; his declaration that he is friendless is palpably inaccurate in view of the change in the government. Newcastle and Henry Pelham were by no means rendered powerless by the cabinet shift, but Walpole, with whom Steele was closely associated, had become very powerful indeed. In the letter to Pelham it appears that Steele was engaging in some gratuitous self-effacement, possibly seeking to hasten his reinstatement at Drury Lane by a display of courtly humility and by avoiding any allusion to the political change in his favor. His reference in his journal to his application to Sunderland and Walpole shows that he himself was aware of his improved position. Steele evidently believed that his task would be easier if Newcastle did not violently resent his restoration.

The Earl of Sunderland, to whom, with Walpole, Steele applied for assistance, was in a very different political position from that of Walpole in the spring of 1721. He was one of the ministers tried on charges arising out of the South Sea disaster,[80] and, al-

---

[79] Ibid., pp. 541, 162.

[80] Steele had defended Sunderland and the other implicated ministers in the parliamentary trials.

though in March, 1721, he was acquitted, he was compelled by public opinion to resign his post in the government. He remained nevertheless a powerful man whose assistance could be of value to Steele in regaining Drury Lane. That he was benevolently disposed toward Steele is implied by his support of Steele the following year in his election to Parliament from Wendover, Buckinghamshire, support tantamount to giving him the office.

The details of the action by which Steele was restored to Drury Lane are not known. Certainly Walpole, and possibly Sunderland, took Steele's side against Newcastle, forcing him to reverse his former position; but there is no record of precisely what occurred. Genest makes an interesting comment on this gap in our knowledge of the theatrical dispute:

Steele's restoration was owing to the interference of his friend Mr. Walpole, who had just been made Chancellor of the Exchequer—(Dr. Drake)—it does not appear what legal steps Steele took to obtain redress—as the validity of the Patent and the authority of the Lord Chamberlain had been fairly at issue, it would have been most desirable to have had the question fully argued in a Court of Law.[81]

Steele himself recorded merely that he was reinstated after he protested the legality of the lord chamberlain's action.[82]

It is unfortunate that after the strenuous debates over the respective authorities of the patentee and the lord chamberlain no

---

[81] [John Genest], *Some Account of the English Stage from the Restoration in 1660 to 1830* (Bath, 1832), III, 20. "Dr. Drake," whom Genest cites as his authority, was Nathan Drake. In *Essays, Biographical, Critical, and Historical, Illustrative of the Tatler, Spectator, and Guardian* (London, 1805), I, 149–150, Drake writes: "His [Steele's] great friend and patron Mr. Walpole, who, on the 10th of April, 1717, had resigned his place of first commissioner of the treasury, (an event which had, without doubt, laid the immediate foundation for all our author's subsequent misfortunes) was, on April the 2d, 1721, appointed chancellor of the exchequer; Mr. Aislaibie, his predecessor, having been disgraced as a participator in the frauds and profits of the South-sea bubble. The almost instant consequences of this elevation was Steele's restoration to his office and authority at Drury-lane. Animated by such unexpected good fortune, his dramatic genius, which had slept for many years, revived with additional lustre. . . ."

[82] P.R.O., C11/2416/49 (Steele's deposition of June 23, 1726, in answer to the managers' bill of complaint).

open decision on the points at issue was rendered. The controversy was terminated, not by a settlement of the fundamental differences over the jurisdiction of the stage, but by a change in the political fortunes of the participants. External political issues had so injected themselves into the controversy that the questions concerning the government of the stage could not be settled on their own merits. Presumably the patent itself was not affected by Newcastle's action; certainly its authority was respected until three years after the death of Steele, the originally stipulated term of its duration. The other questions are not answered for us, and probably they were not answered for Steele and his contemporaries.

Newcastle's order to the actor-managers terminating Steele's suspension, dated May 2, 1721, is brief and to the point:

> Whereas Application has been made to me in behalf of Sr. Richd. Steele on Occasion of the Regulation under which his Mat.'s Company of Comedians has been lately placed Exclusive of the said Sr. Richd. Steele and his pretentions. I do hereby Order and Direct You to Account with the said Sr. Richd. Steele for all the past and future Share arising from the Profits of the Theatre as he would have been Entitled to by an Agreement between You and him, if the said Regulation had never been made, and to Pay him hereafter from time to time his said Share till further Orders from me, or Determination of that point be made by due course of Law. For wch. this shall be your Sufficient Warrant....[83]

The dispute was over and Steele had scored a personal triumph. Newcastle's order contains an intimation that legal action against Steele might follow, and in later court records there is a hint, though no more, that some subsequent action was taken.[84] However, Newcastle's order is a repudiation of the stratagem of ignoring the patent which Pengelly had suggested. Victory was clearly with Steele. He was again governor of the Royal Company of Comedians, though he was to take the duties of the position less seriously than before.

---

[83] P.R.O., L.C. 5/157, fols. 415–416. Aitken, *Life*, II, 262.

[84] In their deposition of October 13, 1725, the actor-managers testify cryptically: "... and these Defts said Complt Sr Richard Steele was sometimes since [1721] suspended of his Maties Sign Mannuall but Deny that they ever took Advantage thereof...." P.R.O., CII/300/38. I know of no confirmation of this statement.

4 | Journalistic Controversy

NOT THE least important result of Newcastle's action against Steele was the airing it provoked of contemporary opinion on stage government. Midway between the outburst of indignation against the stage at the turn of the century and the decisive legislative action of 1737, Steele's dispute brought to a preliminary focus the ideas that ultimately led to the Stage Licensing Act: many of the same arguments were marshaled against Steele and his colleagues at Drury Lane that were used a decade and a half later in support of the Licensing Act. The major issue in dispute in 1720—rigid control by the chamberlain or freedom of the managers—was again a major issue in 1737. For a brief period during Steele's suspension the chamberlain exercised the comprehensive and absolute control of Drury Lane that became the rule after the Licensing Act passed. The long agitation for a closer regulation of the stage, clamorous since late in the seventeenth century, came, then, to a climax, though an inconclusive and abortive one, with the lord chamberlain's seizing operational control of the theater. Because the chamberlain's action was climactic—arising from years of complaints—and was recognized thus, it produced, along with many bitter personal recriminations, journalistic reviews of the fundamental problems associated with control of the stage.

The surest indication of the contemporary interest in the dispute is to be found in the mass of the journalistic writing occasioned by it: at least two periodicals, nearly a dozen published pamphlets, and a series of newspaper articles were lavished on the controversy. Readers were informed of the successive stages of Newcastle's campaign to humble Steele and his colleagues, and they were supplied with editorial comment, both sympathetic and unsympathetic to the managers, on the significance of the separate events. Newcastle's action seems to have been regarded as the initial step in a decisive change in the mode of theater government—as a reassertion of the government's right to supervise the patent companies.

It is not difficult to discover reasons why Newcastle's action would have been so regarded. For years dramatic critics had deplored control of the stage by actors and had urged some strong supervision by an outside authority; indignation at the actor-managers had frequently expressed itself in demands for closer regulation of the theater. The dissatisfaction with the existing form of theater government was, as has been noted, a chief reason for the initial appointment of Steele to Drury Lane; but the hopes engendered by his appointment, as also noted, were blasted. Under him the actor-managers controlled the theater more firmly than before, provoking a steadily mounting chorus of complaints.[85] Steele and his colleagues, to be sure, had sympathizers—a substantial number of them—and a few entered the journalistic controversy in their defense. Sympathizers and detractors alike, however, recognized Newcastle's suspension of Steele as a major step in the government effort to control the stage.

Steele's major vehicle for defending himself in the dispute was, of course, the *Theatre,* a journal printed on the usual half sheets, appearing twice weekly, on Tuesdays and Saturdays, from January 2, 1720, until April 5, 1720. It by no means ranks with Steele's great periodicals, but it nevertheless represents a substantial literary achievement—in several of the essays may be seen the qualities for which Steele's major periodicals are famous. Even those numbers in which the light-hearted humor of Steele's best writing is displaced by controversial bitterness have, for the most part, a strong compensating historical appeal. The most objectionable quality of the journal is the strong note of self-pity evident in many of the papers; Steele complained, often in a childish whine, of the accumulation of misfortunes with which he was afflicted. But whatever the limitations and palpable inferiorities of the *Theatre,* copies of the essays were eagerly bought and read as soon as they appeared, as shown by a letter written by Dr. Thomas Rundle: "I am sorry I could not get for you a whole set of *Theatres;* the very best are wanting. The demand for them was so great,

---

[85] See above, pp. 79–82.

that even his fiercest enemies bought them up, and enjoyed the author, while they persecute the man."[86] The periodical was popular, not only for its partisan reporting of the theatrical dispute; Steele's ability to write engaging essays had not completely left him.

In its introductory numbers, the *Theatre* reveals no trace of Steele's trouble with Newcastle. The paper begins conventionally with "Sir John Edgar's" introduction of himself, his son Harry, and a circle of friends who meet regularly at the tea table of "Sophronia," a circle interested in the theater. Edgar, an elderly man who has had his youthful interest in the stage rekindled by his son, undertakes the journal, at the request of Sophronia, that it may be of service to the stage. All this, of course, is the familiar fictional machinery of the eighteenth-century periodical.[87] In the third number, the machinery is extended to include "a new scheme for the government of the public diversions," one providing for the election of a board of auditors who in the name of the town will have absolute power to accept or reject, to praise or condemn, the productions of the actors. The actors themselves are to have representatives on the board, as is also each of the social groups who frequent the different parts of the playhouse. But after this elaborate exposition of the framework of the periodical, Steele made no use of it; in his subsequent papers he ignored Sophronia's tea table and the board of theatrical auditors, his preoccupation with the Newcastle quarrel doubtless preventing the maturing of his early plans for the *Theatre*.

Not until the seventh paper did Steele refer to the dispute. Beginning with that number, in a bitter series of seven numbers, he reviewed in righteous indignation all the issues raised by Newcastle's action. His temper cooling thereafter, the South Sea Bill received some of his abuse. In a few of the later numbers, notably in No. 21, he wrote legitimate theatrical criticism and news of the stage.

It is as a controversial document that the *Theatre* is most interesting: Steele, veteran of many paper wars, employed all his gifts

---

[86] Rundle, *Letters,* pp. 11–12.

[87] Cf. Robert J. Allen, *The Clubs of Augustan London* (Cambridge, Mass., 1933), pp. 218–219.

in his own defense. What he did, apart from erecting a smoke screen of personal vituperation, was essentially to insist vigorously on three major points: the dignity of acting as a profession—and hence indirectly the wisdom of his turning over the routine management of Drury Lane to the actor-managers; the flourishing condition of the English stage, more specifically of Drury Lane; the lawlessness and imprudence of Newcastle's intervention in Drury Lane affairs. His case rested on his demonstration of these points, as the more astute of his opponents recognized, and it was on these points that they attacked him.

From the first number of the *Theatre,* before he even mentioned the Newcastle affair, Steele championed the actors and their conduct of the stage. "I doubt not," he observes in No. 1, "but I shall bring the world into my opinion, that the profession of an Actor, who in the other part of his conduct is irreproachable, ought to receive the kind treatment and esteem, which the world is ready to pay all other Artists." It was the old note of Squire Bickerstaff, to be sure, but it had gained new relevance. When, in No. 7, he spoke of the wisdom of his resigning the routine management to the actor-managers, everyone could see the drift of his argument. The undervalued players, according to Steele, had brought the English stage to a point of excellence superior to any of the contemporary foreign ones, and promised to lead it in the future to greatness rivaling the Greek and Roman stages[88]—a brave boast, not allowed to pass without challenge.

The tone of the *Theatre* changes abruptly with No. 7, when Steele introduces the dispute with Newcastle. In thinly disguised allegory virtually charging the duke with perverting royal justice, Steele is bold indeed in his attack; and in a fable of a glass beehive, he suggests not very subtly that if the duke erroneously believes that he can direct the affairs of Drury Lane, he will suffer for his indiscretion. In No. 10 Steele is quite explicit in asserting the illegality of Newcastle's action. "I cannot but think," Sir John Edgar observes, "his [Steele's] adversaries are well aware of it [the legality of the patent], or else they would not attack him in a way so invidious to themselves, as that of denying him the due course of law. . . ." Such lawlessness as that demonstrated by Newcastle, if

[88] The *Theatre,* No. 1.

it became widespread, Edgar warns, would destroy the safeguards of property and justice in England. But, Edgar observes maliciously, "What comfort can the deprived person have greater, than in the reflection upon his own part, against the late bill of Peerage?" There are many such sallies, many of them telling, scattered throughout the *Theatre,* but there is no extended legal argument. For that Steele employed a pamphlet that he published separately in March, his *The State of the Case Between the Lord Chamberlain . . . and the Governor of the Royal Company of Comedians.*

Of the replies to Steele, the two most conspicuous are easily the two parts of John Dennis's *The Characters and Conduct of Sir John Edgar . . . ,* in which, with mingled vituperation and logic, vindictiveness and informed analysis of theatrical problems, Dennis stoutly challenged Steele's defense of the actors and the state of British drama. Though he clearly wrote from intellectual conviction, Dennis was moved to undertake *The Characters and Conduct* by his personal grudge against Steele and the actor-managers.[89] He remembered bitterly the failure of his *The Invader of His Country* when it was presented at Drury Lane in November, 1719, a failure for which he held the actor-managers, and indirectly Steele, responsible. Not only had the managers contributed to the failure of his play, Dennis believed, but they had also insulted him by appending an epilogue to it, written by Cibber, containing derisive allusions to him. Dennis had first publicly expressed his complaints about the Drury Lane management in the dedication to Newcastle of *The Invader,* which had drawn a reply from an anonymous defender of the managers on December 1, 1719, in a little pamphlet called *A Critick no wit: or, Remarks on Mr. Dennis's Late Play, Called the Invader of his Country,* containing harsh and frequently unreasonable criticism of the play. The pamphlet no doubt increased Dennis's anger. These personal considerations, then, added vehemence to his arguments in rebuttal to the *Theatre,* if they did not determine the direction the arguments assumed.

[89] There is no evidence to support Aitken's assumption (*Life,* II, 231) that *The Characters and Conduct* was a "hireling" pamphlet. Cf. Hooker, *Dennis,* II, 476; see also II, xxxi–xxxiv, for an account of Steele-Dennis relations.

In the *Theatre*, No. 11 (February 6, 1720), the fictional author remarks: "A Pamphlet was yesterday put into my hands by an hawker, which bears for its title, 'The Characters and Conduct of Sir JOHN EDGAR, called by himself sole Monarch of the Stage in Drury Lane; and his Three Deputy Governors. In Two Letters to Sir JOHN EDGAR.'" Steele's reference is to the first of Dennis's two pamphlets, the pamphlet to which he replied in this same *Theatre* and in the following one. In No. 11, apparently not knowing who wrote the "Letters" (they were published anonymously), Steele could only defend himself and his colleagues against the charges made against them; but in No. 12, having discovered the identity of his opponent, Steele assumed the offensive and made counter-charges.

The Characters and Conduct (Letters 1 and 2) is an abusive answer to Steele's defense of actors and of the contemporary stage in the *Theatre*. Dennis, understanding clearly that control of the stage by actors was at issue, argued their incapacity for the responsibility. An actor lacked the training of a liberally educated gentleman, he insisted, the training requisite to the proper government of a theater. An actor's personal interest, his desire for large profits, was at variance with the national interest in encouragement of drama: to succeed, a playwright had to have his plays produced; yet an actor in control of the theater would frequently refuse even good new plays because he could make more money from old ones. The employment of an actor itself, the constant exposure to plays good and bad, rendered him an incompetent judge of drama; his sense of discrimination was dulled by overexposure, Dennis maintained, just as a drunkard lost his ability to distinguish between wines. Dennis used also a historical argument. The incapacity of actors had long been recognized; for centuries and in many countries they had been carefully supervised.

Nor did he confine himself to impersonal argument. He became very personal, very direct, in an appraisal of the Drury Lane management. Has the stage made any progress since it has been under the direction of the actor-managers? he asks; has it not "vilely degenerated"? Is there any promise of amendment in the future?; any hope of a future actor or a future poet? Dennis answers the questions himself: "No; all is going to Ruin: The Stage is sinking under you; and there is no Hope of saving it, but by getting it out of the Hands of the Separate Ministry." The increased crowds at the theater count for nothing—they are by no means an indication that there has been an improvement in the quality of performances. The audiences are larger because a series of great public events has increased the size of the city, not because the entertainment is better. To demonstrate the absurdity of Steele's claims for the English theater, Dennis draws the characters of the actor-managers; and enraged, he reaches the height of his bitterness in his description of Cibber, who had abused him in the epilogue to his own play. Becoming more temperate thereafter, Dennis argued that Steele's criticism of French drama in the *Theatre* revealed an ignorance of the rules of drama and hence an incapacity to govern the stage.

Apart from Steele's own answer to *The Characters and Conduct* in the *Theatre*, Nos. 11 and 12, at least one other appeared—the anonymous *An Answer to a Whimsical Pamphlet, Called the Character of Sir John Edgar* (dated January 26, 1720, but not published until February 11, 1720).[90] "Written by Sir JOHN EDGAR's BAKER, mentioned in the *Third* THEATRE" and "Humbly inscribed to Sir TREMENDOUS LONGINUS," the pamphlet exhibits a cleverly sustained irony in which Dennis is ridiculed through misdirected praise. The satire is mildly amusing but largely inconsequential. Only at one point does the author approach a major issue in the controversy: Steele and the actor-managers, he asserts, have brought the stage, by their ability and industry, to its present prosperous condition; the crowds who flock to the theater and the frequent attendance of the royal family attest the managers' success at Drury Lane. Lincoln's Inn Fields enjoys no such prosperity, he argues; it lacks full audiences even when no plays are acted at Drury Lane. Although the argument had a certain effectiveness, Dennis had already pointed out a fundamental weakness in it—a prosperous stage is by no means always one favorable to the development of good drama.

Dennis appears also to have been attacked—and perhaps more effectively—in another pamphlet published early in February entitled *A New Project for the Regulation of the Stage*. Advertised

---

[90] Aitken, *Life*, II, 234n.

as "By Mr. D–nis and Mr. G–don,"[91] it was actually a satire on those two critics. Because no copy appears to have survived, all that is known of the work is gleaned indirectly through Pope and Swift's *Peri Bathous, Martin Scriblerus, his treatise on the art of sinking in poetry* (1728), the final chapter of which is a burlesque scheme for the improvement of the stage, purporting to be a plan made public by Gildon and Dennis in 1720, presumably in *A New Project for the Regulation of the Stage.* In introducing the scheme, Pope and Swift praise ironically Booth, Cibber, and Wilks, but in describing the scheme itself they ignore the managers. The moral depravity of the stage and the intellectual depravity of critics provide the real objects of their satire. Dennis, as the foremost critic of the time, suffers derision, but his name is not associated with those of the Drury Lane managers, nor is there in this report of the lost pamphlet any allusion to Steele's theatrical dispute. Because the pamphlet appeared in February, 1720, however, a time when the journalistic controversy about Steele's suspension was at its height, it seems probable that it contained, directly or implicitly, some comment on what was going on at Drury Lane. It would scarcely have been possible at the time to satirize Dennis's theories on stage government without mentioning his violent quarrel, then in progress, with the managers of the Theatre-Royal. Without the pamphlet, however, we may only speculate.

Dennis was by no means without supporters in the controversy with Steele. Among others an able writer, who called himself "Sir Andrew Artlove," contributed to successive numbers of *Applebee's Original Weekly Journal* (February 13 to February 27, 1720) three letters with the title *A Full Consideration and Confutation of Sir John Edgar,* answering, as their title implies, the *Theatre;* more specifically, the numbers of the *Theatre* that were particularly offensive to Dennis—1, 2, 11, and 12. And as "Artlove" revealed a partiality to Dennis in this choice of papers, so also in the arguments he employed. His arguments paralled closely those of Dennis—especially in his more abusive passages—so closely, in fact, that John Nichols assumed Dennis was Artlove.[92]

Insofar as Artlove's three letters contain reasoned argument,

---

[91] The *Daily Post,* February, 5, 1720: "This day is published. . . ."

[92] The *Theatre,* ed. Nichols, II, 465n.

they are a rebuttal to Steele's defense of the contemporary English stage. Exhibiting a strong admiration for classical regularity in drama, the author finds an inconsistency in Steele's preference of the English stage to the foreign ones and his prediction that the English stage might arrive at as great a perfection as was known in classical antiquity. The English stage, for which Steele has such great praise, Artlove insists, is precisely opposite in its nature to the stage that Steele holds up as the exemplar of the greatest perfection—the classical one. "There, regularity, order, and harmony, were perfectly observed; here, under the specious name of Variety, is nothing but a wandering stage (as BOILEAU calls it). . . ." Artlove, of course, is a firm defender of the Aristotelian rules, finding, like Dennis, in Steele's disdain for the rules further evidence of his incapacity. This author's most telling argument against the contemporary stage is his charge of immorality: without acknowledging any attempt at reform, Artlove thoroughly damns the stage for its moral corruptions. If, as Steele maintained in the second *Theatre,* nations as well as private individuals are known by their pleasures, Artlove fears for the reputation of the English:

I am afraid that Foreigners will entertain a very injurious notion of the People of England, when they find that their public diversion is nothing but confusion; and that they are delighted in Comedies by the lewd intrigues of Prostitutes (who yet in these Comedies are represented as fine Ladies), and where the whole business and plot of the Play are to carry on fornication and adultery; when in their Tragedies they are pleased with rapes, incests, prodigious villanies, and inhuman and shocking murthers . . . and yet such are the Comedies and Tragedies brought on, and encouraged most by the present Managers.[93]

Steele, to be sure, had written in the same vein in the *Spectator;* the rub came in his association with Drury Lane, subsequent to the *Spectator.*

Even more forthright than Sir Andrew Artlove in defense of Dennis and in denunciation of Steele was the anonymous author of a mock-heroic prose satire published March 12, 1720,[94] with the

[93] *Applebee's Original Weekly Journal,* February 13, 1720.

[94] The *London Journal,* March 12, 1720. Professor John Robert Moore has, since my account of the satire was written, offered strong evidence that its author was Charles Gildon: "Gildon's Attack on Steele and Defoe

pompous title, *The Battle of the Authors Lately Fought in Covent-Garden, Between Sir John Edgar, Generalissimo on one Side, and* HORATIUS TRUEWIT, *on the Other.* Strongly antagonistic to Steele and only slightly less so to Cibber, the author makes frequent reference to the theatrical dispute, but the battle he describes is not specifically that fought at Drury Lane between Steele and Newcastle; rather it is the unending struggle between ignorance and enlightenment. In choice of subject as well as in narrative method the author seems to have taken suggestions from Dryden's *Mac Flecknoe* and, more immediately, from Addison's the *Spectator*, No. 63. The affair at Drury Lane is constantly in the background of his battle narrative—Steele becomes the leader of the forces of darkness and Dennis of those of light—though the struggle is not restricted to the theater. Contemporary literary figures, including Defoe and Young, are introduced as contestants in the conflict, and all ignorance and presumption in the domain of polite letters receive a share of the author's scorn. Sir John Edgar remains, however, in the dominant position as butt of the satire.

Beneath its allegorical exterior *The Battle of the Authors* was yet another reply to Steele's defense of the managers' conduct of the stage; it was, above all, a satirical denunciation of the condition of Drury Lane. That theater was the domain of ignorance; Steele and Cibber were distinguished for their service to ignorance. Apart from allegorical denunciation, the author had little that was in any way informative to say about Steele, his colleagues, or the condition of the stage. He made some interesting observations about the legal justification for Newcastle's intervention at Drury Lane, but, as I have said previously, he misunderstood the nature of Newcastle's action. His praise of Dennis is extravagant to the point that it sometimes appears ironic, though evidently irony was not intended.

Dennis himself returned to the controversy, probably sometime in March,[95] with a second pamphlet, *The Characters and Conduct of Sir John Edgar . . .*, Letters 3 and 4. Since his first two letters

in *The Battle of the Authors,*" *Publications of the Modern Language Association of America*, LXVI (1951), 534–538.
[95] Cf. Hooker, *Dennis*, II, 485.

were well received—the pamphlet quickly went into a second edition—it is understandable why he was encouraged to continue. This time he signed his name openly, dedicating the letters to Newcastle, as he had previously the published version of *The Invader of His Country*, with again the obvious intention of associating his grievances against Steele with those of the nobleman. The pamphlet is a reply to Steele's rebuttal in the *Theatre* to the first part of *The Characters and Conduct*: Dennis's Letter 3 replies to the *Theatre*, No. 11, and his Letter 4 to the *Theatre*, No. 12. In this second installment Dennis, less seriously argumentative than before, succumbs to petty name calling—as had, indeed, Steele in the *Theatre*, No. 12. Dennis apparently wrote with Steele's papers before him, answering in turn all Steele's arguments, inconsequential as most of them in Nos. 11 and 12 were. Dennis answered no single important point but a series of trivial ones. To be sure, in Letter 4, in defending literary critics, he rose momentarily to serious argument, but his remarks are only remotely associated with the theatrical controversy. Thus this second installment of *The Characters and Conduct* added little that was significant to the debate. Dennis threatened Steele with still another installment—a threat, however, that he never carried out, nor did Steele reply to these third and fourth letters.

If Dennis was the most conspicuous of Steele's antagonists, the most persistent was easily the anonymous author of the *Anti-Theatre*, who devoted a biweekly periodical to the task of answering Steele. His title describes his purpose; of the series of fifteen essays, only two (Nos. 5 and 11) do not in some way refer to Steele himself or to the stage. The periodical appeared on Mondays and Thursdays, rather than on the Tuesdays and Saturdays of the *Theatre*, to allow time for the author to comment on what Steele wrote. "Sir John Falstaffe," as the author called himself, wished to provoke a journalistic debate with Steele, partly perhaps to create interest in his own paper, and he expressed annoyance that Steele did not give him more attention.[96] Steele mentioned his rival briefly

[96] In the "later" *Theatre*, No. 16, Falstaffe wrote: "I mounted the stage as his Adversary, and he accepted my Challenge; upon which I attack'd him with such Weapons as Men of Learning commonly use against one another, yet he declin'd the Combat."

in the *Theatre,* No. 14, but except for a dubious allusion in No. 17 (which Falstaffe was quick to take up), he thereafter ignored the *Anti-Theatre.* Falstaffe was less harsh in manner than Steele's other antagonists, avoiding, to a considerable extent, the ill-tempered name calling found in some of the writings already examined; but he was nevertheless a determined and able opponent who opposed Steele on all the major issues raised in the theatrical dispute. His journal appeared first on February 15, 1720, between the thirteenth and fourteenth numbers of the *Theatre,* and continued as long as did Steele's journal, the last (No. 15) appearing on April 4, the day before the last *Theatre.* All numbers except the first are extant.

Intermingled in the *Anti-Theatre* with many humorous but innocuous efforts to provoke Steele to controversy are serious discussions of problems implicit in Newcastle's intervention at Drury Lane. In his third essay, for instance, Falstaffe argues historically, exhibiting a substantial amount of erudition, that the stage should be controlled by a strong authority external to it (such as the lord chamberlain). Employing as his starting point Steele's assertion in the first *Theatre* "that it will not be the fault of the persons concerned in it [the English theater], if it does not arrive at as great perfection as was ever known in Greece or Rome," Falstaffe traces briefly, for a directly controversial purpose, the history of the classical stage. In Greece, where drama reached its highest development, the stage was carefully governed by the men who governed the state; in Rome, on the other hand, where drama degenerated notoriously, public officials ignored the stage, permitting actors to govern themselves. As still another historical support for his argument, Falstaffe recalls the success of the French stage when it was closely regulated by Cardinal Richelieu. All precedent, he argues, reveals the folly of allowing self-government to actors. "A controuling power over the Stage ... is absolutely necessary; and then public diversions will not depend on the humour or caprice of those within, but on real judges without the walls of the Theatre."

In his seventh essay Falstaffe expressed the elation he and, we may surmise, a substantial number of literary critics felt in Newcastle's close supervision of Drury Lane, the essay apparently having been suggested by the newspaper notice of the company's submission to an oath of obedience to the lord chamberlain and his subordinates. Falstaffe enumerates quite specifically the abuses the lord chamberlain will correct:

The Town now will begin to have less fear of being ridden too hard by that prevailing Theatre; and, however they may be indulged in proper privileges, which the wisdom of the Crown and its deputies know when to bestow, the Directors must now act with a limited power, and not with the air of being that arbitrary Ministry, which they themselves, or the kindness of their better friends, insinuated they were. Among the benefits, as I conceive, that we shall have in our pleasures, from their being under new restrictions, it is no small one, that the tax of advanced prices must not so often be levied on the Town: it is likely now too, that Plays will be performed to better advantage, and parts assigned with some propriety, and not disposed of from the casual motives of indulgence or resentment; for every good Actor that is aggrieved or depressed has his appeal to the Chamberlain for a redress.

To Steele as an apologist for the contemporary stage, Falstaffe makes a strong protest. Noting Steele's criticism (in the *Theatre*, No. 21) of the French pantomimists at the Haymarket, Falstaffe inquires pointedly in No. 9 why Steele has waited until the French actors appeared in England to complain of the stage's obscenity; two objectionable plays—*The Relapse* and *The Careless Husband*—have been acted by English actors (at Drury Lane) since Steele started the *Theatre*, yet he has taken no notice of them. This choice of plays with which to reproach Steele, two usually considered among the best written during the period, reveals a moralistic preoccupation. More conventional are his objections in the *Anti-Theatre*, No. 12, to a performance at Drury Lane. Ironically heading his remarks "From my own Apartment," he describes a pantomime in dancing presented the previous night consisting "of a story, or plot, acted without speaking a single word, and writ by those masters in *dumb poetry*, whose understandings generally lay below their knees." The point of his comment lies in the fact that ten days before, in the *Theatre*, No. 21, Steele denounced such a performance at the Haymarket—a short time before his own company presented one. In his final number Falstaffe openly laments the condition of English drama: the player's business has become merely to get money; the stage. has been prostituted.

Though he does not mention Steele, the actor-managers, or Drury Lane, the drift of his argument is unmistakable.

This paper, the *Anti-Theatre*, No. 15, appeared as usual on Monday, April 4, containing no indication that the periodical was to be discontinued or was to undergo a change. In the *Theatre*, No. 28, however, which came out on Tuesday, April 5, Steele announced that he was concluding his own journal. On Thursday, his usual day of publication, Falstaffe was silent, but on Saturday he issued a paper that, though it bore the number "16" (the next in his regular series), bore as its title Steele's former title, the *Theatre*.[97] For eleven numbers Falstaffe published, on Tuesdays and Saturdays (Steele's former days of publication), this later *Theatre*, making no attempt, however, to pass the journal off as Steele's, to gain popularity for it through Steele's reputation.

In the later *Theatre*, No. 16 (the first in the new series), Falstaffe provides a fictional explanation, in familiar eighteenth-century terms, of why the title of his paper has been changed: "The Reader will hereby understand that Sir *John* is dead: It is for this reason that I appear in his Dress, that I assume his *Habit de Guerre*, for Sir *John* chose me, from among all Men living, to be his sole Executer." But this fiction of a literary inheritance did not compel Falstaffe to carry on the dispute about Drury Lane; indeed, almost the only references to Steele's quarrel with Newcastle in the later *Theatre* appear in the mock will of Sir John Edgar quoted in No. 16. Edgar leaves a number of bequests to individuals involved in the quarrel, bequests ironically appropriate. To his "indulgent Friend and Patron, his Grace the Duke of ———," Edgar leaves his *"transparent Bee-hive,"* the subject of the allegorical anecdote in Steele's *Theatre*, No. 7, through which Steele had suggested that Newcastle would find his attempt to control Drury Lane a painful experience. It is only in this mock will in the entire later *Theatre* that Falstaffe recalls Steele's difficulties with the lord chamberlain;

---

[97] This "later" *Theatre* was for a long time unknown. For an account of its rediscovery, see John Loftis, " 'Sir John Falstaffe's' *Theatre*," *Journal of English and Germanic Philology*, XLVIII(1949), 252–258. Of the eleven numbers of the journal's run, all but one (No. 19) are preserved in the Folger Shakespeare Library. The journal appeared in the Augustan Reprint Society, Series Four, No. 1 (May, 1948).

except for the bare mention of the word, in fact, only in this mock will does he refer to the stage. Falstaffe, whoever he was, simply used Steele's title for what it was worth, making no attempt to bring the subjects of his essays into conformity with it. The theater and Sir John Edgar himself were excluded in favor of a miscellaneous group of nonrelated subjects—dueling, astrology, social affectations, the South Sea Bubble, the fondness for new projects—all treated with pleasing erudition.

Much less ambitious than Falstaffe's periodicals was an obscure, and similarly anonymous, pamphlet published on March 16, 1720[98] (though bearing a date of four days earlier), with the title *A Letter from Sig. Benedetto Baldassarii, of the Hay-Market, to Sir R——d S——e, of Drury-Lane*. Ostensibly an open letter to Sir Richard from an emasculated Italian singer, the pamphlet was doubtless suggested by the appearance of Baldassari ("servant to the Elector Palatine, lately arrived in England") in a concert at Drury Lane on March 11[99] and by an ironical "defense" of Baldassari that Steele included in the *Theatre*, No. 21 (March 12). In satirizing the singer (Steele called him "Beneditti") and, through him, Italian music, Steele perhaps intended to call attention to the change for the worse in Drury Lane offerings under the lord chamberlain's supervision. The anonymous author of *A Letter from Sig. Benedetto Baldassarii* can scarcely be said, beneath his irony, to defend either the Italian or Steele; rather he amused himself—and his readers—by exploiting a number of humorous possibilities for satire directed at both individuals.

Two essentially political pamphlets deserve brief notice here because of their relations to the stage controversy. Though *The Crisis of Honesty*, published anonymously on March 3,[100] was immediately a reply to Steele's *The Crisis of Property*, the author paid his respects to the Drury Lane dispute, revealing himself in hearty agreement with Dennis about the condition of that theater and the principle of stage government by actors. "I shall hardly

---

[98] Cf. the *Theatre*, ed. Nichols, I, 184n. The pamphlet is quite rare (G. A. Aitken never saw it: cf. *Life*, II, 417). I had access to a copy of it in the Yale University Library.

[99] Latreille calendar (Brit. Mus., Add. MS 32249), fol. 301.

[100] Aitken, *Life*, II, 239n.

mention those Vagabonds," he remarks about the actor-managers, "but I find them more insolent than any People of that sort in any other Nation. And tho' they may encourage and commend your Behaviour; they are not to inform the Nation; they must be here treated as they are all the World over"—an emphatic answer to the *Theatre*. Similarly hostile to Steele was a pamphlet, probably by John Dunton,[101] published on March 29[102] with the title *A Word Without Doors: or, A Paradox, Proving the Honour of Deserving a Knighthood Exceeds the Title*, a pamphlet suggested by Steele's platitudinous reflections in the *Theatre*, No. 19, that symbols of honor such as knighthood are merely mockeries if they are not deserved. Chiefly concerned with reciting John Dunton's claims to party favor, the author accomplishes that purpose by comparing Dunton with Steele, insisting on Steele's ingratitude to his party. He deplores Steele's dispute with Newcastle and his rough and undignified treatment of Pengelly in the *Theatre*, adding little, however, to our information. But he does mention, as no one else in the journalistic controversy appears to have done, Steele's theatrical mortgages, implying not quite accurately that Steele had *sold* the patent. ". . . I will allow the *Knight* in much Grief for the Injuries done to the Purchasers of Shares in the Patent disputed, yet I can by no means excuse his manner of expressing that concern." It is curious that this aspect of Steele's theatrical troubles was otherwise so thoroughly neglected in the voluminous journalistic writings. On one other point the author's remarks are informative: he associates Sunderland with Newcastle as a nobleman who previously gave great assistance to Steele, implying that Steele has shown ingratitude to him as well as to Newcastle, and perhaps suggesting that Sunderland was also concerned in the action against Steele. Certainly in their support of the Peerage Bill, Newcastle and Sunderland, as Newcastle's correspondence reveals,[103]

---

[101] Although *A Word Without Doors* was issued anonymously (except insofar as one of the letters included in it purports to be from John Dunton), the pamphlet is so closely similar, both in purpose and in style, to a series of pamphlets known to be by Dunton that it appears virtually certain that he either wrote it himself or collaborated with someone in writing it.

[102] Aitken, *Life*, II, 235n.

[103] British Museum, Additional MS 32686.

were intimately associated. It may be significant that in the spring of 1721 Steele applied to Sunderland along with Walpole for assistance in gaining reinstatement.

The newspaper comment on Steele's dispute with Newcastle was largely confined to a single paper, *Applebee's Original Weekly Journal*. Although occasional remarks about the actor-managers—or at least about Cibber, the most generally disliked of them—appeared in several of the papers, only in *Applebee's* was there extended and informative discussion of the lord chamberlain's action. What reason *Applebee's* may have had for taking up the controversy, other than the obvious one that it was the subject of substantial public interest, is unknown, but as early as February 13, 1720, the paper opened its pages to attacks on Steele and his colleagues, and, with periods of intermission, continued to receive them until July 9, three months after Steele had given over his own defensive journalistic campaign. I have already noted the first criticism of Steele to appear in the paper, "Sir Andrew Artlove's" three letters entitled *A Full Consideration and Confutation of Sir John Edgar*, written in support of Dennis in his "sub-quarrel" with Steele. The last of these letters appeared on February 27; the week following, the paper ignored Steele and the theatrical dispute—but only in that one issue; in the next number (March 12, 1720) a new section appeared in which Steele and Drury Lane were to be favorite subjects.

This new section, entitled the *Muses Gazette*, is in effect a literary essay inserted into the pages of a journal primarily devoted to political and social news. It runs to eighteen numbers, in by no means all of which the stage dispute is mentioned; frequently the essays, not unlike Steele's own, are on moral subjects; but Steele's theatrical affairs provide the most popular single topic. Scattered throughout the series are brief, abusive allusions to him, not remarkably different from scores of others already mentioned, in which he and Drury Lane are made the butts of many amusing but inconsequential jests. Some of the satire, as I have already shown, takes the Censorium for its mark, providing information on the obscure later history of that project. More immediately relevant here, in the *Muses Gazette*, No. 12 (*Applebee's* for May 28, 1720), there appears a serious, intelligent, and surprisingly unbiased discussion of the practical issues at stake in the lord chamberlain's assumption of control of Drury Lane. His jokes at their expense notwithstanding, the author by no means opposes blindly everything for which Steele and his colleagues stand.

In evaluating the lord chamberlain's action, however, the author first arraigns the contemporary stage in uncompromising fashion. Plays are presented "without Order, Connexion or Design," he charges; the distinction between tragedy and comedy is broken down, some plays, called "Tragi-Comedies," incorporating both forms. Recalling the former greatness of English drama, he laments its present condition; audiences congregate at the theater not to see the absurd "Entertainments" but merely to see one another. Obviously a reformation of the stage is needed; and quite specifically, though he employs the fictions of a dialogue and disguised names, he discusses the attempts already made to bring one about. The speakers in the dialogue are Crites, representing Dennis, and Bartonedes, apparently representing Barton Booth. Crites,[104] the author explains, has been active in promoting stage reform and, through his writing, has brought about a resumption by the Camerario (the lord chamberlain) of supervision of the theater. Bartonedes, in an effort to dissuade Crites from continuing his journalistic campaign, argues that the end desired by Crites—the improvement of drama—will not be accomplished by the change in theater government. All this is conventional enough. What is arresting about the discussion is the clear formulation by Bartonedes of the players' reasons for distrusting control of the theater by the chamberlain:

If therefore you have no prospect of reforming the Stage by our Hands, which I confess you have not, how have you mended the matter, by putting the whole Power into the Hands of one Cacavento [a peer], who professes it only while he is Camerario, and who generally knows no more of the matter than the most ignorant of us Players; how should he therefore only favour such Writers as are capable of bringing this great Work about. . . .

---

[104] Charles Gildon, in *The Complete Art of Poetry* (London, 1718), assigned Dennis the name "Crites": perhaps Gildon wrote this essay in the *Muses Gazette*. The views expressed are consistent with those we would expect from Gildon.

... if you would gain a Cacavento to any point of Truth, it must be done by a most artful Management, and daily Repetition of the grossest of Flatteries; but there is still another Difficulty, which you know not, which is by keeping always in Fee with his chief Favourites; and to compass this, we need be at not other Charge than what that share of the Profits will supply, which was taken from one of us Managers.

Does the chief actor imply that in order to obtain the favor of the lord chamberlain it is necessary to bribe his favorites with amounts of money equal to the share of the profits formerly paid to Steele? It would seem so. This anonymous author writes realistically of the taste in dramatic literature usual in high court officers and of the barriers necessarily placed in the way of an effective administration of the stage by them. If the *Muses Gazette* was displeasing to Steele and his former colleagues, it must also have been, after this twelfth number, to Newcastle and his subordinates. The implied charge that the duke's subordinates had to be systematically bribed is nowhere corroborated.

Though the lord chamberlain is here indirectly criticized, Dennis receives the utmost respect; it is indeed implied that he was responsible for the lord chamberlain's intervention at Drury Lane—by no means an accurate representation of the facts. Elsewhere in this same number of the *Muses Gazette* the partiality to Dennis is expressed even more directly in the author's praise of him as a poet. As formerly in the letters of Sir Andrew Artlove, *Applebee's* revealed itself to be his firm partisan.

The many answers to the *Theatre,* so far reviewed, largely ignored the legal problems raised by Newcastle's action, as Steele himself, in the *Theatre,* had neglected them. In a pair of pamphlets, however, one by Steele himself and the other by an unidentified but obviously well-informed writer, the legal issues were exhaustively debated.

Steele argues, in his *The State of the Case Between the Lord Chamberlain of His Majesty's Household, and the Governor of the Royal Company of Comedians* (March 29),[105] that his patent is a freehold, that it is a good grant in fee, and that hence it cannot be taken from him except by due process of law. The lord chamberlain has violated his property rights, he insists, by an illegal

---

[105] Aitken, *Life,* II, 229n.

application of a sign manual—illegal because of the nature of the grant to him. Steele is consequently at pains to establish the nature of the grant in the patent itself, citing, to support his assertion that the patent is a freehold, a series of legal opinions rendered not on his own patent but on that by which John Rich operates Lincoln's Inn Fields. Steele argues that since the two patents are alike as to powers conveyed (except for the limitation in his own to the term of his life and three years thereafter), legal opinions respecting the one apply validly to the other.

As earlier in the *Town Talk*, Steele quotes the entire text of his patent, this time remarking that when he first received the grant, "the then Solicitor-General Mr. *Lechmere* . . . used this Expression: *Sir, the King has here given you a Free-Hold; and if from it you can prove you receive Six Hundred Pounds a Year, you are qualified to be Knight of any Shire in* England." Lechmere referred to the requirements established by the Landed Property Qualification Bill, enacted in 1711, making the possession of property a necessary condition to election to Parliament. Thus he asserted that in the eyes of the law the patent was a grant not different in kind from a grant of land. Just as other property is exempt from arbitrary interference without due process of law, so, Steele insists, his patent rightfully is also.

His patent is legal and, Steele argues, of equal authority with the other one. He too could have had the patent perpetually for himself and his heirs, as had D'Avenant and Killigrew, but he requested it only for the length of his life and three years after, the limited term in no way restricting the powers conveyed. He thus identifies his patent with those granted to D'Avenant and Killigrew, and in effect rests his case on the demand that he be granted the protection that they and their heirs and assigns received.

Steele is wide of his mark, however, using authority to establish points not in dispute and neglecting others crucial to the controversy. He is silent—or nearly so—on the question of the authority of the lord chamberlain. Although he obviously believed that the power of the chamberlain did not extend into the domain of the patent, he says little about the matter directly. Cibber, he observes, "submitted to a Disability of appearing on the Stage, during the Pleasure of one that had nothing to do with it," and his meaning is clear; but he makes no reasoned distinction between the authority of the chamberlain and that of the patentee. Another omission is even more grave. Steele all but ignores the significant fact that it was his license rather than his patent that was revoked. The fundamental theme of the pamphlet is a declaration of the inviolable nature of the patent; yet the patent itself was not directly affected by the king's order of revocation. Steele, to be sure, acknowledges briefly the ambiguity of the order of revocation, but having acknowledged it, he continues his argument, the tenor of which is that his patent has been violated. He understood that Newcastle's maneuver was one to deprive him of any benefit from the patent, and he doubtless considered the distinction between the revocation of the license and that of the patent to be merely a quibble, as in many ways it undeniably was.

One of his adversaries was quick to remind him of the issues he neglected. The most carefully reasoned of all the answers to Steele, the most convincing of the statements in support of the lord chamberlain, appears in the anonymous *The State of the Case Between the Lord Chamberlain of His Majesty's Household and Sir Richard Steele, as represented by that Knight, re-stated, in Vindication of King George, and the Most Noble the Duke of Newcastle* (April 7–9, 1720).[106] Like Steele himself, the author of this pamphlet makes much of the similarity between Steele's patent and those granted to D'Avenant and Killigrew, but for a different purpose. Where Steele insisted on the similarity to demonstrate that his patent was entitled to the same protection as that accorded to the others, his antagonist insists on the similarity to show that Steele's patent is subject to the same regulation as that traditionally imposed by the lord chamberlain on the other grants. He cites a series of cases of intervention by chamberlains in the internal affairs of patent companies, cases, for example, when chamberlains have silenced players just as the Duke of Newcastle silenced Colley Cibber. His point is telling—that if, as Steele insists, his patent is not essentially different from those granted by Charles II, his

---

[106] *Ibid.*, II, 230n. Aitken thought it "probable" that John Dennis was the author of *The State of the Case . . . Restated* (cf. *Life*, II, 231). Professor Hooker, however, considers the authorship unknown (cf. *Dennis*, II, 477).

authority must have the limitations traditionally associated with the earlier patents.

There is one other basic argument in *The State of the Case ... Restated:* Steele cannot legitimately complain of the violation of his patent, because it has not been affected by Newcastle's action and the king's order of revocation. The author explains, as there has already been occasion to observe, that the patent was not affected by the "oblique" attack to which Steele refers in *The State of the Case,* and that, whatever the status of the license, Steele is free to present plays if he can get actors to "enlist under his banner." There has thus been no property violation. This author, however, though his interpretation of the action against Steele is more complete than that of any of his contemporaries, is not completely accurate. He insists that the managers acted by the license all along, that they did not participate in the authority of the patent—a view we know to be mistaken. The author was misinformed in this detail—and it is a detail of some importance—but the mistake does not invalidate his entire argument. As he points out, the patent could not compel anyone to act against his wishes; if the managers were violating a contract with Steele, he was free to enter suit against them. It will be recalled that Steele did write a threatening letter, though he seems never to have carried out his threats. Whoever this unidentified author was, he obviously understood Newcastle's position very well.

Part Four | LAST YEARS

The Genesis of
The Conscious Lovers

1

THE RESTORATION of Steele to Drury Lane prepared the way for the production, in November, 1722, of *The Conscious Lovers,* in Benjamin Victor's phrase, the "last blaze of Sir Richard's glory." His acute political entanglements back of him, Steele was free to appear again as a playwright—to offer to London audiences a dramatization of a number of ideas and precepts with which, in only slightly different forms, they were already familiar. Knowing that the comedy was written by Steele, few well-read playgoers could fail to associate it with the *Tatler,* the *Spectator,* and the *Guardian,* to which in ideological content it bears a close resemblance.

Like many of the earlier essays, the play is obviously didactic in intent: it presents a pattern for virtuous living, and particularly a pattern for the conduct of the "fine gentleman," a character in whom Steele had long been interested. Rejecting in *The Conscious Lovers,* as he did in the periodicals, the satirical theory of comedy implicit in the plays of the principal Restoration dramatists, Steele provides in Bevil, Jr., a direct model for emulation, endowing him with the qualities of filial obedience, faithfulness and generosity in love, nobility in friendship, and reasonableness in affairs of honor, all of which were recommended time and again in the *Tatler,* the *Spectator,* and the *Guardian.*[1] Steele avoided the error into which he believed many of the earlier dramatists had fallen— that of making vice agreeable—by presenting his single degraded character, Cimberton, in so ridiculous a light as unquestionably to

[1] See especially the *Spectator,* Nos. 65 and 75. Professor Hooker describes Steele's prolonged interest in the character of the "fine gentleman" (*Dennis,* II, 497).

183

arouse contempt. Nor are the resemblances between the ideas in *The Conscious Lovers* and those in the earlier essays restricted merely to matters of characterization. In the play, as earlier, the problem of dueling is reviewed; Bevil, Jr., and Indiana discuss the opera in familiar terms; Bevil, Jr., discusses the relations between masters and servants in a manner that suggests the *Spectator;* Bevil, Jr., meditates on Addison's "Vision of Mirza." In writing the comedy, Steele was clearly under the influence of the opinions that led to many of his earlier lucubrations.

These similarities between the play, first produced in 1722, and the essays, published between 1709 and 1713, have always been common knowledge; they are almost inescapable; but it has not been generally known that *The Conscious Lovers* was planned and perhaps in part written while Steele was writing the essays that appear in the major periodicals.[2] Though modern scholars have known that Steele worked on the play for a long time, they have not known that he was working on it almost certainly by 1713 and was probably planning it as early as 1710.[3] The great similarities between the periodicals and the comedy have been accounted for merely by the supposition that Steele was actively interested in approximately the same ideas for a number of years—and indeed there is no reason to assume that he was not.

Perhaps the most important evidence that Steele was working on *The Conscious Lovers* during the years before 1716 (that is, before the date indicated by his correspondence) is in a poem by Jonathan Swift, published in January, 1714. In this poem, *The First Ode of the Second Book of Horace Paraphras'd; And Address'd to Richard Steele, Esq.,* one of the group of abusive political lam-

---

[2] Cf. Aitken, *Life*, II, 275n; *Correspondence*, pp. 314–315, 520n; F. W. Bateson, *English Comic Drama*, 1700–1750 (Oxford, 1929), pp. 53–54.

[3] Professor Hooker remarks: "That Steele in writing *Spectator*, no. 65 [1711], was deliberately paving the way for *The Conscious Lovers*, is unlikely. But there is no doubt that the idea of the hero in this comedy was being formed within Steele's mind for many years before the comedy was written." It has always been known that the Tom and Phillis episode is taken from the *Guardian*, No. 87, and that a character by the name of Myrtle is prominent in *The Lover* (1714); but it has been assumed that Steele writing years later merely made use of some of his earlier literary materials—as in these cases he may have.

poons directed at Steele during the last months of Anne's life, Swift chides him in doggerel verse for meddling in politics. Continuing, Swift mentions a play that Steele is writing:

> But since thou'rt got into the Fire,
> And canst not easily retire,
> Thou must no longer deal in *Farce*,
> Nor pump to cobble wicked Verse;
> Until thou shalt have eas'd thy Conscience,
> Of Spleen, of Politics and Nonsense,
> And when thou'st bid adieu to Cares,
> And settled *Europe's Grand Affairs,*
> 'Twill then, perhaps, be worth thy while
> For *Drury-lane* to shape thy Stile:
> "To make a pair of Jolly Fellows,
> "The Son and Father, join to tell us,
> "How Sons may safely disobey,
> "And Fathers never shou'd say nay,
> "By which wise Conduct they grow Friends
> "At last—and so the Story ends."[4]

Printed in the left-hand margin beside the summary of the play's action is a statement that Steele had been working on, or at least talking about, the play for some time. "This is said to be the Plot of a Comedy with which Mr. St——le has long threatned the Town." The name of the play is not mentioned, but from the six-line summary it may be assumed that it is substantially the one that was ultimately presented as *The Conscious Lovers.* The relations between the Bevils, father and son, conditioning as they do the younger Bevil's relations with Indiana, provide the controlling

---

[4] *The First Ode of the Second Book of Horace Paraphras'd: And Address'd to Richard St–le, esq.* (London, 1714), p. 5. In 1808 John Nichols observed in a note appended to this passage: "In some particulars it would apply to 'The Conscious Lovers' " (*The Works of the Rev. Jonathan Swift,* ed. Thomas Sheridan and John Nichols (London, 1808), XVI, 165n). Mr. Harold Williams quotes this note but makes no comment other than adding that *The Conscious Lovers* was produced at Drury Lane in 1722 (*The Poems of Jonathan Swift,* ed. Harold Williams [Oxford, 1937], I, 181). Aitken describes Swift's poem and actually quotes the lines summarizing the plot of the play, but he does not associate the allusion with *The Conscious Lovers (Life,* II, 3–4).

action of the play: young Bevil demonstrates how a son can have his own way without actually disobeying his father. In this brief summary also the comedy's didactic purpose is suggested as well as the exemplary nature of the characters. By 1714, then, and long enough before for word of the play to be noised about, Steele had determined at least the central idea of the play—the idea he took in part from Terence's *Andria*.

Two brief allusions in letters written by George Berkeley in 1713 provide still earlier glimpses of Steele working on a comedy, though they contain no hint of its nature. Berkeley wrote, on January 26, 1713, that "he [Steele] is confined with gout, and is, as I am informed, writing a play since he gave over the 'Spectators.' "[5] And again on March 27, 1713, Berkeley remarked, "A play of Mr. Steele's, which was expected, he has now put off to next winter,"[6] an allusion that helps to identify plausibly the play with the one to which Swift referred the following year. The manner in which Berkeley mentions having heard of the play implies that Steele's plans for it were known by a number of the literary men then in London.

Three years earlier than Berkeley's references there is a passage in Steele's own writings that probably refers to *The Conscious Lovers*, though the identification can be made with less assurance than in the allusions of Swift and Berkeley. The *Tatler*, No. 182 (June 8, 1710), is one of Steele's many essays devoted almost entirely to the theater: Bickerstaff acknowledges his delight in plays and he praises the actors, especially Robert Wilks and Colley Cibber. Of particular interest, he speaks paternally of a young playwright now working on a comedy who can probably be identified as Richard Steele:

I have at present under my tutelage a young poet, who, I design, shall entertain the town the ensuing winter. And as he does me the honour to let me see his comedy as he writes it, I shall endeavor to make the parts fit the genius of the several actors, as exactly as their habits can their bodies: and because the two I have mentioned [Cibber and Wilks] are to perform the principal parts, I have prevailed with the house to let "The Careless Husband" be acted on Tuesday next, that my young author may

---

[5] Rand, ed., *Berkeley and Percival*, p. 106.
[6] *Ibid.*, p. 112.

have a view of the play which is acted to perfection, both by them and all concerned in it, as being born within the walls of the theatre, and written with an exact knowledge of the abilities of the performers. Mr. Wilks will do his best in this play, because it is for his own benefit; and Mr. Cibber, because he writ it. Besides which, all the great beauties we have left in town, or within call of it, will be present, because it is the last play this season. This opportunity will, I hope, inflame my pupil with such generous notions from seeing this fair assembly as will be then present, that his play may be composed of sentiments and characters proper to be presented to such an audience. His drama at present has only the outlines drawn. There are, I find, to be in it all the reverent offices of life, such as regard to parents, husbands, and honourable lovers, preserved with the utmost care; and at the same time that agreeableness of behaviour, with the intermixture of pleasing passions as arise from innocence and virtue, interspersed in such a manner, as that to be charming and agreeable shall appear the natural consequence of being virtuous. This great end is one of those I propose to do in my Censorship; but if I find a thin house, on an occasion when such work is to be promoted, my pupil shall return to his commons at Oxford, and Sheer Lane and the theatres be no longer correspondents.[7]

There are several reasons for believing that Steele here alludes to his own composition of *The Conscious Lovers*, the principal one being his description of the young playwright's plan for the play. Like the comedy projected by the young man, *The Conscious Lovers* portrays "all the reverent offices of life, such as regard to parents, husbands, and honourable lovers . . . ," exhibiting a preoccupation with these "offices" almost to the exclusion of everything humorous. Young Bevil's relations with his father, as previously noted, provide a major theme in the play, a theme that offers some justification to John Dennis's charge that "the filial

---

[7] In annotating this passage, Aitken comments merely on *The Careless Husband* (the *Tatler*, ed. George A. Aitken [London, 1899], III, 357). In 1786 John Nichols suggested, with strong reservations, that Steele here alluded to Leonard Welsted's *The Dissembled Wanton*, a comedy that was not performed until 1726, four years after *The Conscious Lovers* (the *Tatler*, ed. John Nichols [London, 1786], V, 103). The suggestion has little to recommend it except that Welsted was literally Steele's protégé–though not necessarily Isaac Bickerstaff's. There is no evidence that *The Dissembled Wanton* was planned as early as 1710, nor does it fit the description in the *Tatler* as well as *The Conscious Lovers*.

Obedience of young *Bevil* is carried a great deal too far."[8] And young Bevil, supporting Indiana but rigorously refusing to acknowledge his own love for her or to take advantage of her dependent position, is an extreme type of the honorable lover. Less is made in *The Conscious Lovers* of a wife's regard for her husband—in Mrs. Sealand, Steele presents a woman who is not entirely respectful toward her spouse—but the tone of the comedy is unmistakably one of conjugal fidelity; the indifference toward the marriage tie exhibited in many of the earlier comedies is noticeably absent here. Certainly in intention and design *The Conscious Lovers* resembles the play that Bickerstaff's protégé was writing.

The young man's play, it appears, like *The Conscious Lovers,* is to be an exemplary comedy: its moral precepts are to be conveyed primarily by providing models for conduct rather than by making folly ridiculous. Bickerstaff explains that "agreeableness of behaviour, with the intermixture of pleasing passions which arise from innocence and virtue," are to be "interspersed in such a manner, as that to be charming and agreeable shall appear the natural consequences of being virtuous," an explanation suggesting the theory of comedy of which *The Conscious Lovers* is a preeminent example; it was precisely this theory that was debated most heatedly in the literary controversy precipitated by the acting of the play. "How little do they know of the Nature of true Comedy, who believe that its proper Business is to set us Patterns for Imitation . . . ,"[9] wrote John Dennis in opposition (in an essay immediately occasioned by *The Conscious Lovers*). The comedy projected by Bickerstaff's protégé, then, was one planned in accordance with the theory of comedy of which *The Conscious Lovers* was a controversial example. Though it would not be accurate to describe it as the first exemplary comedy,[10] *The Conscious Lovers* was the play that was first generally recognized as such—it first brought into the open the clash between the proponents of the two different comic theories. To Steele the play represented a

---

[8] "Remarks on . . . The Conscious Lovers," in Hooker, *Dennis,* II, 263.

[9] "A Defence of Sir Fopling Flutter," in Hooker, *ibid.,* 245.

[10] Cf. John Harrington Smith, "Shadwell, the Ladies, and Change in Comedy," *Modern Philology,* XLVI (1948), 22–33.

studied attempt at providing the English stage with a comic form that could be an effective stimulant to virtuous action.[11] Hence, when Bickerstaff describes an exemplary comedy (a form of comedy that Steele thought to be his own innovation), there is strong reason to believe that he is referring to the one on which it is known that Steele was working some three years later.

There are other examples of Steele's introducing in his essays disguised references to his own affairs; indeed, in the *Theatre*, No. 19 (March 5, 1720), there is an allusion to the still unfinished *The Conscious Lovers* as a comedy being written by a friend of the suppositious conductor of the periodical, "Sir John Edgar." In the *Theatre*, No. 3, moreover, several of the play's characters are introduced.

Bickerstaff makes a definite statement about the condition of the play he describes: it "has only the outlines drawn." Assuming that the outlines are those of *The Conscious Lovers*, a number of scattered allusions over a period of years may refer to Steele's efforts to complete the comedy.[12] From Berkeley's allusion in the spring of 1713 comes a hint of Steele's procrastination—the play that had been expected was postponed until the next season. In 1714 Swift suggests Steele's preoccupation with politics as the reason for his failure to finish the play—and in 1714 Steele was busy indeed with political journalism. Two years later, on March 26, 1716, Steele wrote to his wife that he would stay at home because he found his "hand in," hoping "this Evening to finish what I have deferred from day to day for two months last past," a remark that Professor Blanchard interprets as a possible allusion to *The Conscious Lovers*.[13] More definite is a statement in a letter he wrote on July 16, 1717. "For I must keep my self to my self and have

[11] Cf. the *Spectator*, Nos. 65, 75; the *Town Talk*, No. 6; the *Theatre*, Nos. 19, 28; the preface to *The Conscious Lovers*.

[12] In the *Muses Mercury, or The Monthly Miscellany* for January, 1707, appears the following: "... had not the death of a dear friend hindered Capt. Steel from finishing a Comedy of his, it would ... have been acted this Season" (quoted from Aitken, *Life*, I, 151). In the complete absence of information about the comedy, it is futile to conjecture whether or not Steele planned *The Conscious Lovers* this early.

[13] *Correspondence*, pp. 314–315.

my Play ready this ensuing Winter, in Order to be quite out of Debt."[14]

Steele did not have his play ready by the winter of 1717–1718 as he hoped, but he seems to have largely completed it by the winter of 1719–1720, some of the writing possibly having been done in Wales.[15] *Applebee's Original Weekly Journal* of November 21, 1719, reported that "a new Comedy, call'd, The Gentleman. Written by Sir Richard Steele" would soon be presented at Drury Lane, without much doubt referring to *The Conscious Lovers*;[16] three months later the *Orphan Revived* noted that this play, which had been anticipated, probably would not appear during the current season.[17] In the *Theatre* (January 2–April 5, 1720) Steele made a number of specific references to the comedy, implying that it was almost ready for presentation.[18] However, a remark in the *Theatre*, No. 19, suggests that it was still to undergo some drastic revision: "Sir John Edgar" praises the duel scene, referring obviously to the first scene of the fourth act; but he says that it is in the third act.

The production of *The Conscious Lovers* was delayed, it appears, by Steele's dispute with Newcastle, perhaps by an order from the duke prohibiting the players from acting it. In the *Theatre*, No. 19, Steele remarks that the play would have already been performed "had not some accidents prevented," and in *The State of the Case* (March, 1720) he lists as a loss he has sustained by the lord chamberlain's action against him "The Profit of acting my own Plays already writ, or I may write,"[19] perhaps referring to *The Conscious Lovers*. More specific is a statement of Dr. Thomas Rundle in a letter written March 24, 1720: "It is said a most excel-

[14] *Ibid.*, p. 361.

[15] *Ibid.*, p. 410n.

[16] The final title of the play was apparently not chosen until a short time before it was presented on the Drury Lane stage. Dennis calls it "The Fine Gentleman" in "A Defence of Sir Fopling Flutter" (Hooker, *Dennis*, II, 250). It is called "The Unfashionable Lovers" in a newspaper advertisement of October 2, 1722 (cf. Nichols, ed., *The Epistolary Correspondence of Richard Steele* [London, 1809], II, 62n).

[17] The *Orphan Revived* for February 13–20, 1720.

[18] See especially Nos. 19, 28.

[19] In *Tracts and Pamphlets*, p. 607.

lent comedy of Sir Richard Steele's is to be prohibited acting, lest it should draw away good company, and spoil the relish for operas, by seducing them with sense, wit, and humour. . . ."[20] Still more convincing, in a brief statement in the *Theatre*, No. 28, Steele refers directly to his inability to produce a play, which in all probability was *The Conscious Lovers*. In summing up his case against the lord chamberlain, he says:

> It is, I think, incumbent upon me to shew that I was not wholly negligent; but, as far as greater duties would give me leave, writ for the Stage, in order to introduce agreeable characters in opposition to the false customs and habits which have prevailed amongst us.[21] To manifest further the injury done me by robbing me of the means of bringing on my own performances in an advantageous manner, I shall forthwith print a new Comedy called Sir JOHN EDGAR; and hope proper allowances will be made; and due consideration had, that a Play is not designed so much for the Reader as the Spectator.

Steele did not then publish the play, however, as he here promises to do.[22]

Although Aitken believed that Steele in this essay referred to a play that "never saw the light,"[23] we may be virtually certain that the "new Comedy called Sir JOHN EDGAR" was *The Conscious Lovers*—that Steele merely applied to it the name of one of its principal characters, who at the time was called "Sir John Edgar" (the name of the fictional author of the *Theatre*) rather than "Sir John Bevil." The evidence for this assumption is no less than a memorandum about the play in Steele's handwriting in which the character we know as Bevil has the name Edgar.[24] The final title of

[20] Rundle, *Letters*, p. 19. Aitken quotes Rundle's statement, but he does not associate it with *The Conscious Lovers* (*Life*, II, 236n).

[21] Note the similarity between this statement and Bickerstaff's description in the *Tatler*, No. 182, of his pupil's projected comedy.

[22] In a rough memorandum dating from September, 1720, Steele wrote cryptically: "about Permits of my Play" (Brit. Mus., Add. MS 5145C, fol. 163).

[23] *Richard Steele*, The Mermaid Series, ed. George A. Aitken (London, n.d.), p. lvi.

[24] British Museum, Additional MS 5145C, fol. 198. Printed by Nichols in *The Epistolary Correspondence of Richard Steele* (London, 1809), p.

the play was not chosen, as we know, until a short time before it was acted. Steele doubtless altered the character's name to avoid the unpleasant associations of the dispute with the lord chamberlain that would necessarily have been called up by the name of Sir John Edgar.

Two seasons after these references to it appear in the *Theatre, The Conscious Lovers* reached the stage—though not without undergoing revisions by Colley Cibber. Several conflicting statements make it difficult to determine accurately the extent of Cibber's aid. Steele himself acknowledged his obligation in the preface to the play, implying that Cibber's help was rather that of a stage manager than of a collaborator: "Mr. Cibber's zeal for the work, his care and application in instructing the actors and altering the disposition of the scenes, when I was, through sickness, unable to cultivate such things myself, has been a very obliging favour and friendship to me." At the suggestion of Cibber, he writes, he discarded the incident of the funeral that is in the Latin original. When several years later in the course of his lawsuits with the managers he was less kindly disposed to Cibber, he asserted in a deposition that in this acknowledgment he intended to thank Cibber only for his instructing the actors, not for any help in writing the play; Cibber had indeed made several changes in the play, but, so Steele insisted, the changes were injurious.[25] Cibber himself expressed a contrary view in 1728, remarking that the managers paid Steele well for *The Conscious Lovers,* "though, in writing that Play, he had more Assistance from one of the Menagers than becomes me to enlarge upon, of which Evidence has been given upon Oath by several of our Actors. . . ."[26] According to Theophilus Cibber, the parts of Tom and Phillis were intro-

---

648n. The memorandum obviously refers to *The Conscious Lovers:* "Mem. That the character of Sir John Edgar be enlivened with a secret vanity about Family. And let Mrs. Coeland, the Merchant's wife, have the same sort of pride, rejoicing in her own high blood, despising her husband's pedigree, and affecting to marry her daughter to a relation of her own. . . ."

[25] P.R.O., C11/2416/49. Aitken, *Life,* II, 314.

[26] *Apology,* II, 206 (from Cibber's address to the law court at the combined hearing of the suit and countersuit of Steele and the managers).

duced after Colley Cibber had cautioned Steele that, as originally drafted, the comedy was too serious for an English audience;[27] perhaps so, but one of the conversations between Tom and Phillis—about their first meeting—Steele took, with little alteration, from the *Guardian*, No. 87.

Such then is the history of the composition of Steele's most famous play. It was not a product of his middle age, of the years after his health had broken and he had encountered serious personal reverses; rather it was conceived, and perhaps in part written, during the vigorous years when he was writing the essays on which his fame rests. *The Conscious Lovers* was planned under the stimulus of the ideas that led to the many essays on the character of the fine gentleman and to the essays denouncing the type of comedy represented by *The Man of Mode*. It was planned, at the time Steele was writing about comic theory, as an example of the new type of comedy he was advocating—exemplary rather than satirical comedy. What is new and most significant about *The Conscious Lovers*—its exemplary characters—thus represents a bond with the essays he conceived contemporaneously.

2 | *The Conscious Lovers* at Drury Lane

WRITTEN and revised though it was over a number of years, the play was an enormous, unprecedented success, bringing more money to the company than any previous one presented there—an amount specified by Steele in his deposition of May 11, 1727, as £2,536/3/6.[28] For eighteen successive performances it was acted to enthusiastic audiences, and, according to the *St. James's Journal* (December 8, 1722), it would have continued to attract large audiences had not the managers substituted another play before the town became weary of it.

[27] Theophilus Cibber, *The Lives of the Poets of Great Britain and Ireland* (London, 1753), IV, 120.

[28] P.R.O., C11/2416/49. Aitken, *Life*, II, 314.

Steele modestly attributed the great success to the excellency of the actors,[29] who were, indeed, the best in the company. All three of the managers were in the cast—Booth as Bevil, Jr., Wilks as Myrtle, and Cibber in the comic role of Tom—and Mrs. Oldfield had the female lead as Indiana. The play was elaborately staged, moreover, with new clothing and scenery (the handsome staging provided an excuse for advancing the prices of admission). The company gave their best, and their governor was pleased with the result, Benjamin Victor recording that "All the performers charmed him, but Griffin, in the character of Cimberton."[30]

Steele enjoyed large profits from the play, both as author (he had three benefits) and as patentee: Cibber reported his receipts as about £600;[31] Steele himself, in his deposition of May 11, 1727, said that he received about £329/5s from his benefits[32]—to which, of course, his share of the profits added substantially. This large return was still further augmented by a gift of £500 from the king, to whom Steele dedicated the published version (it appeared December 1, 1722),[33] the size of the gift suggesting the importance attached to the play. Whatever the dramatic merits or faults of *The Conscious Lovers,* financially it was a great success.

The warm reception given the play was not occasioned entirely by its own qualities: a publicity campaign, perhaps previously unequaled in the history of the English stage, had prepared the way for it.[34] I have already discussed the early records of the play, some of which appeared publicly in print years before it was produced. Dennis observed sarcastically, a few days before it reached the stage, that the play "has trotted as far as *Edinburgh* Northward, and as far as *Wales* Westward, and has been read to more Persons than will be at the Representation of it, or vouchsafe to read it, when it is publish'd." He himself added to the publicity by publishing *A Defence of Sir Fopling Flutter* (where he made this statement) several days before the first performance, an essay that,

---

[29] Preface to the published version of the play.

[30] *Original Letters* (London, 1776), I, 327.

[31] *Apology,* II, 206.

[32] P.R.O., C11/2416/49. *Aitken,' Life,* II, 314.

[33] It was published, however, with the date 1723. Aitken, *Life,* II, 276.

[34] Cf. Hooker, *Dennis,* II, 495.

even though hostile to the play, contributed to the general curiosity to see it. On October 22, 1722, a newspaper advertisement, presumably paid for by the managers, announced the comedy for the following month with the remark that "It is thought that this play is the best modern play that has been produced."[35] Such a bold statement provoked comment that increased still further the public interest. The *Freeholder's Journal* summarized the matter succinctly on November 14, 1722: "The Play of the *Conscious Lovers* had such a Reputation before it was known, that a Man of no very great Curiosity would have ventur'd to squeeze into the Crowd that went to see it the first Night."

That the spectacular success derived in a measure from the publicity can scarcely be doubted. But the play itself pleased; Steele had once more accurately gauged the public taste. *The Conscious Lovers* gained a favored position in the repertory, which it held for the rest of the century, and it remains one of the few early-eighteenth-century plays that are still read.

3 | Critical Controversy

To THE modern student *The Conscious Lovers* belongs to the number of plays that are rather more interesting as dramatic landmarks than as drama. It is usually read not because of any dramatic excellence but because it illustrates an important change in the history of comedy. Nor is this modern reputation of the play as a landmark without strong eighteenth-century precedent. Steele himself and his contemporaries considered it a pronounced departure from English comic tradition—as something new, as a studied attempt to break away from the pattern of earlier comedies. This conviction explains partly, of course, the magnitude of the critical commentary evoked by the play; Steele's long campaign

[35] Quoted from Nichols, ed., *The Epistolary Correspondence of Richard Steele* (London, 1809), II, 62n.

in preparation for it let everyone know that it was to be different, and put them on their guard to look for innovations. His prominence and his controversial career, moreover, added intensity to the interest in comic theory; other authors had written plays embodying critical principles more original than those in *The Conscious Lovers*, only to be greeted by complete indifference. But a play by the celebrated Richard Steele on principles enunciated in the *Spectator*, a play some ten or twelve years in preparation, was one precisely calculated to bring to public attention conflicting views about comedy that previously had lacked articulate statement.

The Conscious Lovers is generally considered the prime exemplar of "sentimental comedy," the name usually applied to the form of comedy that emerged in association with the early-eighteenth-century reform movement. Yet, as applied to *The Conscious Lovers*, the term "sentimental comedy," implying an emphasis on appeal to the emotions of sympathy, is inadequate to explain what Steele and his contemporaries found to be new and most controversial about the play.[86] Steele did, in his preface, defend the inclusion of pathetic incident in comedy, and John Dennis and Benjamin Victor, among others, debated its propriety. The quality of *The Conscious Lovers* that was felt to be most original and that proved to be most controversial, however, was not the appeal to pathos but the employment of admirable characters providing models for conduct—notably Bevil, Jr., the "fine gentleman"—rather than the traditional witty yet debauched characters familiar in Restoration comedy. It is the insistence on the exemplary characters that most conspicuously differentiates *The Conscious Lovers* from Steele's earlier plays (though *The Funeral* possesses such characters less fully developed) and from the plays, for example, of Cibber, who shares with Steele in popular opinion the leadership of the movement toward sentimental comedy; and it is assuredly the nature of the characters that was responsible for the frequent comparisons of Dorimant and Bevil, Jr., during the critical controversy stirred up by the play. This is not to say

[86] I am heavily indebted at this point to John Harrington Smith, "Shadwell, the Ladies, and Change in Comedy," *Modern Philology*, XLVI (1948), 22–33; *The Gay Couple in Restoration Comedy*, pp. 193–232.

that Steele inaugurated exemplary comedy—Professor John Harrington Smith has conclusively shown that its beginnings are to be found at least as far back as 1688 in Shadwell's plays—but it remained for Steele in his periodicals to make the principles of exemplary comedy the current coin of dramatic criticism, and in *The Conscious Lovers* to provide an embodiment, at once successful and controversial, of those principles.

I would recognize three different, though related, aspects of Steele's comic theory as finally embodied in *The Conscious Lovers:* the employment of exemplary characters; the appeal to the emotion of sympathy; the self-conscious avoidance of licentious dialogue. (The third is, of course, a negative quality that was scarcely controversial.) These are the qualities that in combination represent the dramatic formula Steele evolved, and only one of them (the appeal to sympathy) was a uniform characteristic of earlier "sentimental" comedy. Charles Harold Gray's remark, "Over the production of ... *The Conscious Lovers* ... arose the first open discussions of the antagonism between the dominant tradition of the comedy of manners set by Wycherley and Congreve and the new sentimental comedy,"[87] is somewhat misleading, because what chiefly was discussed was not the "sentimental" (pathetic) element—though it received attention—but the exemplary characters.

Consider, as a demonstration of the inadequacy of the term "sentimental comedy" to describe what was distinctive about *The Conscious Lovers,* the sharp differences between it and Cibber's *The Careless Husband*—the most conspicuous of the earlier sentimental plays. In Cibber's play the humanity of Lady Easy's concern for her husband's health is, of course, abundantly evident, and the strong appeal it makes to the sympathy of the audience is perhaps not different in kind from the emotion evoked by Indiana's distresses. But here alone—in the pathetic appeal—have the plays anything in common. *The Careless Husband* has in spirit much in common with the Restoration tradition. The play exhibits licentious characters (slightly subdued) preoccupied with adulterous sexual relations; it was censured for its lasciviousness—by, among others, the author of the *Anti-Theatre*. Far from employ-

---

[87] Charles Harold Gray, *Theatrical Criticism in London to 1795* (New York, 1931), pp. 64–65.

ing characters who provide models for conduct, Cibber supports explicitly in the dialogue of the play the satirical theory, to which Steele so strongly took exception, by which Restoration dramatists sought to defend their employment of depraved characters. "Tis Hard, indeed, when People won't Distinguish between what's Meant for Contempt, and what for Example," Lady Easy observes, in a direct thrust at the reformers. Dennis would have agreed completely with Lady Easy—witness *A Defence of Sir Fopling Flutter,* written in oppostion to *The Conscious Lovers.* In short, to identify *The Conscious Lovers* as merely a preëminent exemplar of the type of comedy represented by *The Careless Husband* is to ignore differences that are quite as important in the evolution of drama as the similarities.

In the contemporary controversy over *The Conscious Lovers* the two distinct principles—employment of exemplary characters and appeal to sympathy—were debated, no one assuming that they were indivisible; and of these two principles, the one that differentiates *The Conscious Lovers* from most earlier "sentimental" comedies received decidedly the larger share of attention.

There is, of course, a logical relationship between these two principles, one that was acknowledged in some of the contemporary discussions of the play. It is not merely by chance that exemplary characters so frequently appear in "sentimental" action. A moment's consideration will reveal that an exemplary character cannot, without damage to his effectiveness as a model for conduct, be placed in a ridiculous situation; if he appears in hilarious action at all, not he but someone else must have the experiences that arouse the spectators' laughter. The anonymous author of a pamphlet in defense of Steele explained the matter:

[Dennis] tells us, that the Principal Characters of Comedy should be always ridiculous, and gives some Instances to prove it: But if this were granted, where the finest Gentleman is to be expos'd to View in a Character upon the Stage, how ridiculous must it make a Fine Gentleman appear to the World. To my Understanding, a Fine Gentleman, and a Ridiculous Character, are wholly inconsistent; so that this Character must be banish'd the Stage: Or you may as well make a Buffoon a Fine Gentleman, as a Fine Gentleman a Buffoon.[88]

[88] *Sir Richard Steele, And . . . The Conscious Lovers, Vindicated* (London, 1723), p. 16.

If the playwright, then, desires to present a fine gentleman, he must find some means other than the traditional resource of comedy—ridicule—by which to interest his audience. That substitute was, of course, frequently found in pathos.

Pathetic situations, moreover, provide a means of demonstrating the benevolence and humanity of exemplary heroes. A man is tried not by prosperity and its attendant gaiety but by misfortune, his own or another's, and its attendant sorrow. By emphasizing a character's magnanimous response to his own adversity or generous response to the adversity of someone else, a playwright could show him to be a fit subject for the spectators' emulation.

Though there are thus cogent reasons why exemplary characters and the appeal to sympathy are frequently associated, the exemplary and the sentimental by no means always appear together. Exemplary characters cannot, as I have already said, be made to appear ridiculous. Yet ridiculous characters can assuredly be employed to elicit a sympathetic response—Young Bookwit in *The Lying Lover,* for example. To state the relationship another way, "sentimental" comedy is by no means always exemplary comedy; but exemplary comedy can scarcely be laughing comedy without loss of didactic effectiveness. In short, sentimental comedy and exemplary comedy are frequent companions, but they are not identical.

Perhaps the relationship between these two principles—the sentimental and the exemplary—in *The Conscious Lovers* can best be perceived in terms of the critical controversy precipitated by the play. In the development of this controversy, as I believe will become apparent, the two principles remained substantially independent.

Steele had expressed long before *The Conscious Lovers* the rationale of laughterless comedy—as in the epilogue to *The Lying Lover:*

> For laughter's a distorted passion, born
> Of sudden self-esteem and sudden scorn;
> Which, when 'tis o'er, the men in pleasure wise,
> Both him that moved it and themselves despise;
> While generous pity of a painted woe
> Makes us ourselves both more approve and know.

An appropriate epilogue to a play that had so freely called on the spectators' sympathy. In *The Funeral* also Steele had exploited the sober appeal of magnanimous altruism—as in the loyalty of the old servant Trusty—though he subordinated pathos to the merriment of two pairs of young lovers. John Hughes, himself an active literary theorist who had probably discussed the play with Steele, praised especially the humanity of Trusty's reflections when alone at the lodgings of the disinherited young Lord Hardy. "Everyone will own," Hughes added, "that in this Play there are many lively Strokes of Wit and Humour; but I must confess I am more pleas'd with the fine Touches of Humanity in it, than with any other Part of the Entertainment."[39] In Steele's own periodicals there are expressions of a similar preference for sober emotions, as in his praise in the *Tatler*, No. 68, of manly tears as a mark of humanity, and in his disparagement in the *Tatler*, No. 219, of misdirected ridicule. Addison too distrusted laughter, associating it in the *Spectator*, Nos. 47 and 249, with a selfish contempt for and feeling of superiority over the person provoking it (he acknowledged his debt to Hobbes).

It was consistent with Steele's defense of pathos in comedy that he admired Terence, believing, as Professor Krutch has pointed out,[40] that in Terence he had found a precedent for his own comic theory, in which laughter was relegated to a subordinate position. Praising *The Self-Torturer* in the *Spectator*, No. 502, he found it a merit in the play that it did not provoke laughter; rather it was remarkable for "worthy Sentiments." Such admiration for the Roman dramatist's humanity doubtless led to his selection of *The Andria* as the source for *The Conscious Lovers*, the Roman play providing ample incident for displaying tender emotions.

The Conscious Lovers was indeed but a modernization of Terence's play, the major characters, the relationships between them, and the plan of action being derived from it—a fact of which Steele's contemporaries were acutely aware. When reproached for following Terence so closely, Steele insisted that he considered the faithfulness of his adaptation a merit. "I am extremely surprised to find . . . that what I valued myself so much upon—the transla-

---

[39] The *Lay Monk*, No. 9 (December 4, 1713).
[40] *Comedy and Conscience After the Restoration*, p. 249.

tion of him [Terence]—should be imputed to me as a reproach."[41] In an age of authoritarian criticism, the good name of the Roman dramatist was welcome support in literary controversy.

Steele's desire to gain respectability for his inclusion of pathos in comedy perhaps accounts also for the presence on the title page of the first edition of *The Conscious Lovers* of a quotation from Cicero in which the dramatic formula Steele employed is described with surprising accuracy.

Illus genus narrationis, quod in personis positum est, debet habere sermones festivitatem, animorum dissimilitudinem, gravitatem, lenitatem, spem, metum, suspicionem, desiderium, dissimulationem, misericordiam, rerum varietates, fortunae commutationem, insperatum incommodum, subitam letitiam, jucundum exitum rerum.[42]

No distinction is here made between tragedy and comedy, a distinction that became a central issue in the controversy over *The Conscious Lovers*. But Steele did not ignore the distinction. Meeting the charge that he had confused the two genres, he argued, in a famous statement appearing in his preface, that anything with "its foundation in happiness and success must be allowed to be the object of comedy; and sure it must be an improvement of it to introduce a joy too exquisite for laughter, that can have no spring but in delight. . . ." This was an extension of the subject matter of comedy not acceptable to orthodox critics in that it confounded the laughing reaction evoked by traditional comedy with a benevolent participation in the happiness of the dramatic characters— but more of this when I come to John Dennis's arguments in rebuttal.

So much for Steele's theoretical justification of the pathos in *The Conscious Lovers*, a quality that was present in all his earlier plays and one that he had publicly defended as early as 1703. Consider now his exposition of the principle of exemplary comedy.

Bevil, Jr., the exemplary hero of the play, is a direct descendant of Steele's Christian hero of 1701 and of the many fine gentlemen in the *Tatler*, the *Spectator*, and the *Guardian*;[43] and, as I have al-

---

[41] Preface to *The Conscious Lovers*.
[42] Cicero, *Rhetor. ad Herenn.* Lib. I.
[43] Cf. Hooker, *Dennis*, II, 497.

ready said, he is a close relation of Lord Hardy of *The Funeral*. He is, and was recognized to be by Steele's contemporaries, an embodiment of precisely the contrary moral qualities of those exhibited by the Restoration gallants who people the comedies of Etherege, Dryden, Wycherley, and Congreve; he owes his existence to Steele's conviction (shared with a multitude of other reformers) that, theory to the contrary, the display of debauched characters on the stage was damaging to the morals of the spectators.

Steele had, of course, employed a modified exemplary method in at least one of his early comedies, a method in which he was anticipated by a number of dramatists led by Shadwell; but apart from affirming his desire to write morally inoffensive plays, he had not, before he began his periodicals, insisted on the exemplary method. Rather, it was while he conducted his major periodicals (and in all likelihood he then planned *The Conscious Lovers*) that he self-consciously evolved the exemplary theory. His method was both negative and positive: he denounced characters of Restoration plays, Dorimant of *The Man of Mode* most conspicuously, and praised the display in comedy of "all the reverent offices of life." Dennis openly charged that in condemning Etherege's play he was purposely preparing the way for *The Conscious Lovers*. "The Knight certainly wrote the fore-mention'd Spectator [No. 65], tho' it has been writ these ten Years, on Purpose to make Way for his fine Gentleman, and therefore he endeavours to prove, that Sir *Fopling* is not that genteel Comedy, which the World allows it to be."[44] In all essentials Dennis's charge seems to have been just. Steele's papers in the *Spectator* on the characters proper to comedy were, as I have previously argued, written under the stimulus of the ideas responsible for *The Conscious Lovers*.

Not until the *Theatre*, however, did Steele openly associate the theory of exemplary comedy with his forthcoming play; and nowhere is he more explicit about his didactic method than in the *Theatre*, No. 19, in which he explains that the play would already have been produced had not "some accidents" prevented.

The third act of this Comedy . . . has a scene in it, wherein the first character bears unprovoked wrongs, denies a duel, and still appears a man of honour and courage. This example would have been of great service; for

---

44 "A Defence of Sir Fopling Flutter," in Hooker, *ibid.*, 244.

since we see young men are hardly able to forbear imitation of fopperies on the Stage, from a desire of praise, how warmly would they pursue true gallantries, when accompanied with the beauties with which a Poet represents them, when he has a mind to make them amiable!

This puff represents, of course, an early stage of the publicity campaign that preceded the play's production, a campaign in which the admirable nature of the leading character was uniformly insisted on—it is significant that the play was called, before it appeared, "The Fine Gentleman." Everyone in London remotely interested in the theater knew before the play was first acted, in November, 1722—if he knew nothing else about it—that its leading character was a young man of extraordinary virtue. Such was the popular reputation of the play (deliberately fostered by Steele in the *Theatre*) responsible for the conviction that it represented a new kind of comedy; the advance talk about sober comedy (receiving no direct support from Steele as applied to *The Conscious Lovers*) was subordinated to discussion of characters proper to comedy.

Early in 1721 Steele reopened the Dorimant–"fine gentleman" antagonism by introducing into an epilogue (designed to have been spoken at Lincoln's Inn Fields but published separately with a prologue by Leonard Welsted when it was not used) a renewed attack on Etherege.[45] In a prefatory note Welsted recalled frankly Steele's earlier attempt to discredit the plays of Etherege, these having, in Steele's opinion, "a tendency to corrupt Chastity of Manners, and introduce a wrong Taste." As the plan of Steele's forthcoming comedy was already known, the epilogue must have appeared little less than an invitation to compare Etherege's debauched gallant with Steele's young Christian gentleman.

Dennis, in the name of orthodox criticism, accepted the invitation. His attack on *The Conscious Lovers* gained vehemence from the remembered wrongs of three seasons earlier, but from settled conviction Dennis opposed the comic theory that Steele had developed.[46] In his opposition he agreed with the many critics of the

---

[45] *A Prologue to the Town ... Written by Mr. Welsted. With an Epilogue on the same Occasion By Sir Richard Steele* (London, 1721).

[46] Professor Hooker summarizes the background in critical theory for the opposition between Dennis and Steele (*Dennis*, II, 495–496; 500–502).

time—Drake, Vanbrugh, Gildon, Theobald, among others—who argued that comedy, through foolish and depraved characters, should present admonitions against misconduct, this argument having been the fundamental one employed in defense of the dramatists against Jeremy Collier. In the ensuing debate over *The Conscious Lovers,* in fact, Dennis repeated many of the arguments used earlier in the century in rebuttal to Collier, just as Steele and his defenders used Collier's arguments.

It was five days before *The Conscious Lovers* was first acted that Dennis, honestly contemptuous of Steele's theory of comedy and of his publicity campaign, in an effort to curb the enthusiasm for the new play, published *A Defence of Sir Fopling Flutter.* Because Dennis had not read *The Conscious Lovers*—his information about it was gained only from the newspaper reports and from friends who had heard it read—he could attack only the dramatic principles upon which the play was based. His arguments, however, are not for that reason the less compelling, because it was, of course, the principles—which Dennis already understood with perfect clarity—that were chiefly at issue. Dennis could not be misled here, as he was in a portion of his later *Remarks on . . . The Conscious Lovers,* by relatively unimportant considerations of detail. In *A Defence of Sir Fopling Flutter* he puts unequivocally the case against exemplary comedy, and conversely the case for satirical comedy. Freely acknowledging the degeneracy of characters in *The Man of Mode,* he insists, citing Aristotle and Horace as authorities, that such characters are the proper subjects of ridicule and that ridicule alone is the proper concern of comedy. " 'Tis its [comedy's] proper Business to expose Persons to our View, whose Views we may shun, and whose Follies we may despise; and by shewing us what is done upon the Comick Stage, to shew us what ought never to be done upon the Stage of the World."[47] Virtuous characters presented as models for imitation are out of place in comedy, he explains, "For all such Patterns are serious Things, and Laughter is the Life, and the very Soul of Comedy." Comedies of Molière and Ben Jonson are the ones he finds most admirable, laughing comedies in which the principal characters are absurd and ridiculous by reason of faults exhibited as admonitions to the spectators.

[47] Hooker, *Dennis,* II, 245.

Dennis insists on instruction by laughter, and he implies, in no uncertain terms, that Steele's new comedy will be deficient in laughter; but he does not discuss the inclusion of pathos in comedy. He acknowledges that exemplary comedy must necessarily be deficient in laugh-provoking characters, but he says nothing, in this essay, that articulates the contemporary critical expectations of Steele's new play, about the pathetic elements in it. His attitude is negative, not positive: he anticipates the absence of laughter, not the presence of pathos. In short, what Dennis was led to expect as the distinguishing feature of *The Conscious Lovers* was its exemplary characters rather than its sentimentality (or pathos).

Far from prejudicing the town against *The Conscious Lovers* and decreasing its popularity as he intended, Dennis's attack, a few days before the play was first presented, increased public interest and contributed indirectly to its success.[48] *A Defence of Sir Fopling Flutter* contains much sound criticism—the objections to Steele's comic theory are cogent ones—but critical arguments were not in themselves sufficient to counteract the widespread curiosity to see the play.

Because of this curiosity it is understandable that the play attracted a large amount of attention in three of the newspapers, the *Freeholder's Journal,* the *Weekly Journal* (Mist's), and the *St. James's Journal.* The two former were mainly hostile, the *Freeholder's Journal* even more than the *Weekly Journal,* whereas the *St. James's Journal* assumed the position of a neutral, sometimes defending, sometimes attacking the play. In the *Freeholder's Journal* and the *St. James's Journal* there were serious attempts at critical appraisals of *The Conscious Lovers;* personal animosity, though sometimes evident, was subordinated to reasoned critical argument. In the *Weekly Journal* criticism of the play, except in a single "letter" printed in the paper, provided merely a medium for further attacks on the group in charge of Drury Lane.

Like Dennis, the *Freeholder's Journal* began its comments on the play before its production; and, also like Dennis, the newspaper emphasized the importance to Steele's design of his leading character. "We flatter ourselves," the unidentified author wrote on

[48] Benjamin Victor, *An Epistle to Sir Richard Steele, On his Play call'd, The Conscious Lovers* (London, 1722), pp. 5–6.

October 31, "that the Drama we expect will . . . afford a compleat Model to that leading Pattern of Life, *The Gentleman*." There is not a word in this preproduction discussion of the play about the appropriateness or inappropriateness of pathos to comedy; there is not even, as there was in Dennis's essay, an insistence that comedy provoke laughter. Even in the series of articles in later numbers of the paper,[49] after the play had appeared, the character of Bevil received most attention (much space was devoted to comparisons of him with Pamphilus, his prototype in *The Andria*). In some of the later articles, to be sure, appear comments about the sorrowful denouement; the writer objects, Steele's statement to the contrary, that the emotions aroused are not appropriate to comedy: "The Discovery at last is entirely Passionate, Melting and Tragi Comical: The Audience are sent off with a sorrowful impression, and Tears in their Eyes, not to be wip'd off by the final event."[50] But he does not associate the appeal to the spectators' sympathy with the admirable nature of the hero.

The *St. James's Journal* was kinder to Steele, devoting a generous amount of space in three different numbers to sympathetic discussion of the play—first in a letter signed "Townly"[51] (where the

[49] Cf. the issues for November 14, 21, 28, December 5, 12, 1722.

[50] November 28, 1722.

[51] This letter, included in the *St. James's Journal* for November 15, 1722, bears an elaborate title, printed in a way that has given rise to a misunderstanding among modern scholars. Because it is separated from the body of the letter by a brief, satirical poem, this title to the letter itself has been mistakenly assumed to be "an announcement of a piece called 'A short defence of two excellent comedies, viz., "Sir Fopling Flutter," and "The Conscious Lovers"; in answer to many scandalous reflections on them both, by a certain terrible Critick, who never saw the latter, and scarce knows anything of comedy at all'" (Aitken, *Life,* II, 284. Cf. Hooker, *Dennis,* II, 496). That the letter itself is the "piece" to which this descriptive title applies appears from a comment in the following issue of the paper (November 22). It is observed—the statement will also indicate the contents of the letter—that "one of your Correspondents, in the Title of his Letter, promis'd us a short Defence of the *Conscious Lovers;* but it seems afterwards utterly forgot it, and diverted *us* with his Severities upon the *Old Critick,* and his Panegyricks upon his good Friends (As I suppose 'em) the *Triumvirate.*" "A Short Defence," then, was not a pamphlet published separately, but Townly's letter.

actor-managers are praised as well as the play), and later more judiciously in two letters signed ironically "Dorimant."[52] The first letter is of little interest here, but the Dorimant letters warrant attention as discriminating contemporary appraisals of the comedy, although in them the controversial principles with which I have been chiefly concerned receive only subordinate attention. Dorimant believes *The Conscious Lovers* to be inferior to the Latin original; he finds improbabilities in the action and unnecessary episodes; he considers the character of Cimberton gross; he believes Steele represented the character of the old servant better in *The Funeral;* and though he does not find fault with Tom, he observes that the character is less closely related to the design of the play than was Davus, his prototype in Terence's comedy. On the other hand, this writer is complimentary on the subject of the relations of the Bevils, father and son: "The tender, and at the same time prudent Concern of old *Bevil,* for his Son's Interest and Satisfaction in Marriage, is very well hit; so the filial Fondness and Duty to the Father, with the Struggles of Love and Generosity to the Lady." The author thus indirectly commends the employment in comedy of exemplary characters, in this instance of characters who exhibit a "sentimental" sensitivity to the afflictions of others. He is more direct in his defense of Steele's tearful conclusion. It is significant, however, that he does not consider the inclusion of pathos in comedy (as distinct from the employment of exemplary characters) as in any way an innovation:

... the tender Scene upon the Father's discovery of his Daughter, has received the most reasonable and natural Applause of eighteen successive Audiences, their Silence and their Tears. A Pleasure built upon the most sincere Delight, which no sensible Mind would exchange for the momentary *passant* Transports of an inconsiderate Laughter. An Applause which a Masterly Writer prefers to a thousand Shouts of a tumultuous and unreasonable Theatre. Some of our best Comedies, *The Fool in Fashion, The Lady's Last Stake, The Careless Husband,* have wound up their Catastrophe in this tender manner with great Success, and never-failing Applause.

[52] November 22, December 8, 1722.

Little need be said about the comments on *The Conscious Lovers* in the *Weekly Journal.*[58] Except for a judicious appreciative essay in the issue for March 30, in which Steele's moral purpose is applauded, they represent merely another phase of that paper's long campaign against Drury Lane. Mixing derogatory judgments about the play with satirical allusions to the managers, the paper for the most part made damning pronouncements without offering substantiating arguments. Not all the allusions to the comedy are hostile, but none, except that in the issue for March 30 (and that only tangentially), provides informed comment on the critical problems posed by it. Typical of the remarks is one that anticipates Parson Adam's famous pronouncement of a later day: the writer charged that Steele wrote the play to determine "how the Publick would like *Sermons* work'd up into *Comedies.*"[54]

Steele himself did not answer the hostile criticism, but he encouraged Benjamin Victor, then a young man who had only recently made his acquaintance, to do so.[55] Victor's *An Epistle to Sir Richard Steele, On his Play, call'd, The Conscious Lovers* (November 29)[56] is, in comparison with Dennis's *A Defence of Sir Fopling Flutter,* to which it purports to be an answer, a lame performance. His comments about *The Man of Mode* lack pertinency; he argues over irrelevancies not important to the fundamental question of the opposition between the two theories of comedy, the propriety, for example, of Dennis's identification of Dorimant with Rochester. Similarly he is distracted by the comparison of Bevil, Jr., with Pamphilus that had appeared in the *Freeholder's Journal:* he is at pains to demonstrate Bevil's greater virtue. But he does not neglect completely the major issues.

Is it possible, Sir [he asks], that *De——s* can be so void of Shame to attempt to prove, that vicious Characters is the only Business of Comedy, and

---

[58] Cf. the issues of January 19, February 9, 16, March 30, 1723. Some of these remarks on *The Conscious Lovers* may well have been written by Daniel Defoe.

[54] January 19, 1723.

[55] Cf. Victor, *Original Letters,* I, 328; *The History of the Theatres of London and Dublin* (London, 1761), II, 99–101.

[56] A second edition was called for on December 4. Aitken, *Life,* II, 281.

that their corrupt Examples have the same design'd Effect upon the Audience as a virtuous honourable Character. . . .[57]

The separate principle (and Victor considers it separately) of the inclusion of pathetic incident in comedy he also defends. "It was the Opinion of all the Antients, that Love (the usual Argument of all Comedies) is there best written where it is most distress'd, and in despairing Passion; that Part of Comedy seeming best which is nearest Tragedy."[58] At no time had Steele suggested that the pathos of comedy should approximate that of tragedy: the disciple was more devout than the master.

The defense of Steele was further strengthened by an anonymous pamphlet appearing December 13,[59] bearing the bold title, *Sir Richard Steele, and his New* COMEDY, *call'd* THE CONSCIOUS LOVERS, VINDICATED, *From the malicious Aspersions of Mr.* JOHN DENNIS. WHEREIN *Mr. Dennis's vile Criticism's, in Defence of Sir* FOPLING FLUTTER, *are Detected and Expos'd*. The unidentified author answers Dennis's arguments systematically, proceeding from point to point through Dennis's essay; but, like Victor, he often fails to discriminate between what is important to Dennis's case and what is extraneous. Some of his remarks, however, are directly pertinent, as when he explains lucidly why exemplary characters cannot be employed to arouse laughter, at the same time affirming their didactic effectiveness in comedy as models for conduct. "But cannot Comedy instruct by Virtuous Characters? Will nothing but Vice and Ridicule please; and shall Ridicule only be the Standard of Wit?"[60] Tacitly acknowledging that Bevil's virtue somewhat exceeds probability, he defends the dramatist's right, citing Aristotle as authority, to draw characters beyond life. At this point he, of course, ignores the distinction made by orthodox critics between the characters proper to comedy and those to tragedy; but later in the essay, facing the objections made to the pathos in Steele's last act, he specifically defends the play as a comedy. Tragedies, he insists, have a fatal catastrophe; *The Conscious*

---

[57] P. 17.

[58] P. 11.

[59] The date 1723 appears on its title page. Aitken, *Life*, II, 285.

[60] P. 16.

Lovers, in contrast, ends happily, notwithstanding the emotion aroused in the fifth act. Employing the argument Steele had advanced in the preface to the play, he affirms the appropriateness of the emotion to comedy by reason of its origin in joy. With all his logic, however, this author seems not completely to have convinced himself. "Sir Richard Steele's new play," he concludes, "if it be not in the strictest Sense throughout a Comedy, it is an Entertainment superior to it."[61]

The replies to Dennis in defense of Steele were thus somewhat stronger than they had been in the dispute three years before—stronger probably than Dennis had anticipated. He was angered by the town's hostile reaction to his effort to reveal the fraud he believed *The Conscious Lovers* to be, and he displayed his anger in his second attack, *Remarks on a Play, Call'd, The Conscious Lovers, a Comedy* (January 24, 1723).[62] To this pamphlet he prefixed a dedication to Robert Walpole and a preface, in both of which, in a manner reminiscent of *The Characters and Conduct of Sir John Edgar,* he denounces roundly the actor-managers and the "easy Patentee," reasserting his charge that they exercise a stifling, inhibitory effect on the production of dramatic poetry. It is in his "Remarks on the Preface to The Conscious Lovers," however, that he advances his most relevant and his most telling arguments. In *A Defence of Sir Fopling Flutter* his chief mark was Steele's exemplary hero, but here it is the pathos of Steele's final act—the pathos that Steele defended in his preface. Dennis's charge is, fundamentally, that Steele confused two genres by introducing into comedy emotions proper only to tragedy. "When Sir *Richard* says, that any thing that has its Foundation in Happiness and Success must be the Subject of Comedy, he confounds Comedy with that Species of Tragedy which has a happy Catastrophe."[63] Steele's argument that comedy would be improved by introducing "a joy too exquisite for laughter" is untenable because comedy cannot be dissociated from the joy that does produce laughter: joy itself is an undifferentiated emotion common to all forms of literature; only when it is expressed as laughter is it characteristic of

---

[61] P. 19.

[62] Aitken, *Life,* II, 28n.

[63] Hooker, *Dennis,* II, 259.

comedy." So goes his argument—and it is a strong one—the conclusion of which is that *The Conscious Lovers* is no comedy at all.
Here he says nothing directly about the exemplary characters.
They are, to be sure, the agents through whom the spectators'
emotions of pity are enlisted, and, as Dennis doubtless understood,
their deficiencies in laughter-provoking qualities required the sub-
stitution of some appeal in place of the traditional comic one. It is
significant, however, that he does not openly associate the pathos
with the model characters.

That portion of *The Remarks on the Conscious Lovers* devoted
to the play itself, because it is specific rather than universal in
application, adds little to the debate on comic theory. Many of
Dennis's objections to improbabilities of plot and character are,
nevertheless, strong ones: he finds inconsistencies in action and
inadequacies in motivation. Most vehemently he objects, as would
be anticipated, to Bevil, Jr., charging that his character is "made
up of Qualities, either incoherent and contradictory, as Religion
and Dissimulation, Morality and Fraud; or most ridiculously consistent, as Circumspection and Folly."[65] Some of his supporting
arguments are, it is true, unreasonably dogmatic, but others of
them are compelling.

Indubitably the longest of the critical essays on *The Conscious
Lovers* was the last of the contemporary ones, the anonymous *The
Censor Censured: or, The* CONSCIOUS LOVERS *Examin'd: in a*
DIALOGUE *between Sir* DICKY MARPLOT AND JACK FREEMAN.
INTO WHICH MR. DENNIS *is introduced by way of* POSTSCRIPT:
with some CONVERSATIONS *on his late* REMARKS. The author re-
peats in mediocre dialogue the current criticisms of the play, chiefly
those hostile to it, adding little that is new. Following the *Freeholder's Journal* and Dennis's *Remarks,* he compares *The Conscious Lovers* at length with its Roman original, to the disadvantage
of the modernization. "Sir Dicky Marplot" is an enthusiastic, naïve
fool, who cannot tolerate criticism of this play on which he has
worked for three years. Dennis is introduced only to repeat the
objections to the comedy's inconsistencies and improbabilities that
he had presented in his *Remarks.* The pamphlet is repetitive in this,

[64] *Ibid.,* II, 260.
[65] *Ibid.,* II. 272.

as in nearly all its parts; but it does emphasize anew that the pre-production expectations of *The Conscious Lovers* chiefly concerned the exemplary characters, the author recalling in his preface that

we were taught to expect, that Vertue, long banish'd the Scenes, was once more to make a flourishing Figure on the Stage, adorn'd with all the gay Simplicity of sprightly Innocence. Thus she was to have the force of Precept and Example too; and thus at once she was to instruct and please.

The fact of the pamphlet's ambitious scale—its eighty-eight pages of dialogue—is striking testimony to the critical interest aroused by the comedy.

Few plays have attracted more attention on their first appearance than *The Conscious Lovers;* certainly few have aroused critical controversies that were sharper and more clearly defined. To dismiss that controversy as one merely over sentimental comedy—even sentimental comedy known by another name—is, as I hope I have demonstrated, seriously to oversimplify. What gave the play its advance reputation as a new form of comedy was Steele's insistence that his chief character would provide a pattern for the conduct of the Christian gentleman. Only after the play appeared was there discussion of the "sentimental" element, the appeal to the spectators' sympathy, and never were the exemplary characters and the pathos identified as a single indissoluable unit.

The production of the play marked the virtual end of Steele's attempts to reform the English stage, the task for which, as he insisted, he was appointed to Drury Lane. In the play he presented his final plea for a reformed drama—a plea that was not without great effectiveness, as the comedy of the later part of the century bears witness. Whatever had been his failures as an administrative head of Drury Lane, he accomplished one of the theatrical objectives he had set for himself in providing the stage with an enormously successful play that was without moral offense. The condition of the stage had been deplored in his patent: "instead of exhibiting such representations of human life as may tend to the encouragement and honour of Religion and Virtue, and discountenancing Vice, the English STAGE hath been the complaint of the sober, intelligent, and religious part of our people. . . ." Steele had been commanded to make the drama an incentive to virtuous be-

havior. *The Conscious Lovers,* in which there appear "representations of human life" that certainly were intended for "the
encouragement and honour of Religion and Virtue, and discountenancing Vice," was his most effective answer to that command.[66]
The method he employed provoked serious criticism, but his play,
nevertheless, represents an effective attempt at moral reform of the
stage.

4 | # Steele and the Management, 1721-1729

RESTORED nominally to the governorship of Drury Lane
by the lord chamberlain's order of May 2, 1721, Steele in fact never
resumed his former close relations with the company; Wilks,
Booth, and Cibber were compelled to readmit him to a share of
the profits (they devised an expedient to reduce the amount he
received), but they continued to control the theater's affairs. Before
his suspension Steele had by no means assumed a measure of responsibility for the company in any way equivalent to that borne
by the actor-managers, but often—insofar as his political, financial,
and literary undertakings permitted—he had taken a direct and
active part in the theater's business. After his suspension, and even
after his subsequent reinstatement, matters were emphatically
otherwise. The actor-managers, in their deposition of January 11,
1726, asserted that beginning January 28, 1720 (the day after they
received a license exclusive of Steele), he had "altogether absented
himself" from the management.[67] Though demonstrably an ex-
aggeration—there are records of his participation in Drury Lane
affairs during the later years—their statement was substantially
accurate. From his restoration in 1721 until his death in 1729, with
the exception perhaps of the interval when *The Conscious Lovers*

---

[66] In his dedication of the play to the king, Steele associates ·*The Conscious Lovers* with his performance of his duties at Drury Lane.

[67] P.R.O., C11/2416/49.

was produced, Steele's interest in Drury Lane was almost solely a financial one.

Steele's personal relations with Cibber, Wilks, and Booth, as may be surmised from scattered innuendoes, were never cordial after his reinstatement; he no doubt resented the actor-managers' having placidly submitted to the lord chamberlain's direction, and they certainly found it a substantial inconvenience to pay him his share of the back profits for a season and a half. They, to be sure, produced *The Conscious Lovers* handsomely—with an unprecedented profit to themselves—in a manner that earned his public thanks, Cibber even helping him prepare the play for the stage; but that event appears to have been merely a truce in a prolonged period of strained relations.

The order of May 2, 1721, by which the managers were directed to account to Steele for the share of the profits "he would have been Entitled to" had he not been suspended, came near the end of the regular theatrical season. On June 6 the company suspended its normal routine and, except for a few irregular performances during the summer, did not resume acting until September 9. About the time this new season started, Steele and the managers settled accounts—after a fashion rather unfavorable to Steele. Protesting that they had lost heavily in the South Sea Bubble and that Steele had not borne his share of the costs of scenes during his suspension, the managers persuaded Steele to accept a large deduction from the amount due him—a deduction variously described as £1,200 and £1,400.[68] Steele was lawfully entitled to the money, he later said;[69] as an act of good will, he forfeited his claim to it, only to help his colleagues.

The sum Steele actually received seems to have been reduced further by a stratagem that, unknown to him, the managers employed to reduce the amount of their clear profits and hence the amount of Steele's share. Commencing January 28, 1720, they deducted £5 a day in compensation for their own work, the sum being divided among the three of them. Previously, scholars have

---

[68] Described as about £1,200 in Steele's deposition of June 23, 1726 (P.R.O., C11/2416/49); as £1,400 in Steele's letter of December 7, 1721, to Wilks (*Correspondence*, p. 169; cf. also pp. 170-171n).

[69] Cf. *Correspondence*, p. 169.

assumed that they did not begin this deduction until June 18, 1723: both Aitken and Professor Blanchard cite this later date.[70] However, the legal records of the subsequent lawsuits over the deduction support clearly the earlier date; the significance of June 18, 1723, is merely that, not knowing about the deduction, Steele then signed a receipt in full for his Drury Lane profits, establishing the date as one before which, so the actor-managers insisted, the division of the profits should not be contested. A deposition of the actor-managers explains the matter:

... And Yr. Oratrs. [Cibber, Wilks, and Booth] shew that ever since the sd. day of Janry 1719/20 aforesd being the time the sd. Sr. Richd. Steele began to absent him self from the business of the sd. Theatre Your Orators have had reced and taken to their own ye Use respectively 1.13.4 apiece for every day there has been a play Acted at the sd. Theatre in Consideration of such their attendance and Actings as aforesd. and the same has been always Entred in the daily Charge of the Accots. of the sd. Theatre ... and he the sd Sr Richd Steel was so conscious to himself that Your Oratrs. Deserved a much greater sume ... that he the sd. Sr. Richd. Steele allowed the Accots. of the sd Theatre wherein the sd 1.13.4 p Diem was Charged and never made any Objection thereto and in particular the sd. Sr. Richd. Steele upon the 18th of June 1723 passed and setled ye Accots. of the sd. Theatre & reced his proportion of the profits thereof and gave a receipt. ...[71]

Steele and the actor-managers differed in a number of details about the deduction, but they agreed that it began in January, 1720—witness the following deposition of Steele:

And this deft. saith that from the time of the said first mentioned order [Newcastle's license to the actor-managers exclusive of Steele] the Comlts in an extraordinary manner thought fitt to increase their own allowance from one pound a night each which they had before that time allowed them in the said constant paybook equally with this deft. they placed and allowed to themselves one pound thirteen shillings and four pence apiece for each night and have continued to deduct and take to themselves for each night the like allowance ever since exclusive of this deft. of which this deft. saith he had no manner of notice or was in the least made acquainted with untill ... very lately that he was informed thereof by a person noe ways concerned in the said Theatre. ...[72]

[70] Aitken, *Life*, II, 303. *Correspondence*, p. 171n.

[71] P.R.O., C11/2416/49.

[72] *Ibid.*

There was no disagreement about the date when the deduction began, then, but about the date when Steele was informed of it. The actor-managers insisted that they made the deduction openly (in his *Apology* Cibber maintains that they told Steele about it in the beginning),[73] whereas Steele insisted that he learned about it only accidentally several years later. Probability here seems with Steele. The managers would scarcely have informed Steele in the beginning, as Cibber reports, because Steele was then excluded from the theater by Newcastle's action. The managers began the payment to themselves, we may surmise, as an accounting procedure growing out of Steele's suspension, only after Steele's reinstatement employing the argument of "salaries" to justify their withholding sums from him. It will be recalled that they, with Steele, had attempted unsuccessfully to employ such a stratagem against Thomas Doggett. That Steele, in fact, was not openly informed of the deduction is suggested by a personal memorandum he drew up in April, 1724 (not intended for publication), in which he described it as a "clandestine alienation."[74]

Obscure and conflicting though the records are, it appears that Steele received relatively little money from the actor-managers in September, 1721. He was no match for them in the complexities of theatrical finance.

The same month that they settled accounts, Steele and the actor-managers took steps to clarify their respective property rights in the theater, executing on September 19, 1721, two separate sets of articles of agreement.[75] In the first they agreed that the profits or losses of the theater should be divided equally among the four of them (there was no mention of "salaries" to the actor-managers); that on the death of Steele, his heirs should be paid one-fourth of the profits for three years and should in addition be paid £1,200 for his share in the clothes and scenes; and that no one of the four should sell, mortgage, or in any other way part with his share in the patent without the written consent of the other three. This agreement was thus much like that by which they had previously

---

[73] II, 197.

[74] British Museum, Additional MS 5145C, fols. 132–133. The memorandum is quoted in Aitken, *Life*, II, 298–299.

[75] Land Registry Office, Entry 1724, 5, 275–276.

operated; only the provision that no one of the four should without permission alienate his share—a provision obviously directed at Steele—was new. The second set of articles drawn up that same day apparently grew out of the difficulties occasioned by Steele's suspension. It will be recalled that Newcastle's order restoring Steele to the management contained a hint that further action would be taken; Newcastle had ordered the managers to pay Steele his share of the profits until they received further orders or until the legal complexities of Steele's case should be settled by law. Wilks, Booth, and Cibber probably insisted on this second set of articles, which were designed to protect them from financial loss and prevent controversies and misunderstandings if the implied threat was carried out. If Steele was again suspended, it was agreed, he should not be paid his share of the profits; his interest in the clothes and scenes, however, would not be affected.

Two days later Steele, again acting in concert with the actor-managers, wrote to Newcastle requesting his "Influence and Protection" for Drury Lane. The letter suggests that he and the duke were reconciled.[78] Steele had two specific complaints, both of which concerned the rival playhouse, Lincoln's Inn Fields. First, an actor, formerly employed at Drury Lane and in debt to the company, had deserted to the other house; the lord chamberlain, Steele observed, had two traditional methods of dealing with such an offense: he could order the actor back to Drury Lane, or he could silence him. Lincoln's Inn Fields, moreover, had usurped the title "theatre-royal," properly applied, according to Steele, only to Drury Lane; in fact, as he subtly hints to the Whig lord chamberlain, the term "theatre-royal" as applied to Lincoln's Inn Fields might be interpreted ambiguously in view of that theater's demonstrated disaffection to the king.

Steele's complaint about the rival company's advertising itself "theatre-royal" produced no discernible result—the title continued to appear in Lincoln's Inn Fields' advertisements; but whether moved by Steele's letter or some other cause, Newcastle took action to prevent John Rich from hiring Drury Lane actors. The duke wrote first, on December 4, 1721, to the Drury Lane managers, directing them not to allow any member of their company to engage

_____
[78] *Correspondence*, pp. 165–166.

himself to any other company without first obtaining a discharge from the managers, to be approved by Newcastle himself;[77] then he wrote sharply to Rich, on December 24, 1721, instructing him not to hire anyone from Drury Lane who did not possess the discharge.[78] For the moment Newcastle, perhaps at Steele's request, sided with Drury Lane.

The brief interval of coöperation between Steele and his colleagues ended abruptly when in December, 1721, he quarreled with them over a financial matter—as shown in letters he wrote to all three of them on December 7.[79] The letter to Wilks contains the clearest statement of Steele's complaint:

I am sorry that the Gift of fourteen hundred pounds, for what was mine before, could not prevail so much as to let what I had stand as a deposit for a Contingent in Case an impudent cheat is not determined to be such in Wilbraham, who detains my Writings contrary to the order of Minshull, to which he is obliged under his hand to deliver them.

But the Business of this Letter is in particular to speak to you not to persist in so unreasonable a thing as the Denyal of payment of the Sum which remains above what there is any Claim or pretence against my Receiving.

In the letter to Booth he further identifies the sum he requests as "the fifth of the fourth heretofore demanded, and to which there is no claim."

Steele's request (which has not previously been fully understood by scholars)[80] requires an explanation. At the time he wrote the letters he had not yet entered suit against Wilbraham (Minshull's attorney) to regain the assignment of the theatrical patent, but, believing that he had redeemed it, he had attempted unsuccessfully to induce Wilbraham to surrender it. Wilbraham still employed the assignment to obtain a large portion of Steele's share of the profits directly from the treasurer of the company. Having no success with Wilbraham, Steele, it appears, attempted to persuade the managers not to honor the assignment, proposing that they consider the large sum of money deducted the previous Sep-

---

[77] P.R.O., L.C. 5/158; L.C.7/3. See below, p. 247.

[78] P.R.O., L.C.5/158; L.C.7/3. See below, pp. 247–248.

[79] *Correspondence*, pp. 169–173.

[80] Cf. *Correspondence*, pp. 169–170n.

tember (when they settled accounts after his suspension) from the amount due him, as security against any loss resulting from their refusal to honor Wilbraham's claim. Not only had the managers refused his request; they carried their refusal, so Steele charged, to the point of withholding even that portion of his share of the profits not covered by the assignment. In the letter to Booth he specifies "the fifth of the fourth . . . to which there is no claim," referring to the unassigned twentieth portion of the patent. It will be recalled that when Steele first mortgaged his share, he held and thus could mortgage only one-fifth of it because Doggett's claim still had not been settled; when in December, 1716, Doggett was by court order finally excluded from any claim to the patent,[81] Steele's share was increased to one-fourth. Thus the difference between a fifth share and a fourth share (one-twentieth of the whole) remained unencumbered and in the undisputed possession of Steele. On the reverse side of the contemporary copy in the British Museum of the letter Steele wrote to Booth on December 7, 1721, is a computation of "the Neat profits of the Theatre in the Year 1721" in which Steele's twentieth part ("the fourth of the fifth" which, of course, equals a fifth of the fourth) is calculated separately for September, October, and November.[82] If, as Steele charged, the actor-managers refused to pay him this unassigned twentieth part, it would seem that his anger was justified.

Our information about this episode, it must be remembered, comes only from Steele; the actor-managers' action was probably less unreasonable than it appears from his letters. The clue to the episode may indeed lie in Cibber's account of the managers' refusal to advance money to Steele before it became due.

Sir Richard . . . was often in want of money; and while we were in Friendship with him, we often assisted his Occasions: But those Compliances had so unfortunate an Effect, that they only heightened his Importunity to borrow more, and the more we lent, the less he minded us, or shew'd any Concern for our Welfare. Upon this, Sir, we stopt our Hands at once, and peremptorily refus'd to advance another Shilling 'till by the Balance of our Accounts, it became due to him. And this Treatment (though, we

[81] P.R.O., C33/327, f. 226; C33/335. Land Registry Office, Entry 1724, 5, 275. See above, pp. 40–41.
[82] British Museum, Additional MS 5145C, fol. 106.

hope, not in the least unjustifiable) we have Reason to believe so ruffled his Temper, that he at once was as short with us as we had been with him; for, from that Day, he never more came near us. . . ."[83]

As Cibber mentions no date, it is impossible to determine whether or not he presents his own version of the episode that prompted Steele's letters of December 7, 1721. But whatever the date of the quarrel Cibber describes, his report offers a corrective to the view that Steele suffered unprovoked wrongs from the actor-managers.

Steele himself, replying on January 30, 1722, to a complaint by Henry Davenant that Drury Lane delayed in accepting a play for production, alluded to his break with the managers, declaring that he was "only on a doubtful footing at the theatre."[84] Leonard Welsted was also offended at the company's neglect of a play, Steele observed, explaining to Davenant that he could be of no assistance whatever. When sometime the same year Steele scribbled some rough notes preparatory to writing the preface to *The Conscious Lovers,* he recorded, in terms that suggest ill-humor, his alienation from the management: "As for Power in the Playhouse I cannot imagine where it came into anybody's head I desired it."[85]

However, his break with the theater was not, in 1722, complete. On February 9, 1722, he wrote to Castleman, the treasurer of the company, requesting, as he would scarcely have done if he had not retained an active interest in the Drury Lane repertoire, a "Catalogue of Our Stock of plays".[86] On April 12, 1722, he joined the actor-managers in signing an agreement with John Rich (which possibly grew out of Steele's request to the lord chamberlain the previous September and the lord chamberlain's subsequent order) that the two theaters not employ the other's actors under penalty of £20.[87] The previous November a similar agreement, which did not include Steele's name, was drawn up though not executed[88]— presumably because without Steele the articles would not have been binding. The delay until April was perhaps occasioned by

[83] *Apology,* II, 201.
[84] *Correspondence,* pp. 173–174.
[85] Quoted from Aitken, *Life,* II, 277n.
[86] *Correspondence,* p. 174.
[87] British Museum, Additional MS 12201, fols. 13–24.
[88] Aitken, *Life,* II, 274n.

the animosity between Steele and the managers, revealed in the letters of December 7 and January 30.[89]

On January 19, 1722, the month after he complained to the actor-managers about their withholding his share of the profits, Steele entered suit against Wilbraham, Minshull's attorney, to regain the assignment he believed he had redeemed.[90] Because the details of this very complex case have been considered before, it is necessary to add now only that it was apparently settled out of court by a compromise.[91] Steele certainly did not pay the full amount demanded by Wilbraham, but he was forced to continue some payments on the original debt; as late as June 17, 1723, more than a year after initiating this suit against Wilbraham, he paid £300 and executed an assignment of £200 a year from his theater profits to William Woolley, who by a complex series of transfers had become the beneficiary of his original mortgage. The assignment, it was agreed, should remain in effect until the £900 residue of the original debt was made up with interest at 5 per cent; the original mortgaged deed, however, was returned to Steele upon his presenting as security for the £900 his share in the company's stage properties.[92] The difficulties following in the wake of his financial entanglements of 1716 and 1717 thus continued to plague Steele and certainly contributed to the friction between him and the actor-managers.

The alienation of Steele from the managers was by 1722 common knowledge[93]—or so it appears from an open letter to Steele

[89] On September 22, 1722, Cibber, Wilks, and Booth signed an agreement providing that each of them and Steele should have twelve free theater tickets a week for their friends. Aitken, *Life*, II, 274n. The document is now in the Folger Shakespeare Library. Cf. *Correspondence*, p. 397n.

[90] P.R.O., C11/1424/35.

[91] Aitken, *Life*, II, 105.

[92] British Museum, Additional MS 5145C, fol. 134. P.R.O., C11/66/22. Aitken, *Life*, II, 291.

[93] Steele's name nevertheless continued to be linked occasionally with those of the actor-managers in references to the management of Drury Lane. Cf. the preface to *The Impertinent Lovers* (London, 1723); *To Diabebouloumenon: Or, The Proceedings At the Theatre-Royal in Drury-Lane* (London, 1723), pp. 15, 29.

"From about twenty gentlemen of the temple" which appeared in the *Weekly Journal* (Mist's) on January 13 of that year. The "letter" reveals the animus against Drury Lane responsible for the decade-long campaign of abuse against the theater waged by Mist, but it is not for that reason the less informative:

> We chuse to address you in this publick Manner, because it is upon a publick Occasion, You being Monarch of the Stage (if you are not a King of Straw) tell us, we beseech you, why you suffer your Ministers to abuse your People? They have revell'd long in the Sunshine of your Graces, and being grown Rich, have a Mind to grow Arbitrary.... Prithee, dear Sir Dick, change your Ministry, for between us, they are vile Statesmen ... and if you neglect this, we shall suppose your Government is like Trinculo's in the *Tempest,* that you are King, but they are Viceroy's over you.

A little more than a year later, on March 16, 1723, another comment, similarly informative, appeared in the same paper:

> One would think, that since there has been a SUPERINTENDANT appointed over *that* Theatre of a different Character [from the actor-managers], these Abuses could not happen; but *that* Gentleman, it seems, looks upon his Employment to be no more than a *Sine-Cure;* and tho' it is supposed he has no Aversion to the *Profits,* yet it is plain he is more of a Gentleman than to concern himself in the *Business* he is *paid for.* ...

This report—except, of course, for the partisan interpretation of Steele's motive—seems to be an articulation of current opinion; and indeed the account of Steele's indifference to Drury Lane affairs is consistent with other records dating from the same time.

    Steele's health in 1723 and thereafter would have prevented his doing much in support of the theater even if the personal animosity between him and the actor-managers did not exist. Uncertain for several years (he suffered a stroke of apoplexy as early as January, 1721),[94] his health virtually gave way during 1723; from the summer of 1723 until his death he was little more than an invalid, unable physically to carry on any sustained work. Sir John Vanbrugh observed in a letter to Newcastle written July 30, 1723, that Steele, whom he had recently seen, seemed to be "in the declining way I had heard he was."[95] Vanbrugh took the occasion to remind New-

---

[94] The *Daily Post*, January 23, 1721.
[95] Vanbrugh, *Works,* IV, 150–151.

castle of the duke's promise to favor him in the reversion of Steele's "Sinecure." Though Steele held the "sinecure" for six more years (three years longer than Vanbrugh lived), he performed no more duties than the term implied.

Recognizing apparently that his health would not markedly improve, Steele in the spring of 1724 set about putting his affairs in order for his retirement. As an effort presumably to increase the value of his estate, he attempted in March, 1724, to secure a new theatrical patent that would subsist in perpetuity to his heirs and assigns, in contradistinction to his existing one, which was, of course, limited to his lifetime and three years thereafter. When in 1715 he had first petitioned for the patent, he purposely avoided requesting for his heirs an office that required a specialized skill to execute;[96] but in 1724 he came to feel otherwise. In a letter to the lord chamberlain, still the Duke of Newcastle, he enclosed his petition to the king, citing as grounds for the request, "That Your Petitioner by writing the Comedy of the Conscious Lovers, has found by Experience, that more Regular and Vertuous Entertainment would take place if he had duration of time in which to Establish Rules and make Contracts accordingly."[97]—testimony to his belief in the didactic efficacy of his play, perhaps, but certainly not the reason he wanted the patent in perpetuity.

In the letter to Newcastle that accompanied the petition, Steele, writing plaintively of his poor health, made what was almost an apology to the nobleman for past deeds, the submissive tone of his letter providing a marked contrast to the defiance evident in *The State of the Case* and in the *Theatre.*[98] He informed Newcastle that he was presenting his petition with the support of Lord Townshend (then one of the secretaries of state), and he acknowledged his willingness that any clauses be included in the patent necessary to subject it to the lord chamberlain's authority. Nothing beyond the single statement in this letter is known of Townshend's part in the matter.

In May, 1724, Steele requested the assistance of Mrs. Charlotte Clayton, woman of the bedchamber to the Princess of Wales, with

[96] The *Theatre*, No. 8.
[97] The petition is printed in *Correspondence*, pp. 533–534.
[98] *Correspondence*, p. 182.

some petition—perhaps this same one for a new patent. Steele wrote to her twice, first on May 26, requesting that she intercede with the princess, and again the following day, thanking her for espousing his cause.[99] Apparently Mrs. Clayton undertook to help him by recommending his case to Princess Caroline. Nothing came of her help, if she gave it for the patent; nothing more is heard of Steele's attempt to procure the perpetual grant. The original grant remained in effect.

Among his preparations for retirement, Steele, on April 23, 1724, drafted a detailed proposal for the payment of his debts—largely from his Drury Lane income.[100] He made David Scurlock (his wife's cousin) his trustee, authorizing him to examine periodically the account books of Drury Lane to insure that he was paid his just portion of the profits; and he instructed William Plaxton, his secretary, to pay his creditors in an established order of priority. Steele noted, in a memorandum appended to the proposal, that the payment of his debts might be accelerated, first, if he obtained his portion of the sums that Wilks, Cibber, and Booth had appropriated in compensation for their services, and, second, if his new play (*The School of Action*, on which he was then working) was produced the next season.

Steele encountered opposition from the actor-managers in implementing this proposal. He drew up on June 3, 1724, an indenture of assignment quadripartite between himself of the first part; Wilks, Booth, and Cibber of the second part; Steele's creditors of the third part; and David Scurlock of the fourth part, by which he transferred his share of the patent to Scurlock in trust for his creditors.[101] The actor-managers refused to sign the indenture, justifying their refusal by the provision in the agreement of Sep-

---

[99] *Ibid.*, pp. 183–184.

[100] British Museum, Additional MS 5145C, fols. 132–133. Quoted in Aitken, *Life*, II, 298–299.

[101] Land Registry Office, Entry 1724, 3, 270. Cf. Aitken, *Life*, II, 299–302. This transfer to Scurlock was legally an absolute sale, though Scurlock became obligated to pay Steele's creditors. It was this negotiation to which the author of the Steele article in the *Biographia Brittannica* (London, 1763) must have referred when he wrote: "... about the year following [the production of *The Conscious Lovers*], being reduced to the utmost extremity, he [Steele] sold his share in the Playhouse...."

tember 19, 1721, that no one of the four partners be allowed to part with his share in any way without the written consent of the other three. The managers, Cibber explained, wished to avoid the serious inconvenience of opening their accounts to strangers; but, as Cibber acknowledged, they could not lawfully prevent the indenture from taking effect.[102]

The reason that Steele and Scurlock were not blocked by the managers' refusal may be surmised from records in the Land Registry Office.[103] The indenture of September 19, 1721, prohibiting the transfer of one of the four partners' shares without the consent of the others, was not registered until two weeks *after* Scurlock, on October 7, 1724, registered the indenture of June 3, 1724. Apparently the actor-managers, upon learning what Scurlock had done, took the earlier indenture to the county hall for registration—but not until October 23, 1724. Thus Steele, it appears, was not legally bound by the earlier agreement—an attorney, in fact, informed him that he was not.[104] Cibber maintained, however, that in honor he was.[105]

Late in the summer of 1724 Steele retired permanently from London. He was evidently there in May, June, and possibly July making preparations for his retirement,[106] leaving about the first of August. "Sir *Richard Steele,* Knight, Member of Parliament for *Wendover,* in the County of Bucks," reads a notice in the *British Journal* for August 8, 1724, "went down last Week to his Estate in *Wales.*"

Until the season before Steele's retirement, Drury Lane fortunes had been consistently at a high level, the theater having maintained its popularity over Lincoln's Inn Fields since the early jockeying for position that followed Rich's opening. Frequent complaints appear in prologues and epilogues spoken at Lincoln's Inn Fields about the town's partiality to Drury Lane, a partiality that

[102] *Apology,* II, 201–202.

[103] Land Registry Office, Entry 1724, 3, 270; 1724, 5, 275–276. These records, not previously known to scholars, were called to my attention by Professor Arthur W. Secord.

[104] P.R.O., C11/2416/49 (Steele's deposition of June 23, 1726).

[105] *Apology,* II, 201–202.

[106] *Correspondence,* p. 407n.

seems not to have been noticeably affected even by the lord chamberlain's action of 1720.[107] The critics, it is true, continued their complaints about the actor-managers, insisting, as before the lord chamberlain's intervention, that their tyrannical and arbitrary management of the theater constituted a cultural bottleneck, stifling drama.[108] Caring little about what the critics said, the town, however, crowded to Drury Lane—until December, 1723.

In that month a decisive reversal of Drury Lane–Lincoln's Inn Fields fortunes accompanied the simultaneous runs at the two theaters of similar pantomimes: *Harlequin Doctor Faustus* at Drury Lane and *The Necromancer* at Lincoln's Inn Fields. Gabriel Rennel, an obscure critic, explains what happened:

When their poor Brethren at the New-House, in order to keep themselves from starving, had set up a Raree-Show, and had picked up a little Money by this low Artifice, the Managers of Drury, out of mere Wantonness, and for the Sake of driving the Enemy from this his last Hold, contrived a Raree-Show of their own, that far exceeded the other in Magnificence and Splendor. But their ill-judged Scheme has proved no less foolish than fatal in the Event. For by introducing new and ridiculous Inventions into the Play-House, and by prostituting the Use and Dignity of the Stage, they have brought their Theatre into Contempt; and what is still worse, they have propagated such a vitious Taste for Raree-Shows, through the whole People, that charmed by the superiour Power of the Sorcerer, they are caried away in Throngs to the New-House; whilst the Actors of Drury-Lane perceive such a sensible Decay of Trade, that they talk of shutting up Shop, and of publishing in their next Bills that THIS HOUSE IS TO BE LET.[109]

[107] The epilogue to *The Compromise* (London, 1723) strikes a familiar note:

> "Ev'n You, Gallants, as to our Cost we find,
> Do all we can t'engage; You, too unkind,
> Old Drury's Hundreds have so often trod,
> Are hardly brought to try the other Road;
> But long accustom'd croud this neighbouring Shop,
> Nor seem concern'd should we all Commerce stop. . . ."

[108] Cf. Aaron Hill, preface to *King Henry the Fifth* (London, 1723). Preface to *The Impertinent Lovers* (London, 1723).

[109] *Tragi-Comical Reflections, Of a Moral and Political Tendency, Occasioned by the Present State of the Two Rival Theatres in Drury-Lane and Lincolns-Inn-Fields* (London, 1723), pp. 12–13. A similar account of

Notwithstanding the color of the narrative, this is not far from being an accurate account of how Drury Lane was plunged into a depression by the great success of Lincoln's Inn Fields initiated by *The Necromancer.*[110] The vogue of pantomime, dominated by John Rich as Lun, mounted steadily for the next several years, leaving Drury Lane a poor struggling second in the race for the town's favor.[111] *Pasquin* reported facetiously on February 18, 1724, that Drury Lane's profits had recently been so low, because of the town's preference for the dances at the other theater, that only the managers could afford clean clothes.

So low, in fact, did Drury Lane fortunes droop that Cibber, Wilks, and Booth wrote to Steele on December 12, 1724, suggesting that they sell the patent.[112] Their profits had always been more than double, they reported, to what they had fallen to; and with Lincoln's Inn Fields, the opera, and the prospect also of the little theater in the Haymarket "exhibiting nonsense of different kinds" against them, the managers saw little hope of improvement. There were several wealthy persons, they believed, who would buy their interests in Drury Lane in order to organize it as an academy—in the managers' opinion, the only form in which the English theater could survive. Needing Steele's assistance badly, they urged him to return to London.

The friendly tone of the letter is surprising in view of the current strained relations between Steele and the triumvirate. It is perhaps to be explained by the managers' need for Steele's and Scurlock's concurrence if they sold the patent. Despite the urgency of their letter, however, Steele evidently remained in Wales.

The managers did not take the extreme step of selling the patent; rather they persisted, experiencing in the spring of 1725 some improvement in their fortunes.[113] They frankly entered into rivalry with Rich in pantomimic entertainments, apologizing for

how the reversal in position between the two theaters came about appears in the epilogue to George Jeffreys, *Edwin: A Tragedy* (London, 1724).

[110] Barker, *Cibber*, pp. 138–139.

[111] Cf. M. P. Wells, "Some Notes on the Early Eighteenth-Century Pantomime," *Studies in Philology*, XXXII (1935), 598–607.

[112] *Correspondence*, pp. 184–185.

[113] Barker, *Cibber*, pp. 139–140.

them but nevertheless featuring them. The epilogue to Cibber's *Caesar in Aegypt* (1725) expresses the somewhat superior attitude that marked their efforts:

> —Since then rank Farce is grown a Taste so new,
> No wonder we exhibit Nonsense too!
> And tho' w'are but Beginners there, we'll drudge,
> And entertain as low as Crowds can judge!

Steele in Wales, of course, had nothing to do with this rivalry. However, on September 4, 1725, his relations with Drury Lane were revived when, through his trustee, David Scurlock, he brought suit against the managers to regain the portion of the profits he had lost through the deduction of £5 every acting day.[114] The issues implicit in this suit and in the countersuit have been considered in detail before;[115] it will be enough merely to review the several stages of the litigation. In his initial bill Steele charged that the managers had wrongfully withheld the money and that they refused to state accounts.[116] Cibber, Wilks, and Booth, together with their treasurer Castleman, answered on October 13, 1725, declaring themselves entitled to the money in compensation for their work, Castleman denying that he had refused to allow Steele to examine the company's books, though he failed to answer directly the charge that he had refused Steele's representative. Upon obtaining a court order, an attorney representing Steele then gained access to the books and determined the amount allegedly owed to Steele; whereupon Steele amended his original bill on February 12, 1726, the managers replying on June 15, 1726.

Before this amended bill was presented, however, Wilks, Booth, and Cibber, on January 11, 1726, entered a cross action against Steele,[117] who replied on June 23, 1726. Modifications were made

---

[114] The *British Journal*, on October 9, 1725, under date October 5, included the following notice: "Sir *Richard Steele* hath exhibited a Bill in Chancery against the Masters of *Drury Lane* Theatre, for a Share of the Profits of that House; which he claims by Virtue of a Patent granted him by his Majesty some Years since."

[115] See above, pp. 57–61.

[116] P.R.O., C11/300/38. Aitken summarizes the successive stages of the litigation in *Life*, II, 303–317.

[117] P.R.O., C11/2416/49. Aitken, *Life*, II, 311.

from time to time in the several bills, and finally, on February 17, 1728, the combined suits came to a hearing before Sir Joseph Jekyll, master of the rolls. Cibber himself addressed the court, explaining at length the nature of the duties of a stage manager (a point at issue because it was for the performance of the duties that the managers claimed their deduction).[118]

The court decided in the managers' favor, ruling that the extra compensation to Cibber, Wilks, and Booth was justified and that they were entitled to an allowance for their expenses.[119] The master instructed an officer to examine all the company's books to determine the amounts due to the different parties in conformity with the decision. When the day after he rendered his report, July 11, 1728, the court confirmed his findings, the case was settled. The managers were ordered to pay Scurlock, in trust for Steele, £1,061/17/2 as Steele's share of the back profits exclusive of the deduction allowed the managers; the debt to Woolley, it was ruled, had already been discharged in full from Steele's account. As Steele was not advised to appeal the decision, "both Parties paid their own Costs, and thought it their mutual Interest to let this be the last of their Law-suits."[120]

A little over a year later, on September 1, 1729, Steele died in Carmarthen. Two daughters survived him and inherited his property rights in the theater, though the younger of them died herself a few months later. The managers fulfilled the terms of the agreement drawn up on September 19, 1721, paying Steele's surviving daughter £1,200 for his share in the properties[121] and paying her also the quarter share of the profits for three years, deducting, as

---

[118] Cibber, *Apology*, II, 196–207.

[119] P.R.O., C38/394. Aitken, *Life*, II, 316–317.

[120] Cibber, *Apology*, II, 208.

[121] *Ibid.* II, 175. *Correspondence*, p. 412. John Nichols records, however, that though the money was paid, it was not received by Steele's daughters: "Sir Richard Steele's interest in Drury Lane Theatre became, after his death, the joint property of his two daughters, and on the death of the younger of them, devolved to Elizabeth, the elder, who sold it for no inconsiderable sum. But as if a fatality attended the business, the attorney who received the money for her ran away with the whole, and she never received a penny" (*The Epistolary Correspondence of Sir Richard Steele* [London, 1787], I, 250).

they were permitted to do by court order, their own salaries for
acting and managerial work.[122]

Wilks, Booth, and Cibber were themselves, on May 15, 1731,
granted a patent for a twenty-one-year period commencing September 1, 1732.[123] Inasmuch as the new patent became effective
exactly three years after Steele's death—on the date that his patent
expired—the legality of his patent obviously was recognized. The
lord chamberlain's threats to the contrary, the grant made on January 14, 1715, was never annulled.

5 | Unfinished Plays

IF PROFLIGATE with his money, Steele carefully preserved at least his personal papers—drafts of letters, notes for
pamphlets and essays, memoranda about his literary and financial
projects—many of which have survived to delight students of his
life and writings. John Nichols bought a large collection of the
papers from the Steele family and, after publishing most of them,
bequeathed the original manuscripts to the British Museum; another large collection found its way in an unknown manner to the
muniments room of Blenheim Palace.[124] In both these collections,
which jointly represent the bulk of Steele's extant manuscripts,
there are fragments of plays that Steele left unfinished; in the
Blenheim collection, moreover, there is also a substantial body of

[122] Theophilus Cibber, in explaining why Colley Cibber and Wilks did
not pay Booth's salary while he was unable through illness to perform his
duties, wrote: "The Salary of £1. 13s. 4d. per Diem, which they had
allowed themselves, and was confirmed by a Decree in Chancery, they
could not continue to him on his Absence from the Stage, as the Heirs,
&c. of Sir Richard Steel had a Right to call him and them in an expensive
Law-suit, and obliged him to have refunded every Shilling of it" (The
Lives of The Actors, p. 57n).

[123] Cibber, Apology, II, 257 (supplementary chapter by R. W. Lowe).

[124] Cf. Correspondence, p. 467n.

notes and random jottings for projected plays. Nichols printed
in his second edition of Steele's correspondence (1809) the two
most considerable fragments, *The School of Action* (perhaps a
third of a finished play) and *The Gentleman* (scarcely a scene in
length); Aitken reprinted both in the Mermaid edition of Steele,
adding some but by no means all the Blenheim notes.

These fragments and memoranda, which reveal Steele again
exploiting a number of the themes prominent in his completed
plays and his essays—including, emphatically, the theme of stage
reform—merit attention as a further expression of his dramatic
interest.

By all odds the most important of the fragments, *The School of
Action* [*Acting*] is structurally a descendant of *The Rehearsal* and
an ancestor of *The Critic*, the plot here combining clever scheming to win a lady from an unscrupulous and selfish guardian with
burlesque of stage absurdities. Mr. Severn, a young gentleman educated at one of the Inns of Court, has with the assistance of his
friend Humber, a scholar from Oxford, set up a school of acting.
To the school Severn brings a northern attorney, his wife, niece,
and servants, leading them to believe the school an inn—all, that
is, except the niece, Severn's beloved, who is partly informed of
Severn's plot to frighten the uncle into repenting of his intention
to withhold half of her dowry. The situation thus provides for burlesque of stage business functionally justified as tricks to frighten
the attorney; and enough of the play is completed to reveal the
effectiveness of the design.

Steele worked on the play, it appears, from 1723 until perhaps a
year or so before his death. The *London Journal*, on September
14, 1723,[125] and again on January 4, 1724, reported that it was expected "this Winter"; Steele himself mentioned it in his deposition of June, 1726, emphasizing, in his customary vein, its reform
purpose:

And this deft further saith that he is at this time preparing as fast as his
health will permit a new Comedy which God willing he hopes to finish
by the next season the plot of which Play is formed for the reformation
of the Theatre and restoring the Creditt and good sense of Theatrical
Entertainmts. which he is sadly sensible was never more wanted[.][126]

---

[125] Aitken, *Life*, II, 293.
[126] P.R.O., C11/2416/49.

One of the Blenheim memoranda for the play (in Steele's handwriting) may be tentatively dated by a reference to a newspaper: "Inquire about Mists Journall whether yt writ by Mr. Welsted abt. Doctor Faustus." On January 11, 1724, the *Weekly Journal* (Mist's) carried a long article on the *Doctor Faustus* pantomimes, then attracting attention at both Drury Lane and Lincoln's Inn Fields; presumably Steele made the note within a week or so of that issue—or at least sometime that winter, when the town was excited over *Faustus*. That he was also working on the play during the summer of 1725 is implied by a letter to him from his secretary, William Plaxton, enclosing a copy of Hamlet's "To be or not to be" soliloquy.[127] Steele employed the soliloquy humorously in *The School of Action* at the expense of the Welsh, whose dialect was doubtless all too familiar to him at the time.

When Steele wrote, in 1726, that *The School of Action* was designed to reform the theater and restore the credit and good sense of theatrical entertainments, he had in mind, we may assume from the play itself, not moralistic reform but rather curbing the "non-rational" entertainments then so prominent on the London stage. Unlike *The Conscious Lovers,* the play makes no calculated assault on iniquity, but it does, with the force of sharp satire, attack theatrical performances in which spectacle overshadows good sense. A memorandum at Blenheim, describing some of the episodes Steele planned, makes his burlesque purpose quite clear:

To ridicule ye whole mechanick of Dr Faustus etc wth. all things of that kind for ye. Theatre—make persons to play tricks break necks and the like for ye Theatre let Pinkethman and the other Comedians fall down like Edipus on the Stage. let a woman Image be Thrown down in a Hoop Pettycoat etc.

In the completed part of the play he ridicules fustian in the person of Buskin, a candidate for the stage who cannot recite his lines when stripped of his plumes. Written at a time when spectacle dominated the London theaters, the fragment, we may be sure, was designed as a good-humored plea for return to orthodox drama.[128]

---

[127] *Correspondence,* pp. 185–186.

[128] Formerly among the Blenheim memoranda for *The School of Action* was the following note in Steele's handwriting: "For the Prologue take

The sympathetic portrayal of the problems of theater management in *The School of Action* must certainly derive from Steele's
Drury Lane experience: the point of view and the values are those
of a manager, not of an outside critic. At a time when baiting the
managers was a major preoccupation of theatrical critics, when to
be fashionable one cursed the managers, he expounded dramat-
ically some of their daily, routine problems, laughing not at them
but at the blockheads who made their work trying: the gentleman
who fancied he could act, the gentlewoman of quality who wished
the manager to engage her daughter without seeing the daughter's
face, the actor who was struck dumb when deprived of his feathers.
Severn and Humber settled of a morning, in a manner surely
reminiscent of Drury Lane, "to hear any person or persons that
pretend to the stage, to examine scenes or goods to be shown or
exhibited there, and to give them their answers."

As always in his writings, Steele defended the profession of
acting, insisting at once on its dignity and difficulty. "It is won-
drous to consider the folly of mankind," observes Humber, "that
think so lightly and so meanly of the faculties of a player.—
Roscius had three thousand scholars, and but one only fit for the
purpose." Making the same point ironically, with a glance at the
multitude of his contemporaries who disagreed with him, Steele
explains through the mouth of his bumptious northern lawyer
that stage players are mere animals and lawful game, "and any man
that has so much a year may kill them."

There are other familiar themes in *The School of Action*—in
the memoranda as well as in the published part. Mrs. Umbrage
(an actress) expresses Mr. Spectator's views on the proper subordination of music to poetry; Severn, his conviction that public
shows are a chief formative influence on the behavior of a people;[129]

---

notice of this play as a *Posthumous Work* according to Dr. Partridge's
Friends". Also at Blenheim was a part of a prologue (not in Steele's handwriting) apparently intended for the play, but in its fragmentary condition
it reveals nothing of the intended attribution to Partridge. The original
manuscripts are inaccessible, having been removed from Blenheim, but
Aitken's transcripts of them are in the University of Texas Library.
[129] Blenheim MSS.

Humber closes the third act with an epigram that might well have
been lifted from *The Conscious Lovers:*

> Would you reform an heedless guilty age,
> Adorn with virtuous characters the stage.

It is precisely in the "virtuous characters," notably in the two
chief young men, that the fragment betrays most clearly its
kinship with Steele's other comedies. Though not so oppressively
virtuous as Bevil, Jr., Severn and Humber are thoroughly admirable young gentlemen benevolently aware of the misfortunes
of others and sensitive to nice discriminations of honor. Humber
is unwilling to second Severn's design to win Dolly until he satis-
fies himself that there is nothing dishonorable in it, nothing that
might injure Dolly. The two are much such a pair as Lord Hardy
and Campley in *The Funeral*, gay—one more than the other—
but not wanton.

In describing the pair, however, Steele seems to have had in
mind closer models than Hardy and Campley: Addison and himself—idealized to be sure, and by no means completely realized,
but recognizable in outline. Severn is the impetuous young man
about town; Humber, the scholar who has studied eloquence
till he is dumb. Were the resemblance merely that, it would, of
course, be commonplace and inconclusive. At the beginning of
the third act, however, there is a dialogue that parallels closely
Steele's famous description in the *Theatre* of the friendship, com-
patible with strong differences in personality, between himself and
Addison. The passages require quotation. First, from the *Theatre*,
No. 12:

There never was a more strict friendship than between those Gentlemen; nor had they ever any difference but what proceeded from their
different way of pursuing the same thing. The one with patience, fore-
sight, and temperate address, always waited and stemmed the torrent;
while the other often plunged himself into it, and was as often taken out
by the temper of him who stood weeping on the brink for his safety,
whom he could not dissuade from leaping into it. Thus these two men
lived for some years last past, shunning each other, but still preserving the
most passionate concern for their mutual welfare. But when they met,
they were as unreserved as boys, and talked of the greatest affairs, upon
which they saw where they differed, without pressing (what they knew
impossible) to convert each other.

Now, Severn and Humber, from *The School of Action:*

Sev. I have often begged you to let me shift for myself, let my character sink or swim. Every man who attempts any new thing must allow mankind to talk of him as they please. I do not regard what the world says, but what they should say.

Hum. It is very odd that we have never happy moments but at midnight, so different are our tempers; and we are made to keep together from no other rule, but that we never expostulate upon past mistakes; to meet again after a misunderstanding, contains in itself all manner of apology, all expostulation. . . .

Have we not Steele and Addison here frankly acknowledging their differences? The contrast in the personalities described is the most obvious resemblance between the two passages, but there are at least two similarities of detail: the metaphor of swimming and the manner of avoiding differences. To insist that Severn is consistently Steele and Humber Addison would be folly, but it does not seem too much to insist that Steele consciously derived his conception of the complementary personalities from the already famous partnership of which he was a member.

The promise of *The School of Action* is substantial: the fragment is humorous and it has point. It would not have followed the sober and patently didactic vein of *The Lying Lover* and *The Conscious Lovers,* but rather would have returned to the laughing temper of *The Funeral* and *The Tender Husband,* providing, even more than those plays, an abundance of farcical situations. Steele persisted, it appears, in a regular alternation of the moods of his comedies.

Among the Steele papers at Blenheim there is a manuscript plan for a play that (so far as I know) has never been described. Aitken's personal papers in the University of Texas Library reveal that he saw it, but he apparently did not consider it Steele's: at the top of his transcription of it he wrote *"Memorandum* for Play (not Steele's)," meaning, according to his usual notation, that the original manuscript at Blenheim is not in Steele's handwriting. Were it not for Aitken's authoritative statement to the contrary, I would assume, from an examination of the manuscript, that it is in Steele's handwriting—the matter will be decided positively only when the Blenheim papers become more easily accessible—but handwriting apart, there is strong internal evidence that the plan was Steele's own.

Since the manuscript has never been published, it will be appropriate to quote from it at length:

Let Mr. Severn Come to the Bath with his pockett full of Bank Bills to the Value of 2000 £ to pretend himself Deaf & Dumb. To come unattended and unacquainted wth a recommendation to an apothecary who' is to provide him with Every Thing and know his Fund of Money. Equipp him with Servts. and all other kind of Necessaries as well as Doctors etc.

Let there be a Consultation of physitians About his hearing & dumbness. The practise and Iniquity of his Servts.

He is in Love with Lady Mary and She with him. She taulks wth him upon his Fingers and not knowing that he heres her not wth ten thousand Languishing things besides.

There is a Table of Gamesters at Hazard wth all the Humours and Blasphemies of that Game. In the Intervals of that Game at wch. Severn and Lady Mary are lookers on and Speak in opposition to the Distraction of Gamesters the fine & tender passion & sentiments of Lovers. . . .

Mr. Afterday an old Rake Carried about in his Chair and placed among the Woemen full of desire and Impotence wth Ketches of Gout and Stone in the midst of the flashes of pleasure. . . .

Prosper a Soniteere take his Character out of The Spectator.

Harrisons room Commending it wth. a design of the Walks etc. Comparing them to the Structures of the old romans made & given to the people. The Bath it self. The Town of Venus made & formed for Love and Luxury wth. all ye Calls upon Humanity and Admonitions to the rich by beholding all the decreeped from all distresses and diseases to administer Comfort to their Fellow Creatures, wch is an Emminent Inclination to ye Heroe & Heroein of the play. Querey [wd.?]

Mr. Stormwell who by his Naturall qualities Experience of the World and despiseing the practise of Modesty and the like Arts makes himself Gouvernor of Bathe. . . . Stormwell to profess to Severn that he likes his Method that himself was the something as deaf & dumb by an University Bashfulness. . . .

The conception of characters, themes, sentiments, and situations evident in these notes bears, I believe it will be readily agreed, a strong family resemblance to that in Steele's known writings. To be more specific: Steele himself was at the Bath for his health in the fall and winter of 1723 and hence might be presumed to have an especial interest in it. At that time he was working on *The School of Action,* in which the chief character has the name Severn, here assigned to the gentleman feigning deafness; indeed, the leading character of the shorter fragment that Nichols printed (*The Gentleman*) has the same name, as has also a character in the *Lover* (1714). The memorandum, moreover, calls for a character ("Prosper a Soniteere") to be taken from the *Spectator*—presumptive evidence that the author considered the periodical his literary property (we recall that Tom and Phillis appeared first in the *Guardian*). These considerations, coupled with the fact of the memorandum's presence among his personal papers, can leave little doubt that the plan was Steele's, whether it exists in his handwriting or in the transcription of an amanuensis.

He envisioned, it seems, a comedy that, in the manner of the *Tatler,* would bring social vices—gaming, lechery, vanity—under a laughing censure, the satire to be accompanied by a warm-hearted but amusing love intrigue complicated by the feigned deafness.

The shorter fragment printed by Nichols and in turn by Aitken bears the title *The Gentleman,* assigned, according to Aitken, by Nichols himself.[130] Aitken, however, is surely mistaken. In the brief biography of Steele that appeared in the *New Political State of Great Britain* for January, 1731, little more than a year after his death, the title appears: "Sir *Richard Steele* had another Play, almost finished, founded upon the Eunuch of *Terence,* which he intended to call *The Gentleman.*" Similarly in the *Biographia Brittanica* (1763): "Among his papers were found the MSS. of two plays; one called *The Gentleman,* founded upon *The Eunuch of Terence;* and the other intituled *The School of Action;* both nearly finished." Though seemingly accurate as to titles, this writer was mistaken about the plays' being almost finished unless large parts of the manuscripts disappeared before John Nichols's time—which seems unlikely in view of the care with which the papers were transmitted.

Whether or not Steele himself intended to use the title *The Gentleman* it is impossible to say. There is no such uncertainty,

---

[130] Aitken, *Life,* II, 293.

however, about the tradition that he used *The Eunuch* as his model. The *London Post,* September 25–27, 1723, reported that among other new plays expected was "a Comedy founded on the Plot of Terence's Eunuch, by Sir Richard Steele." The fragment printed by Nichols, to be sure, bears no resemblance to the Latin play beyond the fact that, like the Latin play, it deals with the pranks of servants: the fragment is a dramatic version of the *Spectator,* No. 88, on servants imitating their masters. Among the Blenheim papers, however, there is still another fragment—and a very witty one—in which the two speakers bear the names of two of the servants in *The Eunuch,* Parmeno and Pythias, the theme of their dialogue being also servants imitating their masters —this time in matters of love. Hence we may surmise that the fragment Nichols printed and the Parmeno-Pythias fragment preserved at Blenheim were intended as parts of the same play, the names not having been Anglicized in the latter. The theme of master-servant relations was, of course, a favorite with Steele. It appears, in varied forms, in *The Funeral,* in the periodicals, in *The Conscious Lovers* (Tom and Phillis), in the notes for the Bath play, and finally in this fragment.

Such, then, are the records of projected plays that Steele did not complete. Probably he planned others—a lawsuit with Christopher Rich resulted in 1707 from a promise Steele made in 1702 or 1703 to supply him with a comedy called *The Election at Gotham.*[181] Whether or not he wrote any of it is unknown: no part of it appears to have survived. A man of multitudinous projects, Steele not unnaturally found the planning of plays easier than the execution.

[181] *Ibid.,* I, 111–123.

Conclusion

THE BORDER LINE between disinterested concern for the advancement of the public good, on the one hand, and selfish opportunism, on the other, is, to say the least, indistinct in Steele's career. Few men have written more about reform than Steele; indeed, if the many testimonials of his contemporaries are to be credited, few literary men have been more effective reformers than he. Yet when records of his association with Drury Lane are closely examined, it is difficult to say in many instances whether he was activated by concern for improvement in drama or by a desire to wring an extra pound from his Drury Lane connection. However, there is no such uncertainty about his accomplishments. Whatever his motives may have been, he certainly did not solve the problem of stage regulation, so troublesome to the government in the early eighteenth century.

Steele's motives, I surmise, were mixed and unsure in his own mind. He seems to have been capable of an unusual degree of self-deception; he had unquestionably a rare capacity for rationalization. Many of the papers of the *Theatre* exhibit a tone of self-righteousness at once repugnant and unconvincing to a reader who has any knowledge of his Drury Lane affairs. His career at Drury Lane was not marked by a bold, energetic administrative effort to reanimate the drama; it was not marked even by the dubious virtue of a rigid, moralistic censorship. When he insisted in the *Theatre* that he had performed his duty as patentee, he seems to have forgotten the bold promises he had made in the *Town Talk*. And when he insisted, in opposition to the lord chamberlain, on his personal authority in the playhouse, he was apparently untroubled by the fact that he had come perilously near to selling his share in the patent. From the contradictions emerges a picture of a man who, possessing strong and frequently conflicting interests in dramatic reform, politics, and his personal fortune, lacked the intellectual integrity necessary to differentiate between the motives that impelled him to undertake a given course of action.

It is then of intellectual dishonesty in evaluating and directing his activities at Drury Lane of which Steele may be accused; not, I believe, of any lack of sincerity in his desire for dramatic reform. The consistency and force of his campaign in support of exemplary comedy—in critical essays and ultimately in *The Conscious Lovers*—are impressive. From the vigorous days of the *Tatler* to the twilight of his prosperity in the success of *The Conscious Lovers,* he campaigned in his writings for the new theory of comedy. It might indeed be argued that it was the intensity of his desire for improvement in the moral tone of comedy that betrayed him into the sacrifice of the traditional merits of comedy to a sober and unenlightening piety.

The record of Steele at Drury Lane has been largely a record of quarrels—with Newcastle, with the critics of *The Conscious Lovers,* and with the actor-managers. The genial, convivial Steele of the coffeehouses—the appealing figure who has won a place in the popular imagination—has had little place here, having been crowded out by the quarrelsome man Steele became after his good humor was soured by age, sickness, political reverses, and comparative poverty. Yet in the very vehemence of the quarrels he aroused—notably those with the lord chamberlain and with the critics of his play—something of his importance can be seen. The articulation he gave to contemporary views on stage government and on exemplary comedy by his disputes are a tribute, if not to his good humor, at least to his rare degree of personal forcefulness.

Appendix | Unpublished Documents Relating to Steele's Theatrical Career

[Opinion rendered by E. Northey and N. Lechmere, January 12, 1714/15, on Steele's petition for a theatrical patent. P.R.O., L.C. 7/3.]

Attorney & Solicitor Generals Opinion upon Mr. Steeles' Petition

1714

May it please your most Excellt Matie

In humble Obedience to your Majestys Comands Signified to us by the Lord Viscount Townshend We have considered of the annext Petition of Richard Steel Esqr. Whereby he Reprsents to yor. Matie That the Use of ye. Theatre has for many Years last past been much perverted to the Great Scandall of Religion & good Government That it will require much Time to Remedy so inveterate an Evill & will expose the Undertaker to much Envy and Opposition That he has duly Considered the prmisses & doubts not but he shall be able to Act therein to yor. Matys Satisfaccon. But yt an Affair of this Nature cannot be accomplished wth. out a Lasting Authority & therefore in Lein of the prsent Licence granted by your Matie to yor. petr. & Robt. Wilkes Colly Cibber Thos. Doggett & Barton Booth to reform & Establish a Company for yor. Matys Service during yor. Matys pleasure He humbly prays yor. Matie will Graciously please to Grant him yor. Letters patents for Forming a Company of Comedians for the Service of yor. Matie during the petitioners natural Life & for three years.

And we do most humbly Certifie Your Matie That the Reformation of the Stage proposed by the petr. is very desirable for the Sake of Religion & good manners, & if effected will very much Tend to ye Honour of yor. Matys Government. And we do further Certifie yor. Matie That the sd. Wilks Cibber & Booth have signified their Consent to the petrs. Desire in the manner annext And yt. yor. Maty may lawfully Grant to the petitioner yor. Lres patents for the purposes aforesd. for his Life & for 3 years afterwds. Subject to such Regulations as have been Usual in Grants of ye like Nature.

All which &c.

E. Northey

N. Lechmere

12: Jan. 1714

[The royal warrant, issued January 14, 1714/15, authorizing the attorney or solicitor general to prepare Steele's theatrical patent. P.R.O., L.C. 7/3.]

Copy of Mr. Steele's Grant to form a Company of Comedians 1714

GEORGE R.

Whereas Our Trusty and Welbeloved Richard Steele Esqr. hath by his Petition humbly represented unto Us, that the use of the Theatre has for many years last past been much perverted to the great Scandal of Religion and good Government, and that it will require much time to remedy so inveterate an Evil, and will expose the Undertaker to much Envy and Opposition; that he has duely considered the Premises, and doubts not but he Shall be able to act therein to Our Satisfaction, but that an Affair of this Nature cannot be accomplished without a lasting Authority, & therefore in lieu of the present Lycence granted by us to him and Robert Wilks, Colly Cibber, Thomas Dogget and Barton Booth to form and establish a Company of Comedians for Our Service during Our Pleasure. He humbly prays us to grant him Our Letters Patents for forming a company of Comedians for Our Service during the Term of his Natural Life, and for three Years after his Death, which Petition having been referred to you Our Attorney or Sollicitor General for your Consideration and Opinion, you have thereupon reported unto Us that the Reformation of the Stage proposed by the Said Richard Steele is very desirable for the Sake of Religion and good Manners, and, if effected will very much tend to the Honour of Our Governmt., That the Said Robert Wilkes, Colly Cibber and—Barton Booth have Signed their Consent to the Petitr's desire, provided that the Authority of the Said Patents be not participated by or assigned—to any other Persons than those Named in Our present Licence; and that you are humbly of Opinion that We may lawfully grant to the Said Richard Steele Our Letters Patents for the Purposes aforesaid for his Life, and for three Years afterwards, subject to Such Regulations as have been usual in Grants of the like Nature. We taking the Premises into our Royl. Consideration are graciously pleased to gratify the Petitr in his Request; And accordingly Our Will and Pleasure is, that you prepare a Bill for Our Royal—Signature to pass Our Great Seal for granting unto Our Trusty & Welbeloved Richard Steele full Power, Lycence & authority together together [sic] form, entertain, govern, privilege and keep a company of Comedians for Our Service to exercise and act Tragedies, Comedies, Plays, Operas, and other Performances of the Stage within the House in Drury Lane, wherein he and the other Persons named in Our Licence—beforementioned do now exercise the Premisses, or within any other House built or to be built, where he or they can best be fitted for that Purpose, within Our Citys of London & Westmr. or the Suburbs thereof. which Said Company shall be our Servants and be stiled Our Royal Company of Comedians and Shall consist of Such Number as the Said Richard Steele, His Heirs or Assigns shall from time to time think meet; and such Persons to be permitted and continued at and during the Pleasure of the Said Richard Steele, his Heirs and Assigns from time to time, to act Plays and Entertainments of the Stage of all Sorts, peaceably and quietly, without the Impeachment or Impediment of any Person or Persons whatsoever for the honest Recreation of Such as Shall desire to see the Same with Power to the Said Richard Steele his Heirs and Assigns, to take and receive of such Our Subjects as shall resort to see or hear any Such Plays, Scenes and Entertainments whatsoever Such Sum or Sums of mony as have been usual or shall be thought reasonable by him or them, in regard of the great Expenses he or they may be at for Scenes, Musick, or—Decorations; and to make Such allowances to the Actors and other Persons imployed in Acting, representing or in any Quality whatsoever about the Said Theatre or any other Theatre or House to be used by him or them for the Purposes aforesaid as he or they—shall think fit; And Our Pleasure is, that the Said Companys shall be under the sole Government and Authority of him the said Richard Steele, his Heirs and Assigns, and that Our Said Grant shall continue to him and them for and during the Term of his Natural Life, and for three Years after his Death. And you are to insert in the Said Bill all Such Powers, Authoritys, Clauses, Regulations and Provisoes as have been usual in Grants of the like Nature, and as you shall think necessary in this behalf. And for so doing this shall be your Warrt. Given at Our Court at St. James's the 14th Day of Janry 1714/15 in the First Year of Our Reign.

By His Maj ty's Command
Townshend

To Our Attorney or
Sollicitor General

[Opinion rendered by Thomas Pengelly and Jo Cheshire, January 20, 1719/20, respecting the course of action to be followed by the lord chamberlain in excluding Steele from Drury Lane Theatre. P.R.O., S.P. 35, vol. lxxiv, No. 43(5).]

Nous avons examiné les lettres Patentes de sa Majesté sous le Grand leau accordées au Chevalier Richard Steele et à ses Executeurs et administrateurs—ayant cause et autres à qui il cedera ses droits pour l'entiere conduite de gouvernement du Theatre de Drury-Lane sa vie durant et trois ans mois après sa mort, Comme aussi certains articles et conventions faites entre le Chevalier Richard Steele, Robert Wilks, Colley Cibber, et Barton Booth pour les introduire et admettre dans la conduite et direction du dit Theatre, et pour y assujetir la troupe de Comediens aux Regles et Directions à la pluralité des voix de ces quatre Personnes; outre cela, une Permission de la Majté. contresignée par la Grandeur le feu Duc de Shrewsbury lorsqu'il étoit Chambellan, accordée au Chevalier Richard Steele et aux Sieurs Robert Wilks, Colley Cibber, et Thomas Dogget, (: qui precede les susdittes lettres Patentes:) par laquelle ils sont chargés du soin et de la Conduite de la Troupe de Comediens de la Majté. sous les ordres de celui, qui sera alors Chambellan de la Maison; et ayans aussi été informée de la mauvaise Conduite, et des abus commis sous l'ombre des dites lettres Patentes, avec toute la soumission possible notre opinion est que de telles lettres Patentes accordees de la Maniere susditte, et contenant un pouvoir extraordinaire,/: lequel nous concievons n'etre pas conforme aux lois:/ ne suffisent pas pour exclüir et empecher sa Majesté d'accorder sa permission Royale a telles Personnes, que sa Majesté jugera capables d'avoir le soin et la conduite d'une Troupe de Comediens pour son service, suivant les ordres et sa Direction du Lord-Chambellan de la Maison de Sa Majté comme il a eté pratiqué et observé jusque à ce que les susdittes lettres Pattentes eussent eté accordées. Et pour mieux reformer et regler la conduite des Personnes on permettra à l'avenir de representer des Comedies, avec toute humilité nous conseillons et recommendons que le Revocation de la Permission susmentionée qui doit etre donnée au Chevalier Richard Steele et autres, soit en premier bien executée selon la forme usitée et leurs lois notifié en donnant à Wilks—Cibber et Booth des veritables copies de la dite Revocation, et en meme tems leur en montrer l'original, et delivrer, et laisser à l'un d'eux une autre Copie pour le Chevalier Richard Steele; apres quoi la Grandeur My Lord Chambellan suivant les ordres de Sa Majesté peux par un ordre signé de la forme ordinaire imposer silence aux dittes differentes Personnes, et leur ordonner de cesser de representer des Comedies etc. Ce qui etant notifié et fait, comme il s'est pratiqué autrefois. Sa majesté peut donner une nouvelle Permission de la maniere susmentionée à ceux qui seront approuver avec les ordres et les Regles, qui leur seront presentes par my Lord Chambellan pour leur conduite future comme il sera trouvé convenable et necessaire. Et si aucun des presens Directeurs ou Acteurs presume non obstant l'ordre qui leur impose silence, et cette nouvelle silence de representer des Pieces sur la representation qui sera faite à My Lord Chambellan la Dejuns ordonnera de prendre telles mesures que la Grandeur jugera suivant les circonstances de l'affaire les plus propres et les plus efficaces pour les reduire à le soumettre conformement aux Lois.

le 20 Janvier 1719
Tho. Pengelly Jo Cheshire

[The lord chamberlain's order to Drury Lane Theatre, issued December 4, 1721, concerning the transfer of actors to other companies. P.R.O., L.C. 7/3.]

Ordrs. to the Theatre in Drury Lane

Whereas I have thought fit for the better Encouragmt. of his Majts. Company of Comedians Acting in Drury Lane, not to allow any of The Actrs. etca. to hire themselves into any other Company. These are therefore Strictly to require You the Manag.rs. of the sd Company of Comedians not to permit any Actr. etca. to hire themselves into any other Company wth. out a discharge first had under the hand or hands of you the sd. Managers and Approv'd of by me as you will Answr. the Contrary at your perill. Given under my hand & Seal this [Breaks off here; dated December 4, 1721, in the Lord Chamberlain's Warrant Book (P.R.O., L.C. 5/158).]

[The lord chamberlain's order to John Rich, issued December 24, 1721, concerning the hiring of Drury Lane actors. P.R.O., L.C. 7/3.]

Orders to the Manager of the Company of Comedians in Lincolns Inn Fields. 1721.

Whereas I have Established the Play House in Drury Lane upon a foot to enable them to Support themselves, and provide for the Entertainment of the Town. And being resolved to continue them under the same Regulations by not Allowing their Players Etca. to be hir'd by any other Company which may Occasion great disorders in the House. These are therefore Strictly to Charge and Require You not to receive, treat, or Agree with any Player, Singer, or Dancer &ca. who is at present in the Service of His Matys. Company of Comedians Acting in Drury Lane, without a Discharge first had under the hand, or hands of the Managers of the said Company and approved of by me, as you will answer the contrary at Your Perill. Given under my hand and Seal this   day of   1721 [sic] in the Eighth Year of His Matys. Reign.

To Mr. Rich Manager of
The Company of Comedians
acting in Lincolns Inn
Fields

[Dated December 24, 1721, in the Lord Chamberlain's Warrant Book (P.R.O., L.C. 5/158).]

Index

Academies: Continental, 99–102, 114, 118; English, 99, 101–102. *See also* Censorium

Academy of Poetry and Music, Baïf's, 100–101. *See also* Academies; Baïf, Jean Antoine de; Censorium

Actor-managers: administered oath of obedience, 152, 170; avarice, 80, 86, 122, 164; complaints against, 72–73, 76–78, 80–82, 86, 121–122, 145, 153, 160, 163, 164–165, 168, 208, 220, 222, 225–227; disaccord with Steele, 56–61, 213–214, 218–222, 224–225, 228–230; friction with lord chamberlain, 121, 122–123, 124–126, 131–149, 152–154; reduction of Steele's profits, 56–57, 92, 213–216, 221, 228–230; sharing of profits, 56, 91, 92, 93 n. 94, 94, 95, 133, 146, 158, 177, 194, 214–217, 218–221, 224–225, 228–230; Steele's relations with, 35, 36, 37, 38, 55–78, 92, 131, 146–148, 213–225, 227–230; Steele's terms of contract with, 56–59, 216–217; supervision by lord chamberlain, 151–154, 158, 168, 170, 173, 214; treatment of playwrights, 69–71, 80–83, 84–86, 122, 133–135, 153–154, 163, 220

Actors: desertion of Drury Lane, 42–43, 64, 217–218, 220, 247–248; status, 22–23, 66, 162, 164, 233; Steele's espousal, 22–23, 66, 162, 164, 233

Addison, Joseph, 1, 11, 21, 51, 69, 71, 72, 82, 84, 90, 91, 102, 109, 125 n. 10, 128, 129, 131–132, 168, 184, 200, 234–235

Afterpieces, musical, 67, 83–84, 88, 122

Aitken, George A., 191, 215, 235, 237

Alexander's Feast (Dryden), 102, 103

All for Love (Dryden), 55

Andria, The (Terence), 186, 192, 200, 206, 207

Anne, Queen, 2, 11, 12, 13, 25, 26, 27, 28, 30, 32, 33, 35, 40, 41, 42, 106, 128, 141, 150, 185

Answer to a Whimsical Pamphlet, An, 165

Anti-Theatre, 77, 79, 133 n. 25, 169–173, 197

Apollo and Daphne (Hughes), 68–69

Apology (Steele). See *Mr. Steele's Apology*

Apology for the Life of Mr. Colley Cibber, An, 33, 58–59, 60, 74–75, 143–144 n. 53, 216

Applebee's Original Weekly Journal, 113–115, 142, 166, 175–177, 190

Arbuthnot, Dr. John, 72, 80

Argyle, John Campbell, second Duke of, 138

Arlequin Columbine, 62

Arlequin Devin, 62

Arlequin Invisible Chez le Roi de la Chine, 62

Arlequin Mahomet, 62

Arsinoe, 102–103. See also Opera

Artlove, Sir Andrew, 166–167, 175, 177. See also *Applebee's Original Weekly Journal*

Baïf, Jean Antoine de, 99–101, 112. See also Academies

Battle of the Authors, The, 142–143, 168

Baron, Mme, 62

Baxter, Mr., 61–63, 83

Beaumont, Francis, 82, 90

Beaux' Stratagem, The (Farquhar), 91, 125

Bedford, Duke of, 39–40

Berkeley, George, 31, 33, 100, 105–106, 107, 108, 186, 189

Betterton, Thomas, 22–23

Bevil, Jr. (*The Conscious Lovers*), 18, 19, 183, 184, 185–186, 187–188, 194, 196, 201–202, 207, 208, 209, 211, 234

Bickerstaff, Isaac, 3, 5, 162, 186–187, 188–189, 191 n. 21

Blackmore, Sir Richard, 4–5, 13, 14

Blanchard, Rae, 105, 106, 189, 215

Blenheim collection of Steele MSS, 230–231, 232, 235–236, 238

Bolingbroke, Henry St. John, first Viscount, 28

Bolton, Charles Paulet, second Duke of, 122–123, 125, 126, 138 n. 39

Bookwit, Young (*The Lying Lover*), 19, 199

Booth, Barton, 29, 33, 34, 40, 41, 43, 44, 45, 50, 58, 59, 68, 70–71, 79, 86, 133, 134, 135, 136, 137, 139, 140, 142, 146, 147, 152, 166, 213, 214, 215, 217, 218–219, 221 n. 89, 224, 227, 228–229, 230, 243, 244, 246

Brereton, Thomas, 14

Busiris (Young), 85, 154 n. 73

Button's Coffee-house, 71–72, 75

Caesar in Aegypt (Cibber), 228

Camply (*The Funeral*), 19, 234

Careless Husband, The (Cibber), 91, 171, 186–187, 197–198, 207

Caroline, Princess, 223–224

Caryll, John, 71, 104, 105

Castleman, Richard, 94, 95, 220, 228

Cato (Addison), 21, 71, 91

Censor Censured, The, 211–212

Censorium: antecedents, 99–102; beginnings, 98, 102–108; bipartisan support, 106–108; expense, 106, 109, 110, 117; explanation of name, 110 n. 139; medal coined for, 100, 109, 110; meetings, 107, 108–110, 113, 115, 117; membership, 99, 100, 101, 105, 108, 110–112, 116; satire on, 113–115, 175; scope, 65, 99–101, 102–103, 105, 106, 108–111; success, 112, 117–118; termination, 117–118. See also Academies; York Buildings

Censorship. See Stage

Characters and Conduct of Sir John Edgar, The (Dennis), 163–165, 168–169, 210

Charles II, 3, 6, 24, 41, 46, 179–180

Cheshire, Jo, 127 n. 13, 138 n. 39, 139, 145, 146, 246–247
Chit-Chat, 66, 111, 112
Cibber, Colley: critical views, 67–69; defense of Steele, 131–132; dispute with Newcastle, 131–132, 134–135; disputes with Steele, 58, 146–147, 192, 215–217, 219–220, 224–225; operatic criticism, 67–69; personality, 80, 86, 122, 175; praise of Steele, 59–60, 131–132; reinstatement, 137, 147; silencing, 131, 135, 137, 178, 179
Cibber, Theophilus, 74, 192, 230 n. 122
Clare, Earl of. See Newcastle, Duke of
Clayton, Mrs. Charlotte, 223–224
Clayton, Thomas, 102–106, 112. See also Censorium
Cleland, William, 38
Collier, Jeremy, 1, 7, 14–25, 47, 65, 204
Collier, William, 33, 35, 37, 39–40, 43, 89, 141
Comedy: characters appropriate, 17–19, 21–22, 24, 47, 65, 167, 183, 186, 187, 188, 191, 193, 196, 198–203, 204–205, 206, 208–209, 212, 234; didactic purpose, 4, 19, 23, 25, 183, 186, 199, 202, 205, 209, 212, 235; exemplary, 4, 6, 25, 47, 186, 188–189, 193, 196–197, 198–203, 204–205, 206, 207, 210–211, 234, 240; "fine gentleman" in, 17–18, 24, 47, 65, 82, 183, 193, 198–199, 203; laughter-provoking, 18–20, 65, 198–200, 201, 204–205, 206, 207, 209–211; moral influence, 15, 16, 17, 18–22, 65, 82, 167, 183, 187, 188–189, 196, 198, 199, 202, 203, 204,

208–209, 212–213, 234, 240; pathetic incident in, 20, 196–201, 205, 206, 207, 209–211, 212; Restoration, 6, 17, 18, 19, 23, 24, 65, 82, 87, 183, 196, 197, 198, 202; satiric, 6, 7, 18, 19, 24, 183, 193, 198, 204, 236, 237; sentimental, 196–201, 212
Commons, House of, 13, 27, 32, 107, 128–129, 138, 150, 151
Companies, theatrical. See Drury Lane; Haymarket; Lincoln's Inn Fields
Congreve, William, 7, 14, 90, 197, 202
Conscious Lovers, The (Steele): characterization in, 183, 184, 186, 188, 191, 193, 196, 198–203, 205, 206, 207, 209, 210–211, 212, 234, 240; controversy over, 19, 187–188, 195–213, 240; didactic purpose, 183, 186, 188–189, 202, 203, 208, 209, 212–213, 223, 234, 235, 240; genesis, 183–193; novelty, 6, 18, 87, 189, 193, 195–196, 212; pathos in, 196–201, 205, 206, 207, 209–211, 212; sources, 183–186, 188–189, 191–193, 200–201, 206, 207, 211; Steele's publicity campaign for, 18, 19, 25, 183–193, 194, 195–196, 202, 203, 204, 211; success, 193–195, 212, 240
Constant Couple, The (Farquhar), 23, 91
Coriolanus (Shakespeare-Dennis), 70–71, 134
Corneille, Pierre, 19
Country Wife, The (Wycherley), 23, 63, 77, 79, 83, 91
Courville, Joachim Thibault de, 101. See also Academies; Censorium

Coverley, Sir Roger de, 11
Cowper, Mary Countess, 13–14
Cowper, William, first Earl, 46
Craggs, James, Jr., 130–131, 138, 155
Crisis, The, 12
Crisis of Honesty, The, 77, 79, 173
Crisis of Property, The (Steele), 150, 173
Critic, The (Sheridan), 231
Critick no wit, A, 163
Crowne, John, 90

Daily Courant, 63, 83, 87, 112, 117
Davenant, Henry, 220
D'Avenant, Sir William, 6, 41, 46, 48, 99, 101, 126, 141, 141 n. 48, 178–179
Dawson, Paul, 113
Death of Dido, The (Booth), 68
Defence of Sir Fopling Flutter, A (Dennis), 194–195, 198, 204–205, 208, 210
Defoe, Daniel, 15–16, 21, 168
Dennis, John: attack on The Conscious Lovers, 187–188, 194–195, 196, 198, 201, 202, 203–206, 208, 209–211; controversy with Drury Lane managers, 133–135, 163, 166; dispute with Steele, 163–169, 175, 210
Desaguliers, John Theophilus, 111, 113
Dieupart, Charles, 102, 104
Dione (Gay), 153
Dissembled Wanton, The (Welsted), 187 n. 7
Distressed Mother, The (A. Philips), 71
Doggett, Thomas, 23, 33, 34, 38, 39 n. 63, 40–41, 45, 56, 89, 92 n. 90, 94, 140, 216, 219, 243, 244, 246

Dorimant (The Man of Mode), 17–18, 24, 196, 202, 203, 207, 208
Drake, James, 204
Drama. See Comedy; Stage; Tragedy
Drummer, The (Addison), 69–70, 87
Drury Lane: audiences, 39, 42, 80, 82, 122, 165, 226–227; competition with other theaters, 6, 39, 41–43, 61–64, 67–69, 78, 83–84, 85, 87–90, 132, 165, 217–218, 225–228; defection of actors, 42–43, 64, 217–218, 220, 247–248; friction with lord chamberlain, 43–44, 48–50, 55, 66–67, 75, 98, 114, 121, 122–126, 130–149, 151, 152–154, 162, 168; improved by actor-managers, 34–35; legal disputes, 39–41, 57–60, 96–98, 216–217, 218–221, 224–225, 228–229; managerial policies, 2, 57, 61–64, 67–69, 69–73, 75, 78, 82–88, 90–91, 152–153, 226–228; possible offer to Steele by Tories, 25–33, 106; profits, 34, 36, 39, 42, 43, 87, 91, 92, 95, 225, 227; prosperity, 34–35, 39, 57, 61, 74, 82, 86, 88–89, 92, 122, 132, 146, 162, 165, 225–226; repertory, 66, 69–73, 78, 79, 80–89, 90–91, 122, 152, 153–154, 220, 226–228; sharing of profits, 5, 33–34, 36, 37, 40–41, 43, 47–48, 91, 92, 94, 95, 133, 146, 158, 177, 213, 214–217, 218–221, 224–225, 228–230; silencing, 137, 144–145, 147; stage properties, 40–41, 48, 49–50, 94, 97, 121, 148, 151, 221; Steele's neglect, 57–59, 61, 75–78, 79, 80, 97–98, 213–215, 219–220; Steele's participation in management, 55, 61–76, 97–98,

213, 217–218; Steele reinstated in governorship, 56, 155, 157, 158, 174, 183, 213, 214, 216–217; Steele's services to, 57, 58, 59–61, 63–66, 214, 217–218; supervision by lord chamberlain, 140, 151, 152–154, 158, 162, 168, 170, 172, 173, 176, 177, 214; suspension of Steele's governorship, 2, 3, 6, 26, 43, 56, 59, 75, 79, 80, 82, 92, 121, 130–149, 151, 152, 154–159, 160, 166, 213, 214, 216–217

Dryden, John, 90, 102, 103, 131–132, 168, 202

Dueling, 20, 173, 184

Dunkirk, 12

Dunton, John, 174

Edgar, Sir John, 136, 146 n. 57, 151, 161, 162–163, 168, 172–173, 189, 190–192. See also *Theatre* (Steele)

Election at Gotham, The (Steele), 238

Elrington, Tom, 134

Englishman, The, 12

Englishman's Thanks to the Duke of Marlborough, The (Steele), 11

Epistle to Sir Richard Steele (Victor), 208–209

Epsom Wells (Shadwell), 23

Estcourt, Richard, 23

Etherege, George, 7, 24, 90, 202, 203

Eunuch, The (Terence), 237–238

Examiner, 27

Falstaffe, Sir John, 169, 170–173. See also *Anti-Theatre; Theatre* (later)

Farce, 62–63, 71–73, 83, 88

Farquhar, George, 82, 90, 125

Fears of the Pretender Turn'd into the Fears of Debauchery with a Hint to Richard Steele, Esq., The (Defoe), 15, 16

Filmer, Edward, 1, 14

"Fine gentleman," 17–18, 24, 47, 65, 82, 183, 193, 198–199, 203

First Days Entertainment at Rutland-House, The (D'Avenant), 101

First Ode of the Second Book of Horace Paraphras'd, The (Swift), 184–185

Fletcher, John, 82–90

Forster, John, 30

Freeholder's Journal, 195, 205–206, 208

French Faith Represented in the Present State of Dunkirk, The (Steele), 12

Full Consideration and Confutation of Sir John Edgar, A, 166, 175

Funeral, The (Steele), 18–19, 196, 200, 202, 207, 234, 235, 238

Gay, John, 14, 15, 71–73, 80, 153

Genest, John, 70 n. 37, 82 n. 67, 157

Gentleman, The (Steele), 231, 237

George I, 2, 3, 11, 12, 13, 25, 37, 39, 41, 48, 50, 51–52, 61, 90, 106–107 n. 134, 108, 109, 110, 123, 128, 132, 141, 244

George, Prince of Denmark, 27

Gerbier, Sir Balthazar, 99, 101. See also Academies

Gery, Charles, 93–98, 122, 126, 148

Gildon, Charles, 1, 22, 166, 167 n. 94, 176 n. 104, 204

Granville, George. See Lansdowne, Baron

Guardian, 2, 12, 21, 83, 105, 107 n. 134, 136, 183, 184 n. 3, 193, 201, 237

Guinguette or Harlequin Turned Tapster, La, 63

Hamlet (Shakespeare), 90–91
Hanover Club, 123
Hanover, Elector of. *See* George I
Hanover, house of, 11, 13, 26, 50, 89
Hanoverian succession, 12. *See also* Protestant succession
Harlequin Hydaspes, 72
Hardy, Lord (*The Funeral*), 19, 200, 202, 234
Harley, Robert, 25, 27, 28, 29–32, 33, 106–108, 129
Harrison, William, 103
Hart, Charles, 23
Haym, Nicola Francesco, 102, 104
Haymarket, 14, 41, 49, 90, 132, 151, 171, 227
Henry VIII (Shakespeare), 74
Heroides (Ovid), 103
Hill, Aaron, 22, 117
Hooker, Edward N, 184 n. 3
Horace, 109
Horner (*The Country Wife*), 24
Hughes, John, 63, 68, 103, 153, 200
Humber (*The School of Action*), 231, 233–235

Importance of Dunkirk Consider'd, The (Steele), 12, 27–28
Invader of His Country, The (Dennis), 70–71, 133–135, 163, 169
Ironside, Nestor, 12

James II, 129
Jekyll, Sir Joseph, 229
Johnson, Charles, 34–35
Joint and Humble Address of the Tories and Whigs Concerning the Bill of Peerage, The (Steele), 129
Jonson, Ben, 82, 90, 204

Killigrew, Thomas, 3, 6, 41, 46, 48, 126, 141, 178–179

Lansdowne, George Granville, Baron, 26, 27, 28–29, 30, 31, 32
Lechmere, Nicholas, 45, 46, 125–126, 178, 243
Letter from Sig. Benedetto Baldassari of the Haymarket, A, 173
Letter to the Earl of O——d Concerning the Bill of Peerage, A (Steele), 129
Letter to Sir M. W. Concerning Occasional Peers, A (Steele), 26, 28
Libertine Destroyed, The, 77
License, theatrical: applied for, 36–37; granted, 37–38; issued exclusive of Steele, 139, 142, 145, 146–147, 151, 213, 215; revocation, 3, 137, 139, 140–141, 143, 144–145, 146, 179–180; terms, 36–37, 38, 46, 67
Lincoln's Inn Fields, 39, 41–43, 48, 50, 61, 64, 68 n. 35, 71, 72, 75, 83, 85, 87, 88–90, 92, 142, 165, 178, 203, 217, 225–227, 232, 247–248
Lord chamberlain: Steele's dispute with, 121, 123–127, 129, 130–149, 151, 154–159, 160, 162–163, 168, 170, 172, 174, 175, 176, 177, 191, 192, 239, 246–247; supervision of Drury Lane, 140, 151–154, 157–158, 159, 162, 168, 170, 172, 173, 176, 177, 214; theatrical jurisdiction, 121, 122–123, 124, 125–127, 135, 136, 138–139, 143, 145, 151, 152–154, 157–158, 159, 160, 168, 170–171, 176, 177–180, 217, 223, 239, 246–247. *See also* Bolton; Newcastle; Shrewsbury
Lords, House of, 128

Love for Love (Congreve), 17, 23, 83, 91

Love in a Veil (Savage), 74

Love's Last Shift (Cibber), 91

Lucius (Mrs. Manley), 70, 84

Lying Lover, The (Steele), 16, 19, 20, 199, 235

Mac Flecknoe (Dryden), 168

Maid's Tragedy, The (Beaumont and Fletcher), 84, 91

Manley, Mrs. Mary, 70

Man of Mode, The (Etherege), 15, 24, 77, 79, 83, 193, 202, 204, 208

Marlborough, Sarah, Duchess of, 37–38

Marlborough, John Churchill, first Duke of, 11, 37–38

Masque, 63, 67, 68, 69

Masquerade, The (Johnson), 81

Master of the revels, 2, 49, 121

Medley, 32 n. 46

Menteur, Le (Corneille), 19

Mills, J., 23

Minshull, William, 93–97, 122, 126, 218, 221

Mistake, The (Vanbrugh), 24

Mr. Steele's Apology for Himself and His Writings (Steele), 12, 13, 16

Mohun, 23

Mortgage. *See* Patent, theatrical

Muses Gazette, 175–177. See also *Applebee's Original Weekly*

Music, psychological effects of, 100, 101, 102–105, 110. *See also* Academies; Censorium

Music, 100–101, 102–105, 110–111, 233. *See also* Academies; Censorium

Myrtillo (Cibber), 68

Nation a Family, A (Steele), 150

Necromancer, The, 226–227

New Project for the Regulation of the Stage, A, 165–166

Newcastle, Thomas Pelham-Holles, first Duke of: becomes lord chamberlain, 124; patronage of Steele, 51, 123–124, 127, 129, 131, 172; Steele's quarrel with, 6, 123–127, 129, 130–149, 151, 154–159, 160, 161, 162–163, 168, 170, 172, 174, 175, 177, 190, 216, 239, 246–247; Steele's reconciliation with, 217, 223; supervision of Drury Lane by, 140, 151, 152–154, 162, 168, 170, 172, 173, 176, 177, 214

Nichols, John, 115, 116, 166, 230–231, 237, 238

Non-Juror, The (Cibber), 81, 84–85, 89

Northey, Sir Edward, 45, 46, 243

Ode for Music on St. Cecilia's Day (Pope), 102, 104

Old Bachelor, The (Congreve), 23, 83, 91

Old Whig, The (Addison), 129

Opera, 41, 45–46, 50, 67–69, 90, 100, 102, 103, 110, 121, 132, 184, 191. *See also* Haymarket

Original Weekly Journal. See *Applebee's Original Weekly Journal*

Orphan Revived, 135, 190

Otway, Thomas, 90

Ovid, 103

Oxford, Earl of. *See* Harley, Robert

Pantomime, 171, 226–228

Parker, Sir Thomas, 60 n. 14, 138

Parliament. *See* Commons, House of; Lords, House of

Passion of Sappho (Harrison), 103

Patent, theatrical: duration, 44, 46, 146, 158, 178, 223–224, 229–230; granted, 3, 46; legal validity, 126–127, 142–143, 155, 157, 158, 162, 177–180, 230; lord chamberlain's jurisdiction over, 121, 122–123, 124, 125–127, 135, 136, 138–139, 177–180; petition for, 26, 43–45, 98, 223, 243; possible early offer to Steele, 25–33; powers conveyed, 126, 136, 139, 141–142, 146, 158, 177–180; rendered ineffectual by lord chamberlain, 139–141, 142–143, 146, 151, 158; royal warrant, 45–46, 244–245; Steele's mortgages, 93–98, 122, 126, 148, 174, 216–217, 218–219, 221, 229, 240; terms, 3, 45–47, 48, 64–65, 67, 146, 147–148, 178, 212–213, 229–230, 244–245

Peerage Bill, 26, 28, 127–129, 130, 131, 135, 138, 150, 155, 163, 174

Pelham, Henry, 136, 138 n. 39, 154, 155, 156

Pengelly, Thomas, 126–127, 127 n. 13, 138 n. 39, 139–140, 145, 146, 147–148, 158, 174, 246–247

Pepusch, Dr. Johann Christoph, 103 n. 119

Percival, Sir John, 31

Peri Bathous (Pope and Swift), 166

Philips, Ambrose, 71

Plaxton, William, 224, 232

Plebeian, 129

Pope, Alexander, 28, 71–73, 80, 102, 104, 105, 109, 166

Present State of Wit, The (Gay), 14

Pretender, James Edward ("The Old"), 12

Protestant succession, 11, 12, 30, 50, 89, 123, 131

Provok'd Wife, The (Vanbrugh), 82–83 n. 66

Rehearsal, The (Buckingham), 73, 231

Relapse, The (Vanbrugh), 83, 91, 171

Remarks on . . . The Conscious Lovers (Dennis), 204, 210–211

Rennel, Gabriel, 226

Rich, Christopher, 41–42, 141, 238

Rich, Christopher Mosier, 39, 41, 42, 45

Rich, John, 39, 41, 42, 43, 44, 45, 61, 73, 87, 89, 178, 217–218, 220, 225, 227, 247–248

Richard II (Shakespeare-Theobald), 81

Richelieu, Cardinal, 170

Rochester, John Wilmot, second Earl of, 24, 208

Roscius, 23, 233

Rover, The (Mrs. Aphra Behn), 77, 91

Rowe, Nicholas, 82, 84

Royal Academy of Music, 90, 132–133

Royal Company of Comedians, 2, 69, 74, 130, 150, 158, 243, 244–245, 246, 247–248. *See also* Drury Lane

Rundle, Dr. Thomas, 160–161, 190–191

St. James's Journal, 193, 205, 206–207

Savage, Richard, 74

School of Action, The (Steele), 224, 231–235, 237

Scurlock, David, 26–28, 30, 32, 224–225, 227, 228–229

Sewell, George, 1, 22, 81
Severn (*The School of Action*), 231, 233–235, 236, 237
Smith, John Harrington, 196–197
Shadwell, Thomas, 197, 202
Shakespeare, William, 70, 82, 90
Sherburn, George, 72
Short View of the Immorality and Profaneness of the English Stage, A (J. Collier), 16–17, 47, 65
Shrewsbury, Charles Talbot, first Duke of, 37, 42–43, 49–50
Siege of Damascus, The (Hughes), 153
Sign manual, royal, 136, 137, 138, 140–141, 144–145, 146, 178
Sir Courtly Nice (Crowne), 91
Sir Fopling Flutter. See *Man of Mode, The*
Sir Richard Steele and his New Comedy, call'd The Conscious Lovers, Vindicated, 209–210
Sir Walter Raleigh (Sewell), 81, 85
Sorin, M., 61, 62–63, 83
South Sea Bill, 149–150, 151, 155, 161
South Sea Bubble, 150, 157, 173, 214
South Sea Company, 149–150, 151
Spanish Friar, The (Dryden), 83, 134
Spectator, 2, 11, 16, 18, 21, 71, 79, 83, 102–103, 104, 106–107 n. 134, 136, 167, 168, 183, 184 n. 3, 186, 196, 200, 201, 202, 236, 237, 238
Spectator, Mr., 5, 233
Spence, Joseph, 72
Stage: abuse, 1, 2, 4–5, 14, 15, 16, 19–20, 21, 23, 32, 47, 77, 82–83, 84, 87–88, 164–165, 166, 167, 171, 176–177, 226–228, 243; control, 1–2, 3, 6, 13, 25, 29, 32, 86, 121, 122–123, 126, 143, 151, 152–154, 157–158, 159,

160, 161, 162–163, 166, 170–171, 172, 173, 176–180, 239, 240, 243, 244–245; moral influence, 1, 15, 16, 17, 18–22, 65, 82, 167, 183, 187, 188–189, 233, 240; reform, 1, 2–5, 13–25, 27, 32, 35, 44, 45, 46–47, 64–66, 77–78, 81, 85–89, 122, 161, 165, 167, 171, 176–177, 212–213, 223, 231, 233, 239–240, 244–245
Stair, John Dalrymple, second Earl of, 61, 62, 78
Stanhope, James Stanhope, first Earl of, 13, 130–131, 138, 155
Stanley, Sir John, 50, 66–67, 68, 78, 121, 122–123, 138 n. 39
Stage Licensing Act, 159
State of the Case Between the Lord Chamberlain and the Governor of the Royal Company of Comedians, The (Steele), 77, 137, 140–141, 163, 177, 180, 223
State of the Case [with] ... the Lord Chamberlain ... Restated, The, 77–78, 79, 83, 130 n. 18, 131, 142, 179–180
Steele, Eugene, 115–116
Steele, Lady, 26, 32, 38, 51, 73, 74, 113, 123, 189
Steele, Sir Richard: active association with Drury Lane ends, 75, 158, 213, 220, 222–225, 228; aesthetic theory of, 67–69, 100–103, 105, 110–111, 113, 233; applies for theatrical license, 37–38; appointed commissioner for forfeited estates in Scotland, 50; appointed to governorship of Drury Lane, 2–6, 7, 11, 13, 25, 32, 43–46, 212–213; attempts to obtain theatrical patent in perpetuity, 223–224; attempts to regain

Steele, Sir Richard (cont'd.)
governorship of Drury Lane, 146, 151, 154–158, 159, 177–178; champions actors, 22–23, 66, 162–163, 164, 233; complains to lord chamberlain about rival theatrical companies, 217–218, 247–248; conducts Censorium, 3, 31, 55, 65, 69, 98–118; controversial journalism, 3, 6–7, 11–12, 13, 21, 27, 63–66, 69, 73, 85, 87, 107, 123–124, 128–129, 136–137, 143–144, 145–146, 148–149, 150–151, 154, 159–163, 166, 167, 168–169, 170–180, 202–203, 240; controversy with Dennis, 70–71, 76–78, 79, 142–143, 163–165, 166, 167, 168–169, 173, 175, 187–188, 194–195, 196, 198, 203–205, 206, 208–209, 210–211; death, 2, 56, 213, 222, 229; defends Cibber, 143–144, 147; dispute with lord chamberlain, 2, 3, 6, 42–43, 48–50, 55, 66–67, 75, 79, 114, 121–149, 151, 154–158, 159–180, 190–191, 192, 239–240, 246–247; dramatic criticism, 1, 2, 4–7, 15, 16–25, 47, 69–70, 87, 161, 183–184, 186–187, 188, 193, 197–203, 207, 209–210, 212–213, 233–234, 240; dramatic theory exemplified in The Conscious Lovers, 183–184, 186, 187–188, 193, 197–203, 205, 207, 209–210, 212–213; enters Drury Lane management, 35–37, 57; expelled from Parliament, 13, 32, 107; excluded from theatrical license, 139, 142, 146–147, 151, 213; financial difficulties, 6, 27, 36, 91–98, 106–107, 110, 117, 214–217, 218–222, 224–225, 228–230, 240; granted patent, 3, 40, 45–48, 121,

244–245; health, 5, 56, 116, 193, 222–223, 240; income from Drury Lane, 5, 36, 40–41, 43, 48, 56, 57, 73, 91–92, 93–94, 95, 97–98, 194, 214–217, 218–221, 224–225, 228–230; inconsistency, 5, 23–25, 62–63, 76–78, 79, 85, 122, 167, 171, 239–240; knighted, 50, 123; lawsuits, 36, 39–41, 57–58, 75–76, 96–98, 154, 214–215, 221, 224–225, 228–229; membership in Parliament, 27, 48, 50, 51, 55, 107, 123, 127, 149; mortgages patent, 91, 93–98, 122, 126, 174, 216–217, 218–219, 221, 240; neglect of duties at Drury Lane, 3, 5, 7, 36, 56–57, 75, 76–78, 79, 85, 97–98, 122, 133, 158, 213, 219–220, 222, 239–240; offered supervision of theater by Tory ministry, 25–33, 106; opposes Peerage Bill, 127–130, 131, 135, 150, 155, 163; opposes South Sea Bill, 149–151, 155; participates in Drury Lane management, 5, 11, 35–36, 39, 55–78, 84, 85–86, 90–91, 97–98, 122, 158, 213–218, 219–220, 222, 225, 227–228, 229, 240; patronized by Newcastle, 123–124, 127, 131, 174; personality compared with Addison's, 234–235; petitions for patent, 26, 43–45, 98, 243, petitions king for protection from lord chamberlain, 139–140; political activities, 5, 11–13, 26–33, 37–38, 50–52, 55, 89, 105–108, 123–124, 127–131, 149–151, 155, 183, 213, 240; as popularizer of reform doctrine, 15, 20–21, 86, 240; presents The Conscious Lovers, 193–195, 213–214; publicity campaign for The Con-

scious Lovers, 6, 19, 25, 194–196, 203; quarrels with Newcastle, 6, 122–127, 129, 131–148, 154–158, 159–163, 168, 174–175, 177–180, 190–191, 192, 216, 240, 246–247; reconciled to Newcastle, 217–218, 223; reformer, 1–7, 11, 13, 14–15, 16–25, 32, 35, 44–45, 46–47, 57, 62–63, 64–65, 76–78, 79, 85–86, 98–101, 102, 110–113, 117–118, 122, 159, 160, 164–165, 167, 171, 183–184, 193, 202–203, 212–213, 231–233, 237, 239–240; relations with actor-managers, 5, 7, 36–37, 39–41, 43–44, 47–48, 55–61, 63–64, 69, 70–73, 74–75, 91–92, 94, 97, 152, 180, 213–217, 218–225, 227–229, 240; resigns commissionership of stamps, 27, 31, 107; resigns pension, 27, 32; restored to governorship of Drury Lane, 92, 157–158, 183, 213, 217; retires, 116, 223–225; suspended from governorship of Drury Lane, 2, 3, 6, 26, 43, 75, 79, 80, 92, 114, 133, 140–141, 143–149, 151, 159–160, 166, 213, 217, 246–247; terms of agreement with actor-managers, 36–37, 57–59, 216–217; unfinished plays, 230–238; views on stage regulation, 3, 6, 7, 43, 48–50, 55, 66–67, 85–86, 121, 124, 130, 140–141, 146, 157–158, 161, 170, 177–180, 239; writes *The Conscious Lovers*, 183–193

Sunderland, Charles Spencer, third Earl of, 128, 155, 156, 157, 174–175

Swift, Jonathan, 30, 31, 166, 184–185, 186, 189

Swiney, Owen, 33, 37

Tatler, 2, 15, 21, 22–23, 24, 35, 60, 66, 83, 86, 102, 106–107 n. 134, 136, 183, 186, 191 n. 21, 200, 201, 237, 240

Tempest, The (Shakespeare), 91, 222

Tender Husband, The (Steele), 19, 91, 235

Terence, 186, 200–201, 207, 237–238

Theaters. *See* Drury Lane; Haymarket; Lincoln's Inn Fields

Theatre (later), 169 n. 96, 172–173

Theatre (Steele), 3, 70, 73, 75, 76, 124 n. 9, 125, 132, 136–137, 143, 143–144 n. 53, 145–146, 148–149, 151, 160–163, 164, 165, 166–167, 169–172, 173, 174, 177, 189, 190–192, 202–203, 223, 234, 239

Theatre-Royal, 25, 81, 89 n. 82, 125, 130, 166, 217. *See also* Drury Lane

Three Hours After Marriage (Gay, Pope, Arbuthnot), 72–73, 80

Theobald, Lewis, 1, 81, 204

Tickell, Thomas, 125

Timon of Athens (Shakespeare), 91

Tonson, Jacob, 151

Tory party, 11, 12–13, 25, 27, 28, 31, 32, 89, 106–108, 128

Town Talk (Steele), 3, 46, 47, 51 n. 93, 63–66, 69, 73, 78, 83, 85, 98 n. 105, 108, 109, 110, 111, 112, 114, 115, 143, 178, 239

Townshend, Charles, second Viscount, 44, 45, 155, 223, 243, 245

Tragedy, 45, 140, 167, 176, 201, 209, 210

Usefulness of the Stage (Dennis), 14

Valentine (*Love for Love*), 17, 18

Vanbrugh, Sir John, 14, 24, 49, 82–83 n. 66, 90, 121, 142, 151, 204, 222–223

Vaudeville-type entertainment, 42, 62–63, 83–84, 88, 226–228, 232
Venus and Adonis (Cibber), 67–69
Victor, Benjamin, 183, 194, 196, 208–209

Wales, Prince of (George II), 90, 128
Walpole, Sir Robert, 13, 129, 150, 155, 156, 157, 174–175, 210
Way of the World, The (Congreve), 23, 24, 83
Weaver, J., 75
Weekly Journal (Mist's), 205, 208, 222, 232
Weekly Packet, 42, 108
Welsted, Leonard, 187 n. 7, 203, 220, 232
Wendover, 157, 225
What D'Ye Call It, The (Gay), 71
Whig party, 11, 25, 26, 29–30, 31, 37, 50–52, 55, 71–72, 89, 106–108, 123, 127–130, 131, 149–150, 174, 217
Whimsical Death of Harlequin, The, 63
Whiston, William, 111

Wilbraham, Ralph, 94–96, 97 n. 101, 218–219, 221
Wilks, Robert, 22, 23, 33, 40, 41, 43, 44, 45, 58, 59, 73, 79, 80, 81, 86, 99, 109, 134, 135, 139, 140, 142, 146, 147, 152, 166, 186–187, 194, 213, 214, 215, 217, 218, 221 n. 89, 224, 227, 228–229, 230, 243, 244, 246
Wolsey, Cardinal, 143, 143–144 n. 53
Woodward, Dr. John, 72
Woolley, William, 93, 96–98, 221, 229
Word Without Doors, A, 174
Wycherley, William, 7, 24, 90, 197, 202

Ximena, or the Heroic Daughter (Cibber), 59–60, 131–132, 134

York Buildings, 31, 55, 65, 69, 99, 102–103, 104, 105, 106, 108, 112–113, 115–116, 117. *See also* Censorium
Young, Edward, 28, 85, 154 n. 73, 168
Younger, Miss, 99, 108

Zara (Hill), 117

CPSIA information can be obtained
at www.ICGtesting.com
Printed in the USA
LVHW100836100922
728013LV00011B/285